PRAISE FOR *A GOO*

"A teenage girl is pressured to marry a much older man and move to a foreign land. If you think you know this story, that it is a stereotype, you are wrong. *A Good Wife* is not the story of an abused woman. This is a memoir of ambition, how the very thing that lured Samra Zafar into an abusive marriage ultimately galvanized her escape and success. With unflinching candour, Zafar dissects the forces constricting her: culture, religion, her parents' difficult marriage, their uneasy complicity in hers, the intergenerational expectations that shackled her in-laws, even her own naïveté. Thorny and surprising, her story is all the more heartbreaking for its complexities. Zafar has penned a rare memoir, a life story worth reading and an emotional roller coaster that will leave you feeling empowered at the end. This is a modern-day fairy tale where the heroine saves her own life."

—SHARON BALA, bestselling author of *The Boat People*

"A thoroughly engaging story of strength, feminism and refusal to conform to societal and familial expectations. I found it difficult to put this book down."

—CEA SUNRISE PERSON, bestselling author of *North of Normal*

"Samra Zafar's harrowing story of escaping her abusive marriage in Canada—arranged when she was just a teenager in Pakistan—might read like a taut domestic thriller, but *A Good Wife* is all too painfully real. I cried while reading this book, but I was also left in awe of Zafar's epic grit and bravery. Her story will stay with you long after the last hope-filled page is turned."

—LISA GABRIELE, author of the bestselling novel *The Winters*

A
Good
Wife

*Escaping the Life
I Never Chose*

DR. SAMRA ZAFAR

with MEG MASTERS

HARPER ⬤ PERENNIAL

Published by Harper Perennial,
an imprint of HarperCollins Publishers Ltd

First published by HarperCollins Publishers Ltd
in an original trade paperback edition: 2019
This Harper Perennial trade paperback edition: 2025

Our lives equip us with unique experiences and perceptions. In the pages that follow,
we explore issues related to a wide range of life situations and circumstances, including some
that may be triggering to some readers. If you encounter material that is challenging
or upsetting for you, or causes you discomfort, I encourage you to seek support.

HarperCollins books may be purchased for educational, business,
or sales promotional use through our Special Markets Department.

HarperCollins Publishers Ltd
Bay Adelaide Centre, East Tower
22 Adelaide Street West, 41st Floor
Toronto, Ontario, Canada
M5H 4E3

Cover design by Lola Landekic

www.harpercollins.ca

Library and Archives Canada Cataloguing in Publication

Title: A good wife : escaping the life I never chose / Samra Zafar with Meg Masters.
Names: Zafar, Samra, author. | Masters, Meg, author.
Description: Previously published: Toronto, Ontario: HarperCollins Publishers, 2019.
Identifiers: Canadiana 20240508831 | ISBN 9781443454889 (softcover)
Subjects: LCSH: Zafar, Samra. | LCSH: Abused wives—Canada—Biography. | LCSH: Arranged marriage—
Canada. | LCSH: Divorced women—Canada—Biography. | LCSH: Women—Pakistan—Social conditions. |
CSH: Pakistani Canadian women—Biography. | LCGFT: Autobiographies.
Classification: LCC HV6626.23.C3 Z34 2025 | DDC 362.82/92092—dc23

Printed and bound in the United States of America
24 25 26 27 28 LBC 5 4 3 2 1

This book is dedicated to the two most important people in my life—
my best friends, my cheerleaders, my partners—my daughters.

CONTENTS

PROLOGUE

I wake to the crackling of bird calls outside my bedroom window, the anemic light of a Canadian spring morning seeping through the curtains. I lie very still, listening. The house is quiet. My in-laws are in the bedroom down the hall. My husband sleeps ten feet below me, in the den. My infant daughter slumbers peacefully beside me. At first, I'm surprised to see her. Why didn't I put her in her crib in the room next door last night? Why is she still here with me? And then I remember. I rub a painful spot on my upper chest. My heart aches almost every morning, but today my ribs are sore as well.

As my drowsiness falls away, another feeling works its way through my body. A frayed, rippling tension, a growing brittleness: anticipation and fear. At any moment, the cold brick house will come alive, and I will be thrown together with the rest of the inhabitants. If all goes well, Ahmed will take his lunch and walk wordlessly out the front door, and I will start on a long, dull day, locked here in the house with his mother and my daughter. The hours will creep by, broken only by chores, television, empty chat.

But perhaps it won't be dull. Yesterday was not dull. Or at least it didn't end that way. And I have come to understand that in this new world of mine, anything other than grey monotony is scary. Anything else is dangerous.

My daughter shifts. I can hear my mother-in-law's slippers as she begins to pad about her room. It is time for me to go in to say salaam. It is time for me to head downstairs with the baby. It is time for me to make my husband's lunch. It is time for me to start my dreary routine.

As I rise, I realize that I am saying a little prayer. I am praying for luck. I am praying for another dull day.

PART
ONE

CHAPTER 1

MEHNDI

Music was drifting up from the tent, but I couldn't find the celebration in it. Instead it sounded haunting and hollow, like a distant echo of happier times. I knew that at any moment the dancing would start. It felt surreal to be trapped up here, all alone, reduced to watching and waiting. I had always loved family weddings, and I loved the dancing most of all. Enthusiastic as I was, I had never been able to resist taking charge of the choreography and hogging the limelight during our little performances.

Sitting in a bedroom in my uncle's house in Karachi, I peered out the window at my family below. They were gathered under a tent, but the sides were open. I could see their brightly coloured clothes and sparkling jewellery. They were talking and laughing. I watched as my little sisters, Warda, Saira and Bushra, helped themselves to mithai and laddoo and other sweets that lined the enormous platters that were being passed from person to person.

Tonight was my mehndi—the pre-wedding music party a bride's parents hold to formally present their daughter to her soon-to-be-husband's family. Earlier in the evening, I had been escorted

3

downstairs to briefly join the festivities. My sisters and cousins had walked with me, holding my yellow dupatta over my head like a canopy. For half an hour or so, I sat on a raised platform, the dupatta draped over my head and my palm outstretched, a large paan leaf in its centre. One by one, all of the adult female guests approached me, putting a dab of henna in the centre of the leaf and a small morsel of mithai in my mouth. I tried to remember to keep my eyes down and not say too much, as for this short while I was the centre of attention. Ahmed's brothers, sisters, aunts and uncles studied me slyly, making comments about my hair, my height and the paleness of my skin. I felt like a new car or shiny watch that was being assessed by its owner's friends. Then I was shepherded back upstairs so the celebrations could continue without the presence of the girl whose modesty needed to be protected. In two days' time, I would no longer be a student, no longer a big sister and beloved daughter, no longer a person with any independence or autonomy. I would be a begum—someone's wife. I was just seventeen.

Sitting on the bed, in my new yellow-and-green dress, my dupatta abandoned beside me, I was seized by panic. I was supposed to be flattered by the proposal of a man eleven years my senior, a man who had a good job and a Canadian home. I was supposed to be relieved that I had avoided the terrible fate of spinsterhood. Most of all, I was supposed to be overjoyed by my impending marriage and the idea of joining my husband's family. But everything about the last few months felt like a terrible, twisted dream.

❧ ❧ ❧

My family and I had arrived in Pakistan several months before and moved into the apartment my mother had bought a few years earlier as an investment. We had left behind in Ruwais, a small town in the United Arab Emirates, our spacious three-bedroom home and a tranquil suburban neighbourhood filled with succulent trees and fragrant blossoms. No one in my family had been happy about the move. My mother had been forced to quit her job. My three sisters and I had been torn from our friends and our school. My father was left to shuttle back and forth between his work in the oil refinery and his wife and children in Karachi. But there was no other way. It was cheaper for us to live in Karachi. And we needed to cut costs to pay for the wedding.

Our new home in Pakistan was a shock. The sweltering summer heat beat its way through the doors and windows, filling the cramped space with fetid, humid air. Used to air conditioning, my sisters and I spent most of our waking hours huddled in my parents' tiny bedroom—the only room that had AC. When we did move about the place, we stepped carefully, watching out for the cockroaches and other bugs that crunched under our feet or scuttled across our toes if we weren't careful. For young girls in Pakistan, there was no playing outdoors or riding our bikes. No tennis or squash or cricket. And when we went outside, we had to leave our jeans and T-shirts tucked in the closet, donning instead the traditional shalwar kameez—a long tunic and flowing pants—our heads and chests covered with a dupatta. The streets, with their emaciated stray dogs, flea-ridden cats and skittering lizards, took us months to get used to.

A week before the wedding, our out-of-town relatives descended upon us. While some stayed with my grandfather and my other relatives, a number wrestled their suitcases into our already impossibly crowded apartment. Once ensconced, they threw themselves into the wedding preparations. My uncles shuttled back and forth to the banquet hall, checking on the arrangements there; my aunts fussed about clothes and bangles and flowers. My sisters and cousins squeezed into the living room to work out the dances they would perform at the two mehndis.

And I stood in the midst of it all, dumbfounded by the activity. It was my wedding, but all the sacrifices people were making, all the expense and exertion they were putting in, seemed to have nothing to do with me. No one sought my input on the flowers or the food we might serve. No one invited me to choose music or even a colour of lipstick. No one asked me if I liked the clothes that they had selected for me to wear at the various dinners and parties. (My actual wedding dress and jewellery were being picked out for me by Ahmed's family and would be presented to my family at *his* mehndi.) It was like standing on the bank of a river, watching the water swell and surge and knowing that I would be pulled into it, helpless, at any moment.

And perhaps the most disorienting thing was that all this effort was focused on attaching me to a man I had never met. A man I had exchanged only a few brief emails with.

But then, a few days before my mehndi, Ahmed appeared.

❧ ❧ ❧

Our first meeting was almost by accident. My family and I had been summoned to his family's home. His relatives needed to get my measurements for the wedding clothes they were having made for me. With the fitting finished, I was ushered into the living room.

"Come here, Samra," called Ahmed's mother. "Our new daughter must sit with us." She gestured to a small space on the couch between her and her husband. I sat down, but my obedience was accompanied by uneasiness. These people did not feel at all like parents to me.

Ahmed's mother's round face was so unlike my mother's soft prettiness. It had a swollen stiffness to it, and even when she smiled her thin lips pressed together and drooped at the edges, as if in disapproval. Yet it was the difference between Ahmed's father and my papa that was the most striking. Ahmed's abba spoke eloquently, giving the impression that he was knowledgeable and enlightened. But no trace of laughter showed in this man's face, none of my papa's teasing or humour dancing in his dark eyes. My mother had been impressed by him, but to me he seemed arrogant. Over the last few weeks I had begun to suspect that the kind words and warm reassurances they both occasionally offered were fabrications. I wasn't sure they were people I could trust, never mind love.

Wedged between these two strangers, I was glad that my dupatta hid part of my face and that my lowered head suggested only proper modesty to them and not avoidance.

For endless minutes, the conversation rippled around me as I studied the dark green silk of my shalwar kameez. And then Ahmed's mother's shrill tone cut through the chatter.

"Ahmed, you're here!"

I heard a deep voice saying salaam to everyone.

My face was suddenly blazing hot, my heart pounding, the air stuck in my lungs. I felt as if I might faint. I couldn't believe Ahmed was actually in the same room. In the months since I first heard his name, since my family had received his family's proposal, Ahmed had been a ghost, a hazy abstraction. I knew almost nothing about him, but everyone told me how wonderful he was. I realized now that I had taken all their vague descriptions and created a tiny cloud of a man out of them, something light and insubstantial that I could carry around in my thoughts. Squeezed between his parents, too frightened to raise my head, I knew how foolish that had been. I couldn't lift my eyes to take a look at him, but I could feel his presence, large and heavy and casting an enormous shadow over the room.

His sister's voice reached me. "Samra, stand up," Fatima said. "Stand up. I want to see the two of you together."

I got up slowly, moving some distance from the sofa, still keeping my eyes down. I could see his frame coming towards me, turning to stand by my side. His shoulder brushed mine. I froze.

Everyone began to talk at once. "They look so great together." "They're both so tall." "They're made for each other!"

Then Fatima's voice broke in. "Look up, Samra," she ordered. "Why aren't you smiling?"

I couldn't make any of the muscles on my face move.

"Oh, sit down," Fatima finally said.

I returned to my place between Ahmed's parents. I could see Ahmed moving to sit across from me, but I still hadn't lifted my head enough to see his face. Now I took a brief glance. *Oh my God*, I thought. *He's a man, not a boy. He looks like a tall uncle.* I dropped my eyes. I couldn't fathom how this man could be in any sort of relationship with me. He was larger than life, powerful and intimidating. I was just a young girl, tall, yes, but an insignificant whisper next to him. I felt as if the life had been sucked out of me, as if somehow in his presence I had ceased to exist.

☙ ☙ ☙

Now, crouched on the bed in my uncle's house with the noisy mehndi celebration going on below me, hammering anxiety was making it difficult to breathe. I wanted to run away, back to my Ruwais bedroom, back to my friends, back to my old life.

I tried to think of what my father had once told me about fear. I had been about ten years old, with my family at an amusement park. My younger sisters and I were trying to make a beeline to our favourite rides when my father stopped and took my hand.

"No, Samra," he said. "You come with me." He marched me over to a towering roller coaster. "I think you are tall enough to ride this now."

For a few seconds I watched as the tiny cars plummeted down the huge metal tangle, children and adults clutching the seats and screaming. I was shaking my head, terrified. Papa bent down and looked me in the eyes.

"Samra, you need to face your fears in order to overcome them. This is how you will love your life."

Reluctantly, I let myself be guided to the entrance and into one of the seats. When the ride jerked into motion, to my surprise, the wrenching twists and sudden drops had me shrieking in excitement rather than horror. I fell in love with the roller coaster.

But *this* was no holiday amusement. This was my entire future. Papa's words were of no comfort. Tears began to course down my cheeks.

Just then my cousin and his wife walked into the bedroom. "How are you doing?" he asked, although my wet face must have told the story.

I took a deep breath. "I'm scared."

"Ah now, beta," he replied, putting his hand on my head. "Everything is going to be fine. This is a woman's destiny, after all."

His wife was standing beside him, nodding. "Yes, Samra," she said. "This is Allah's will."

I had heard those words so often over the last few months. And I'd said them to others. But no matter how many times I told myself that I should follow Allah's direction, that I had avoided the terrible fate of being an old maid, that the marriage would be good for me, the words would not quite work their way into my heart.

It seemed impossible that this was happening to me, that I had gotten to this point. How had I allowed myself to be cajoled into accepting a marriage proposal, and why had I parroted those arguments to others, including my astonished teachers and my reluctant father? After all, I'd never been one of those girls who dreamed about marriage or even thought much about it. When I arrived at school with an engagement ring on my finger all those months ago, the other girls crowded around me to look at my hand. They crowed about how lucky I was, how exciting it must be to be engaged.

But I knew that if this had happened to some other girl, I would not have reacted as they did. I would have tossed my head and told the girl that she was too young. I would have said that she should go to university, should be thinking about her career. And at the very least, I would have said she should marry for love—not because her family wanted her to.

I would have been bold.

This boldness, however, would not only be the sign of an independent mind. I had also been raised this way.

※ ※ ※

"I don't have four daughters," my father said with a laugh. "I have four sons!"

Papa was joking, but my sisters and I knew exactly what he meant. We were out in the street in front of our house in Ruwais. I had a cricket bat in my hand, waiting for the little boy who was bowling to send the ball my way. One of the other fathers on the street had just stopped by to watch the impromptu game.

"Tch, tch, Zafar," he said to my father, "how can you let your girls play like this?"

"Ah yes," said my dad, smiling at our neighbour. "Something is wrong." Then he turned to me. "Samra, move your hands closer together on the bat."

Now it was my turn to laugh. I loved that Papa was teasing this disapproving man. I had no intention of going indoors just because a few neighbours thought that young girls should not play sports. Cricket was my game, after all. I loved to play squash and tennis, too, but ever since my father had started taking me to help out with the local cricket team he managed, I'd wanted to hold a bat in my hand and stand in front of the wicket. And my father encouraged me.

I had always been an energetic child, racing around the house and crashing into furniture. Perhaps that's why my mother let me take squash lessons and climb trees in the park—as a way to expend excess energy. But my father's support of my athletic interests seemed born of other ideas.

Around the dinner table, he would encourage us to dream. "Saira, what career are you thinking of today? A scientist? An engineer?" My eight-year-old sister put her fork down to think.

"*I* want to be a doctor," I proclaimed. It was a game I adored: hospital. As the eldest, I usually took the role of the physician, dispensing jellied candies to treat the various ailments my three younger sisters cooked up. (I suspect that my sisters preferred hospital to my other favourite game: school. For hours and hours every weekend, I assembled them around the blackboard my father had made for us, teaching them all the things I had learned the week before in class.)

"Ah, you have to work hard to be a doctor," said my father. "But you can do it."

My mother sat at the other end of the table, quietly, but she did not disagree.

"You girls can be anything you want," Papa said. "Anything."

And we believed him.

At other times, our dinner conversation centred on what each of us had learned at school that day. Four little voices bubbled up, each of us vying to tell our stories and share our new-found wisdom.

Education and learning were, after all, Zafar family pastimes. As soon as I could read, each day of my childhood started with a ritual. I would take my seat beside my father at the kitchen table. My mother brought me and my sisters eggs and orange juice. Then my father handed me a section of the morning newspaper.

"All right, Samra. Find something interesting to read, and then tell us all about it."

My sisters waited while their baji (elder sister) wrestled with the huge newsprint pages. I dipped in and out of articles until I found something that I could read and digest, then I explained it to everyone else at the table.

"Now we are all learning!" Papa would say with delight.

✳ ✳ ✳

My father encouraged us to stretch our minds, but he had no formal education himself. It was my mother who had moved through the halls of academia and into a professional career. It was my mother who showed us the possibility in all of Papa's promises. It was my mother who was our true role model.

Mama was an elementary school Urdu teacher—and for several years, she was the Urdu teacher at my school. While most of my friends' mothers stayed home and devoted themselves to domestic duties, mine walked out the front door with us each day, her arms laden with student assignments and lesson plans, her expression often lost in thought, as if she were already fully absorbed in the day to come. We parted ways by the time we entered the schoolyard, but I always felt a flutter of pride as I saw her standing in front of a blackboard or chatting earnestly with the other teachers. She was smart, well read and accomplished—and she had at least a small measure of authority. My mother both showed us the rewards of hard work and demanded we put in the same kind of effort as she did. In the two years I had her as a teacher, she always reminded me that she expected me to work diligently, perhaps more so than the other students, because she knew what I was capable of.

And so, from our earliest days, we Zafar girls knew that whatever else happened, education would be in our future. Marriage, well, my father made it clear what he thought about that. When his friends and family teased him about the expense of having four daughters to marry off, he would wave them away. "I don't have to save for weddings. I have to save for university."

ꙮ ꙮ ꙮ

My sisters and I attended a co-ed private school that followed the British system of education and was staffed largely by men and women from the UK. The student population was a lively mix of ex-pat Pakistanis, Arabs from various countries, and a few white students from Europe and elsewhere. With fewer than five hundred children, it was a small, intimate environment, an easy place to get involved or try things out. In my middle school years, I convinced some of my friends to start a girls' cricket team, which the school staff happily supported. And then the following year, in grade eight, I had another idea: a school newspaper. I made posters asking for short stories, articles, poems and jokes. In the end there was no shortage of material to choose from, but as we went through everything we had collected, I noticed that all the poems, stories and opinion pieces were by girls. The boys wrote exclusively about sports. That's when I decided that *I* would be the cricket columnist. I figured I knew just as much about the game as anyone.

After three or four months of hard work, my friends and I photo-copied our first venture into the fourth estate. On the cover, just under the title, it said, "Samra Zafar, Chief Editor." I thought of all those conversations my sisters and I had at the dinner table about our possible future careers. Doctor, lawyer, engineer, teacher. It had all seemed quite a long way off, but now I was holding in my hands a first taste of the world of professional work, perhaps a small harbinger of a glittering future. Samra Zafar, Chief Editor. My fingers tingled.

My middle school years slid happily into high school. There wasn't a class or a course that I didn't enjoy. I worked hard and did well, my love of school only dampened slightly by my hunger for per-fection. Any lost marks, no matter how few, had me scrambling to find out what I had done wrong, vowing to study harder or be more careful next time.

But that need to succeed didn't keep me from an active social life. My friends and I—both girls and boys—would hang out together at lunch and before and after school in the student lounge or the school-yard. Sometimes we'd play tennis or go to the local fast food restaurant after school or on the weekend. We listened to the Backstreet Boys, were fans of *The X-Files*, and watched Bollywood movies and the occasional American blockbuster in the big theatres in Abu Dhabi. Compared to some Western teens and pre-teens, we might have been a pretty tame bunch, but we weren't aware of it. There seemed to be enough excitement and intrigue in our flirting and romantic alliances, even if they were more a matter of status than a reflection of intimate involvement. (I had my first "boyfriend" in grade eight. We didn't even hold hands. The whole thing lasted for two days.)

And while I fit in easily with Ruwais teen society, I was aware that I enjoyed a bit more freedom than some of my friends. By the time I was about fourteen, my parents would give my sisters and me our pocket money, and maybe a little extra for clothes or other necessities, and drop us off at the big malls in Abu Dhabi or Dubai, so we could spend the day shopping and eating on our own. While we knew to choose shirts long enough to cover our behinds and to avoid short skirts, we loved being able to pick out our own clothes.

On our first unchaperoned trip to the mall, my parents squabbled during the whole drive into the city. My mother was annoyed that my father had given us so much spending money. My father was irked that she was once again questioning his financial sense. And then my mother began to fret about our safety. What if we got lost or failed to find our way to the meeting spot at the end of the day? I had promised to watch out for Bushra, but she was only about eight. Were we all a bit too young for this? To this objection, my father responded with reassurance instead of anger.

"They will manage," he said to my mother, as we sped along the highway. "It's important that they learn to do things on their own."

I suspect, now that I reflect upon it, that he thought getting lost—just a little—might do us good. It was like his approach with the roller coaster. He believed that fear could be stifling, and he seemed determined to make us face it.

I came to realize that I had another kind of freedom, too.

It happened during one of our girls' cricket games in middle school. One of the male students was officiating, and he made a bad call. I pointed out what he had missed, but he shrugged me off. "What does it matter? Everyone knows that girls can't play cricket."

I had been annoyed that he wasn't paying attention to the play, but this dismissal of me—and of all my friends out on the field—infuriated me. I let loose and punched him in the nose.

A few minutes later, I was sitting, chastened, in the principal's office, while he phoned my father. "Mr. Zafar, we have a very serious problem here. We would like you to come down immediately."

The minutes sitting on the hard metal chair, waiting for my father to arrive, seemed to go on forever, but the wait was not as difficult as listening to the principal tell Papa how disappointed he was in me. My gold-star-student status was now a little tarnished.

When we finally exited the principal's office, my head was bowed and my shoulders slumped. All of the satisfaction I'd felt at putting that stupid boy right was overshadowed by feelings of guilt and shame. But as we walked outside into the sunshine, my father smiled and bent his head towards mine.

I had forgotten. If fearfulness was to be resisted, so was meekness.

"Way to go," he whispered in my ear.

※ ※ ※

It was hard to believe that a girl who had been congratulated for socking a boy, a girl who had, just a few months ago, taken the bus into Abu Dhabi by herself to go shopping, a girl who had been talking

15

about university with her high school teachers and applying for scholarships was now sitting alone in her grandfather's house, waiting to be married to a stranger.

The night following my mehndi, Ahmed's parents held their party for my family. I was left alone with my grandfather. I watched a movie on TV and dozed on the sofa. I was exhausted. But I was still up when my parents and sisters arrived back at the house much later that night, dragging a big suitcase.

"Your wedding dress," my mother called to me. "Come see."

We all moved into one of the bedrooms, and my mother lifted the suitcase onto the bed. Then she opened it to reveal a long crimson dress with gold trim and embroidery. My mother began to pull out glittering pieces of gold jewellery from the bag as well—bangles and earrings and a teeka for my forehead. My sisters clapped their hands and exclaimed over the beauty of my wedding finery.

All I could think of was my last creative writing assignment. I had completed it just after becoming engaged. It described a young woman sitting on a bed, dressed in red and gold, her arms covered in bangles. The bangles were in the shapes of snakes and serpents, and they were beginning to wriggle and slide, slithering up her arms and around her throat, slowly choking the breath from her.

How had I known? I rushed from the room in tears.

※　※　※

Just a few days later was my wedding. The evening before, miserable and anxious, I slipped out onto the balcony outside my room right after dinner. My sisters and cousins followed me, but I shooed them away. I wanted to be alone.

I started to talk to Allah, praying that Ahmed would treat me well and let me have the kind of future I had always dreamed of. I told Allah that I was trusting he would make the marriage work. But even as I was telling God that I was putting myself in his hands, my eyes were following the scrolling metalwork below me. Would it be possible to climb down? Could I collect what little money I had among my belongings and make my escape? Someone catcalled from the street below, and I pulled back from the railing. If I had been in Ruwais I might just have climbed down, but Pakistan scared me.

I went back inside and crawled into bed. As I thought about my aborted escape, the tears began again. I wondered what would happen if I went into my parents' room and begged them to take me home. Still, I stayed in my room, sleepless and weeping, for the rest of the night.

By the time the sun crept through the curtains, my pillow was a sodden lump. I got out of bed and looked at myself in the mirror. My eyes were as swollen and as red as the henna mehndi tracing up my hands and arms. I picked up the green-and-yellow dress that I had worn at my mehndi ceremony and all the days since. I was to continue wearing it until the legal papers were signed this morning. After that, I would be whisked off to a beauty salon to have my hair and makeup done before I was wrapped up in all that red chiffon.

I slipped the dress on and lay back down. I felt empty. Defeated. My crying and dread had accomplished nothing. I had to hand myself over to my destiny.

I could hear soft footsteps in the hallway. Then my father was standing by the side of the bed. He was wearing his new clothes—a white shalwar kameez—and there were tears in his eyes.

Then Papa said, "Say no, Samra. Just say no if you want to. Even now, there is time."

I sat up and looked at him. He was waiting for me to say the words. Now that he had made this offer, I had to admit that I didn't know what I wanted. I didn't want to get married, but how could I reject something that was the envy of all my friends and young cousins? I didn't want to leave my family and move away, but how could I give up the opportunities that I had been promised in Canada? I didn't want to make a decision I would regret for the rest of my life, but how could I know which decision that was? And even if I wanted to run away from the wedding, I knew I didn't have that kind of rebellious spirit. Hitting a boy in the nose was one thing. Turning my back on this wedding, ruining so many people's happiness, causing such embarrassment to my family—that was another. What I did know was that I wanted to be a good girl. My father took in my silence and then reached over and hugged me. I threw my arms around him and began to sob.

My mother entered the room as we were huddled together. "What's going on?" she asked. Her voice rang with alarm.

"I told her she could say no," my father replied. "I'll take care of it."

"We can't say no, Zafar! Think of the shame and dishonour. Everyone is already here. All the arrangements have been made." My mother sounded more frightened than angry.

My father's eyes turned towards my mother, but to my surprise, he didn't snap at her. Instead he nodded, as if he were acknowledging that his offer to me had not been realistic.

"Samra, you want this, right?" Mama continued.

I nodded.

A look of sadness and relief washed over my mother's face. Tears welled up in her eyes and spilled down her cheeks. She and I both knew she had good reasons for wanting me married. But they weren't all happy ones.

CHAPTER 2

TIME BOMB

I t was a weekend. We were in the kitchen, getting ready for a late morning meal. Papa was already sitting in his customary place as my sisters and I pulled ourselves up onto our chairs. My mother was a flurry of motion, shuttling back and forth between table and stove, putting down glasses of orange juice, a pot of steaming tea, a jar of honey. Sunlight poured through the windows, but despite the brightness, the air in the room was heavy and dark. My parents had been fighting from the moment they awoke.

My father had taken his chair just moments before, issuing a long, loud rebuttal to my mother's previous point. I'm not sure he said anything different than what he had been saying all morning, but everything in his tone broadcast that these words were his closing statement. He was the man of the house. He had spoken. They were done arguing.

My mother paused at this, standing at the table, a plate of paratha in one hand, a spatula in the other. The edges of her mouth were working furiously, as if her facial muscles were pitching their own little battle. Finally, something gave way and her mouth opened, words spilling forth.

"Zafar, no, that's just not—"

Before she could get the rest out, we felt an explosion.

"Shut up!" my father was screaming. "Don't say another word!" He was getting out of his chair, his angry face rising higher and higher like a flame.

My mother did what she was told, yet it seemed that every ounce of restraint she could muster was spent keeping her lips pressed together. There wasn't enough left over to control the fury that was channelling through her hand. She dropped the spatula on the table with more force than was necessary. It made a pronounced snap as it bounced against the Formica.

What happened next was like watching a hurricane blow through the house.

"You want to break things?" shouted my father. "I'll show you how to break things." He bent forward, sweeping his arm across the table. The air burst with noise. The watery crash of the teapot. The metallic clamour of forks against the stony floor tiles. The popping explosion of glass after glass.

My sisters and I scrambled off our chairs and backed away from the table. Papa was at the kitchen cupboards, throwing open the doors.

"No, please, Zafar," my mother begged.

But my father did not relent. His hands fell on plates, bowls, coffee cups. One after another, they took flight, landing with successive blasts, like firecrackers. The kitchen floor quickly transformed into a glinting carpet of china shards, as the cacophony of shouting, crying and shattering dishes continued for several seconds. I looked over at Warda, Saira and Bushra, huddled against the kitchen wall, shuddering with sobs.

"Come, come," I said, holding out my hand. Then I hurried out of the kitchen and over to the hall closet. I opened the door and my sisters bent down to move under the coats. I followed, pulling the door tight behind me.

"There," I said, trying to sound calm and soothing. "Safe."

My sisters continued to sniffle as we hunkered down, now insulated from the destruction by a wooden door and a layer of hanging clothes. The explosive sound of splintering porcelain continued for just a few seconds more, before being replaced by the thunder of my father's footsteps as he left the house. There was a short silence and then the soft swish of a broom across the floor, the tinkling of glass against a dustpan. I opened the closet door and reluctantly moved out into the light, coaxing my sisters to follow.

❄   ❄   ❄

That was not the first time we had hidden in the closet to avoid my parents' fights, nor would it be the last. For as long as I could remember, my parents had argued. Very often, they fought about their finances. My mother felt my father was both impulsive and reckless about money. And as I got older I too could see he didn't believe in saving: his unbridled optimism seemed to have convinced him that whatever he spent could easily be replaced in the future. While my mother returned again and again to her jewellery box, taking one piece of wedding gold and then another to sell to pay our debts, he continued to make extravagant purchases and plan expensive family vacations.

My father, of course, did not react well to my mother's criticism. And he harboured his own grudges and resentments. He often accused my mother of being distant or expressed jealous suspicions of her. When he got angry his rages were ferocious. More than once, he slapped or pushed her.

As we got older, my sisters and I weathered these storms with a certain amount of resignation. We stopped hiding in closets, shed fewer tears and came to accept that home was an unpredictable place. We might return from the calm safety of school to a happy, chatty family dinner or to a meal eaten in stony silence. We might spend the weekends making dolls' clothes with our mother or building a playhouse with our father—or we might spend hours in our bed-rooms, escaping into the comfort of homework as our parents did battle with each other in the rest of the house.

Perhaps it wasn't so surprising that our parents didn't get along. After all, the marriage had not been their choice. My mother and father were cousins, born and raised in the same tight-knit extended family in Karachi—and both sides of this family tree had decided that their marriage would strengthen the branches. The deal had been struck without any input from the prospective bride or groom.

My parents did have their happy times, however. After the worst of their fights, harmony always settled once again. Often, as I watched my father cook one of my mother's favourite dishes or my mother laugh warmly at my father's jokes, I wondered why these moments slipped away so easily.

One of the unfortunate consequences of these frequent marital skirmishes was a deep wound to our family unity. Mama and Papa each looked to their daughters for support and sympathy whenever they had a disagreement. My father had always drawn me into his camp. Bushra, the youngest, had joined me. My two middle sisters cleaved to my mother. But none of us would have chosen this type of rivalry.

Nor did we ever understand how these lines had been drawn. All I knew was that my father had always spent more time with me than my mother had. He taught me to play cricket, to cook and to tend the little vegetable garden he so loved. When he renovated the house, he enlisted me as his apprentice. What's more, he heralded all of my small accomplishments and predicted my future success with such passion that I couldn't doubt it myself.

I knew my mother loved me, and I have many happy memories of the moments we spent together. She taught me how to prepare my favourite dishes, and she spent hours showing me how to hem a dress and sew on buttons. Perhaps our happiest times were the many afternoons we worked on clothes for my baby dolls and Barbies. Yet a quiet but unbridgeable gulf separated us. Even as we moved about the kitchen, or shopped together for clothes on a weekend afternoon, we seemed to travel in concentric circles, only occasionally intersecting to occupy the same space. And when we did close the gap, it would be for unsettling reasons.

※　※　※

I stepped outside into the corridor of the apartment building, our home in the UAE before our white-stuccoed house. The long, empty hallway stretched into the distance, the high white ceiling soared above. To my four-year-old self, it felt as if the whole world were opening up before me.

Just moments earlier I had been in the living room, my father patting me on the head and pressing a few coins into my hand.

"Don't worry, beta. I called Mr. Altaf at the store. He is waiting for you."

"Can I get chips?"

"You can get whatever you want."

My mother was banging in the kitchen, her disapproval wafting in along with the percussive sounds. She did not want me going to the convenience store on the ground floor all by myself. "She's too young, Zafar."

"Nonsense," my papa said. "Samra is so smart and good. It is only one floor down. She knows the way. She can do it on her own."

I knew my father was right. I was his big girl, capable enough to buy cigarettes for him. And he was rewarding me with a treat—the chips of course, but better than that—a taste of independence.

My father had called the shopkeeper to let him know I was coming. Now, I made my way along the hall. At the end, I clattered down the stairs, my footfalls making small echoes in the cavernous stairwell. The building was empty and quiet, the way it always was on Fridays, when so many of the neighbours were at the mosque or otherwise observing Jumma prayers. And then I burst into the little shop.

A few minutes later, I was putting my fils on the counter to pay. Mr. Altaf smiled at me and told me how cute I was. He slipped me a couple of pieces of candy, as he often did. "Say hello to your papa," he said, as I left.

Now back in the hallway, clutching my chips, I headed to the stairwell, feeling taller than I had just fifteen minutes earlier. I knew the way home—up a short flight of steps to the next floor. Then straight to the door with the red garbage can standing outside it, like a squat sentinel.

Just before I reached the stairs, two teenaged girls walked into the corridor.

"Hey there," said one, "why are you taking the stairs?"

"I live on the second floor."

"Why not take the elevator?" The girl was pointing to the blue door at the end of the corridor.

I shook my head. I sometimes took the elevator when I was with my father or mother, but it had no automatic sliding doors. Instead, there was a single metal one with a small window and a big handle at the top of my reach.

"The door is too heavy for me," I said, stepping again towards the stairs.

"Don't be silly. We're going up too. We'll open the door for you." One of the girls pulled the elevator handle. They looked back at me and smiled. It seemed rude to turn down their offer. And it was a bit thrilling, this attention from two older kids.

I walked past the girls and through the open door into the elevator. But before I could turn, I heard it: the metallic thud of the door crashing shut. I spun around and lunged at the door handle. Through the glass window I could see the girls, their mouths opening and their bodies rocking with laughter. They had tricked me and were now relishing their cleverness and daring.

I tugged at the door handle, begging for them to let me out. But they turned from the door and disappeared from my sight. Alone in the elevator, the enormity of what was happening pressed in on me. I could push all the buttons I wanted, but I couldn't get out of this tight metal box. I was four, all alone, and I was trapped. I began to sob.

And then the floor started to shudder. I hadn't pressed any buttons, but the elevator was beginning to move, slowly grinding its way up as I cried and hung on. Eventually it jerked to a halt at the top floor. But the door did not open. Whoever had called it had not waited for the elevator to arrive. I pressed 2 for my floor, and the elevator began to drop. But when it finally stopped, I couldn't budge the door. Then the elevator began to rattle upward again.

When the elevator stopped this time, the door opened, and a man stood before me. I recognized a friend of my father who lived on a floor above.

"Beta, beta, what's the matter?"

Between sobs, I told him.

"I'll take you down to your papa," he assured me. He pressed the button, and we began to move again. I was still sniffling and shaking. The man crouched down and put his arms around me. My head was pressed against his chest; the heat from his embrace was reassuring and calming. Then he pulled back from me. He moved towards me again, kissing me on the cheek before shifting his head slightly. His lips came to rest on my lips. He kissed me once. And again.

I had felt safe and secure for an instant, but now that feeling was tipping away from me. No one had ever kissed me on the lips like that. There was something strange and unsettling about it. I could feel the tears welling up again.

When the elevator stopped my father's friend stood up and opened the door. I could see my papa standing beside the red bin outside our front door. I sprinted towards him.

"Samra, what's the matter?" my father asked as I crashed into his knees.

The man on the elevator explained everything. Well, almost everything. There may have been words to describe what had happened, but at four I did not have any of them.

※ ※ ※

That episode in the elevator is one of my first memories. But in truth it was for many years just a curiosity that took up little space in my emotional universe. My father's arms had received me back into safety. But as the years unfolded, cracks began to appear in that protective embrace. And it wasn't just the domestic discord that made my world less steady.

My family was at a friend's dinner party. The place was buzzing with guests: the adults arguing about Pakistani politics, the children racing through the rooms playing hide-and-seek, their hands sticky with stolen sweets. Eleven years old, I was still young enough to throw myself into the game, and I had darted into one of the bedrooms to find a spot large enough to conceal my lanky, adult-like frame.

Once in the room, however, I heard the soft thud of footsteps behind me. I knew it was not another child—the shadow that loomed over me was too large. My father? No, it was the host. *What is he doing in here?* I wondered. Before I could turn around, the man was at my back. His arm came around me, his hand pressing against my chest, his fingers fondling my breast. Frightened, I froze. In front of me was a mirror. I could see my cheeks burning red with shame and embarrassment. I wondered if I should scream. But what would I say if people rushed in? Once he let go of me, no one would believe me—and everyone would hate me for accusing a loving family man of such a thing. Before I could figure out what I should do, the man released me, and I raced back into the living room, to the security of the crowd. For the rest of the evening,

I was watchful, always making sure I was surrounded by others and keeping as far away from him as possible.

As the hour got later, people began to drift away from the party. Eventually, my family took its leave, too. But I couldn't stop thinking about what had happened. Lying in bed that night, the man's touch played over and over in my mind. My mother appeared at my door to say good night.

"Mama," I said, "can I ask you something?"

She nodded and sat on the edge of the bed. But I couldn't form my thoughts into a question. What did I want to know? Instead, I told her what had happened.

When I finished, I looked up at her face. Her brow was creased, but I couldn't decide whether she was worried or angry. We were both quiet for a few minutes.

Then Mama sighed. "Samra," she said, in a tone that conveyed concern but also disapproval. I felt a lump rise in my throat. Not disapproval of the man or of the incident, but disapproval of me.

"Samra," she said again. "You are growing up too quickly."

❈ ❈ ❈

In some ways, I suppose what my mother said had some truth in it.

I was growing up—physically at least—at a remarkable rate. I hit puberty by the time I was ten, getting my period so early that my mother hadn't gotten around to telling me anything about it. (If a slightly older neighbourhood friend hadn't filled me in, as well as explained the basic mechanics of sex, I would have been taken completely by surprise.) By the time I was twelve, I was five foot eight, with full breasts and the figure of a young woman.

Now whenever we returned to the crowded cities of Pakistan for holidays or family visits, I couldn't walk outside without being assaulted by whistles and lascivious invitations. The streets of

Ruwais were quieter and safer, but unwanted attention was aimed at me in more clandestine ways.

When I was thirteen, my father engaged a local imam to come to the house to tutor me in the Koran. The imam was a stately older man. His white shalwar kameez and skullcap complemented his long white beard and his solemn expression. Even as he pedalled down the street to our house on his rickety bike, his demeanour was as stiff and imperial as if he were arriving on a great white stallion.

The imam and I would sit side by side at the dining room table with the Koran open before us, as the aroma of my mother's curries drifted in from the kitchen. Wearing a long hijab, I recited the passages that I had memorized, while the imam followed along in the text to catch any errors. Whenever I stumbled or made a mistake, he would reach over and tug my ear.

But after a few weeks of these lessons, his hand began to fall after each tug, dropping in front of my chest. Not long after that, his hand began to brush the front of my blouse. It started to linger there for a second each time he tugged my ear. With every touch, once his hand dropped he'd pull himself up straight, his eyes focusing on the holy book before us, a smirk playing across his face. He would continue the lesson with an air of earnest piety and then take his leave.

And then one evening, his fingers swiftly pinched my nipple. With the earlier touching, I had always stiffened and moved back as far as I could in my chair. With the pinching, I jerked upright. I wanted to slap his hand away, but he had moved so swiftly there wasn't time.

I decided I had had enough. As the imam rode off that evening, I went to my father and told him what was happening.

My father's face darkened. "Don't worry," he said. "I will deal with this."

When the time rolled around for my next session, I stayed outside on the front lawn instead of waiting at the dining room table. As the imam cycled up to the house, he looked put out. "What are you

doing out here?" he said as he got off his bike. "You should be ready
for the lesson."

"My father wants to talk to you first—in private." I couldn't keep a
small grin from my face.

The imam disappeared into the house. I heard my father's voice
booming from inside. And then the imam reappeared. His face was
red and his eyes were focused on the pavement. He scurried over to
his bike, clambered on and pedalled furiously away, his white shalwar
kameez flapping in the wind. It was the last I ever saw of him.

The next year, the sports lessons I loved so much had to be
abandoned as well after the teacher leaned towards me one day
and suggested that we might spend some time together doing other
enjoyable "activities."

And then came the summer I was fifteen. My whole family went
to Karachi for the wedding of my father's brother, Ali. In all, we would
spend about two months there, staying with various relatives and
attending a non-stop round of family celebrations. It was a wonderful
time, all the cousins and aunts and uncles enjoying the lengthy family
reunion. There was only one dark spot: Aunt Nasreen's husband, Aziz.

My sisters, my cousins and I had always found the man a bit
creepy. He seemed to pay too much attention to us, to be too interested
in watching the games we played or the dances we choreographed for
the parties. He and my aunt lived next door to my grandfather, and
he always showed up where you least expected him—outside a bedroom door or in a narrow hallway or, once, in a hospital ward.

A few weeks into our visit, I ended up at the emergency room with
dehydration. (The water in Pakistan always made my sisters and me
ill.) I was lying on a gurney, hooked up to an IV, when Aunt Nasreen
and Uncle Aziz appeared in the doorway. My uncle walked to the foot
of the bed and slipped his hand under the sheets to touch my foot.

"How are you doing, Samra?" he said. He had a sly smile on his
face, but my aunt didn't seem to notice anything wrong.

I didn't answer. I was too distracted. His hand had moved from my foot and was sliding up my leg. I pulled my knees up, trying to move my legs out of reach.

"What's the matter, Samra?" His voice was cloying. He moved his hand from under the sheet to pat my arm and then brush his fingers across my cheek. Perhaps it would have seemed innocent to an onlooker, but there was something sinister and insinuating in his touch.

When my mother came by later, I told her about it. "Just cover yourself properly and stay away from him" was her advice.

As the weeks passed, I managed to do that—until one afternoon, when my family was at Aunt Nasreen and Uncle Aziz's house. My aunt was a school principal and teacher, and the two of them had an extensive library on the second floor.

"Are you looking for something to read?" my uncle asked me as we all got up from the lunch table. "You should go upstairs and check out what we've got there."

I was getting a little bored with all the visiting, and the thought of losing myself in a novel was too tempting to ignore. I had just sat down with a book in one of the big upholstered chairs when my uncle appeared. He shut the door behind him.

"Why are you closing the door?" I asked.

"So you won't be disturbed while you are reading." The words were hardly out of his mouth before he disappeared behind my chair and slipped his arm around me, cupping my breast.

I jumped up, shaking him off as I bolted from the room. For the rest of the visit, I made sure we were never alone in the same room.

※　※　※

All these incidents bothered me. But despite my mother's concern that I was growing up too quickly, I resisted feeling that I was somehow to blame. I had seen women in full burkas being groped or pinched while they stood in the crowded Karachi marketplace. They had clearly not invited any advances, and neither had I. And yet, oddly, this did not make me feel in any real danger. Perhaps because I was young and hopeful and felt a certain sense of power and independence, I assumed that if I stayed on my toes in the future, I could avoid the groping and touching—or at least I could stop it in its tracks.

Certainly, by the time Uncle Ali's wedding was over, I was well aware of the need to make sure I was never alone with dodgy men like Uncle Aziz. And I had managed to defend myself more effectively during another incident on that same trip. One afternoon, I was at one of the local outdoor markets with my sisters and cousins. We all crowded around a jewellery vendor's table, choosing which brightly coloured bangles we wanted to wear at the celebration. Suddenly I felt a hand press against my bottom. I whirled around to face the man who had just caressed me. Without a thought, I slapped him across the face—hard. His mouth dropped open as he raised his hand to his burning cheek. His friends burst out laughing as my sisters and cousins gasped in surprise and delight. They had felt the man's touch too but had been too scared to do anything.

All the way home, my sisters and cousins marvelled at my daring. And I had to admit—I was brimming with self-satisfaction. I *could* take care of myself.

My mother didn't seem so sure.

After I told her about the incident at the dinner party, her solution had been to leave me at home whenever my family attended a social gathering with the man and his family. (Eventually, I was allowed to go to the dinner parties and picnics again, but my mother cautioned me against talking to anyone about what had happened.) Now, hearing the story of my uncle in the library, she seemed to realize that protective social isolation wasn't realistic—and that clearly worried her. I noticed that she began to watch me with concern as I headed off on my bike or boarded a bus to the shopping mall.

I tried to assure her that I would be all right.

"You can't be sure of that," she said. "Anything can happen at any time."

It was as if, when my mother looked at me, she saw a time bomb, waiting to go off.

※　※　※

When we returned to Ruwais after our summer in Pakistan, my mother made a new friend.

Her name was Fatima. She was slightly younger than my mom, with four children all a bit younger than me. Fatima almost immediately came to be like family to us. She called my mother bhabhi, or brother's wife, and my sisters and I called her Fatima-aunty. As the months unfolded, Fatima became a constant presence in our home. She was particularly attentive to me, often telling me how tall and beautiful I was, sometimes even stroking my cheek as she complimented me. She chatted with me about my friends and what I was doing in school. When she discovered I had a big art assignment, she confessed that she had always loved art and asked if I wanted her help. We had a great time working together, so I wasn't surprised when she offered to teach me how to make some of my favourite desserts. I baked a cheesecake for the first time under Fatima's watchful eye.

Perhaps because my mother and I were not especially close, I devoured this attention from an older woman and was delighted every time Fatima walked through our door.

My mother seemed perfectly happy that Fatima was taking me under her wing. By the time the new year arrived, Fatima's involvement seemed to create a sort of bridge between my mother and me. I noticed that Mama would often ask me what I wanted her to make for dinner—and even unprompted, she started to serve my favourite foods with surprising regularity. In the evenings, she began to come into my room while I was studying, bringing me snacks or offering to massage my head with oil to help me relax. On the weekends, she took me shopping for books and new clothes.

I had always been jealous of the attention my mother lavished on my younger sisters. I had my father's favour, it was true, and there was some comfort in that. But it had never been enough. I loved the way Fatima sought out my company, but my mother's tenderness was slaking a thirst I'd had for years.

One evening, as I sat at my desk bent over my math homework, my mother walked into the room. She had a glass of juice in her hand. As she set it down beside me, she placed her other hand on my head and gently stroked my hair.

"Can you take a little break, Samra?" she asked softly. "I want to talk with you about a few things."

I pushed my books away and turned to her as she settled on the edge of my bed.

"How are you getting along with Fatima?"

It seemed an odd question. She knew that I liked her friend. I told her about how much fun I had cooking with Fatima, about some of the things Fatima had offered to teach me to make. My mother was nodding and smiling.

"You know, she thinks of you as a younger sister." That made me smile in turn. "Did she mention that she has a brother in Canada?" I nodded. My mother paused. And then, "She says you would make the perfect wife for him."

It was as if someone had knocked me down. For a few moments I was so disoriented that I forgot to breathe. When I could finally get some words out, I realized that I had been sitting there with my mouth wide open.

"What?" I gasped. "What are you talking about?"

"You're so beautiful, Fatima says. And you're both so tall." My mother continued, talking quickly and not looking at me, as if she had rehearsed this little speech.

"I told her when she first suggested the idea that you were far too young. And too ambitious. I told her that this was not a good time, that you had plans for university. But Fatima says that isn't a problem. She says that her brother, her parents, the whole family are very progressive, very broad-minded. She says her mother married at fourteen but continued school afterwards. She says they would never stop your education."

"But, Mama . . . " I started to protest.

"Samra, this would be such a great opportunity for you. I know your teachers say you can get scholarships to schools in England, but what does that matter? How could we send you to a foreign country to live on your own? No girl in our family has ever done that. You couldn't live unchaperoned. If you were married to a Canadian, you could go to a good Canadian university, you could—"

"But Fatima's brother—he's so old . . ."

"He's only twenty-seven," said my mother. "And he earns a very good living. Computers. And—"

"I don't care about that," I said. "I'm not ready to be married—to anyone!"

I still felt shocked by the conversation we were having, but I had found my voice. My mother heard it.

She clasped her hands in her lap and then sighed. "Okay," she said, as she began to stand up. "Don't worry about it. It was just an idea. Maybe it's something you might consider in a few years."

As my mother walked out of the room, I let out a long breath. I pulled my books back in front of me and picked up a pencil, glad to put the absurd conversation behind me.

CHAPTER 3

THE PROPOSAL

My mother left my bedroom that night suggesting I had at least a few more years before I had to grapple with the idea of marriage. But neither she nor Fatima had any intention of waiting that long.

My mother brought up the proposal the very next day. Then the next. And the next. She returned to the idea of university abroad. My teachers had talked to me about applying to the best schools in the world: Oxford, Cambridge, Harvard, Stanford. Now my mother began to sow doubts.

"Even if we could find you a safe place to live in any of those cities, what if you don't get into those schools? You'd be left with Pakistan. Do you really want to go to university in Karachi or Lahore when you could go to an excellent school in Canada?"

My mother knew that the UAE had no prestigious universities we could afford—and that the prospect of attending school in Pakistan, living with relatives, was one I did not relish. And maybe she was right. Why did I feel such confidence that I would get into any of those distinguished places? It wasn't as if I knew of any other students who had gone. Perhaps this was just wishful thinking on my teachers' part.

"Samra, you know what happens when a woman waits too long," said my mother. I understood that she was referring to my aunt, the school principal. Aunt Nasreen had rebuffed all of her family's attempts to find her a spouse when she was a young woman. Instead she went to university, got her teacher's training and started to work.

"Before she knew it, she was forty. And there were no offers!" my mother reminded me. "Look who she ended up with because of that!"

The spectre my mother called forth was a deeply disconcerting one. After the summer months in Karachi, I was well aware of my aunt's dismal predicament. She had her career, but her lack of options had left her locked in a childless, loveless marriage with a man who, it turned out, could not be trusted around young girls.

"No good man is still available to older women," my mother insisted.

Not long after this conversation, Aunt Nasreen herself called to speak to me.

"Listen to me, Samra," she said pleadingly. "Don't give up a marriage proposal to go to school. Look at what happened to me." She reiterated what my mother had told me: "The best proposals come when you are young. You'll get more later, but they won't be as good." I could hear the sadness in her voice.

"Men aren't usually okay with their wives studying after they get married, so if he says you can go to school after the wedding, jump at this chance."

My aunt's words carried the force of bitter experience and regret. But what she said next slipped into my thoughts and could not be dislodged.

"Even if he doesn't let you go, it doesn't matter. The most important thing is that a woman get married."

❄ ❄ ❄

Over the coming weeks, my mother also broached the delicate matter of the male attention I had been getting.

"Think about what happened with your uncle this summer, Samra." My mother's tone was genuinely concerned. I thought of how uneasy and nervous she'd been since I had become a teenager.

"This kind of thing will happen again and again until you are safely married," she said. "Next time you might not be so lucky. It's so easy for a single woman's life to be ruined by a man."

And finally, my mother invoked a higher power. "This marriage proposal is Allah's gift—his way of keeping you out of danger. If you say no, you will be showing your lack of faith in Allah, and you'll surely be punished."

Fatima's approach was a little different but no more subtle. In the weeks after my mother had first told me about the proposal, Fatima's visits to our home became even more frequent. She brought along photographs of Ahmed to show me.

"You see what a beautiful couple you will make," she said. "Both so tall and good-looking."

Fatima also talked about how wonderful her brother was—smart, kind, witty and open-minded. "I'm so sure you will like him, Samra," she said. "Why don't you exchange emails with him? Get to know him?"

I didn't want to appear unreasonable or churlish, so I gave Fatima my email address. She gave me Ahmed's, too, but I wasn't about to write to him first.

When Ahmed's first email arrived, it was friendly and brief. He said that I sounded like a nice girl. He would like to get to know me. He asked what my favourite colour was. What I liked to eat.

I responded even more succinctly. Black. Pizza.

He wrote back to say that pizza was one of his favourite foods, too.

❋ ❋ ❋

Struggling with an onslaught of advice about the proposal, I sought out the support of my friends. I knew that most of these girls were much more interested in the topic of marriage than I had ever been. Every time one of them came back from the wedding of a relative or family friend, our conversations would be dominated for days by descriptions of the bridal dress or jewellery or decorations. But I assumed that, like me, they saw marriage as part of their distant future.

Sitting in the student lounge during our lunch break, I produced a photo of Ahmed that Fatima had given me and told my friends of the bizarre conversations I'd been having with my mother. Their shrieks of surprise were quickly followed by a volley of questions about Ahmed and then expressions of delight and envy.

"You're so lucky!" they said, one after another.

I could barely believe what I was hearing. "I'm only sixteen," I protested.

"But you could go to Canada!" one of them said.

"And he's so tall and handsome," someone else chimed in.

"But I don't want to get married." No one seemed to understand me.

"Are you crazy? If I had a proposal like that, I'd jump at it," said another girl. Everyone was nodding. I looked around at all my dear friends but couldn't find a hint of doubt in their faces. The bell rang.

"Samra, don't be stupid. This is a great thing," said someone, as we collected our books and prepared to go to class. All I could do was smile ruefully at her.

I seemed to be surrounded by a chorus of voices. The song they sang grew louder, with messages from my cousins in Pakistan exclaiming about my good luck and aunties weighing in on the "great news." It was confusing to be so terrified and doubtful while everyone else was cheering my good fortune—as if I were complaining about the weight of gold coins in my purse.

I began to wonder about the future I had predicted for myself. My father and many of my teachers had been telling me for years that I was talented and special. I had become convinced that I would be able to do things a little differently than the women I saw around me—that I could have it all. But what made me think I would escape my aunt's fate? I still didn't believe that marriage was "a girl's purpose," but did I want to be single for the rest of my life? After all, an unmarried, childless woman invited nothing but pity and derision. No matter what else she accomplished, she would be considered a failure. Failure was something I had never been able to handle. The very prospect was terrifying. And yet it seemed that the path I had been carving out for myself might be paved with it.

When my English teacher, Ms. Harr, gave the class a creative writing assignment, I knew immediately what I was going to write about. I had gone to bed almost every night imagining what it would be like if I accepted the proposal. I wrote the piece about sitting on a bed in my red-and-gold silk wedding clothes, with the serpent bangles creeping up to choke me.

The day after I handed it in, Ms. Harr asked to talk with me at the end of class. Once the rest of the students had left the room, she asked me to come with her to her office.

"What's going on, Samra?"

I told her about the proposal.

Finally, someone else looked as shocked as I felt. "You are just sixteen. How in the world can you be thinking about this?"

But Ms. Harr's outrage somehow made me feel defensive. I found myself repeating all the arguments that had been made to me. And I added a few of my own. "His family are very nice people. And he's so similar to me. He's tall, and he likes pizza."

Ms. Harr sighed. Her look of concern had not eased.

"I am very mature for my age. I can handle this," I said defiantly.

"Yes, you are mature. But you are also a child," she said firmly.

※ ※ ※

Despite my mother's excitement and all the talk about "the proposal," my family had not actually had an offer of marriage. That formality would come only once Ahmed's parents had met my family and approved of me.

A few weeks after my talk with Ms. Harr, I learned that Ahmed's parents were travelling from their home in Kuwait to visit Fatima and to meet me.

Our house became abuzz with preparations. My mother thought it would be an excellent idea if I showed Fatima's parents that I enjoyed cooking. She hovered over me as I prepared chicken puffs and samosas, explaining that it was also important that I made myself look as attractive as I could.

The afternoon of the dinner, I put on a shalwar kameez and dupatta. I straightened my hair and put on a little makeup. I had been told that my presence in the living room would not be required immediately. I was to eat in the kitchen with my sisters until I was summoned.

I sat at the table, mute with nerves, as my sisters chatted excitedly about the strangers in the living room. Then Fatima appeared in the doorway.

"Are you excited to meet your future in-laws?" Her voice was teasing, but only my sisters giggled. I tried to smile.

"Don't be nervous—they already like you," she said even though we had not yet met. "Just say salaam when you go in, and make sure that you behave shyly. Don't talk a lot, but be yourself."

I wanted to point out that her last two directives were completely contradictory, but for once words escaped me.

Then I noticed Fatima's brow crease as she stared intently at my face. "You aren't wearing enough makeup," she said. "Come to the bedroom, and I'll do it for you."

In my room, she pulled out eyeliner and put a long, dark sweep across my lids. Then she went through my makeup bag and plucked out the darkest lipstick I had. When she was done, she pulled back and looked at me with satisfaction.

"Now you look older," she said. "Time to take you in."

I stood up and draped the dupatta over my head. We went back to the kitchen, where I picked up the tea tray.

As I followed Fatima into the living room, I felt as if I were an actress walking onto a stage. Fatima had taken care of my makeup and given me direction. Now it was my turn to play the part as convincingly as I could. I kept my head lowered, but as I stepped into the room I could see Fatima's parents. Her mother was sitting by her side in the middle of the sofa. Her father was in a chair next to them. Her mother reminded me faintly of an older version of Fatima. My only thought about her father was that with his white hair and grey complexion he looked vastly older than Papa.

I moved towards them, lowering the tea tray onto the coffee table in front of the sofa.

"Please serve our guests, Samra," my mother said.

I sank demurely onto the floor beside the coffee table and with a trembling hand lifted the teapot. "Aunty, how much sugar and milk do you take?"

As I prepared each cup of tea, I tried to keep my hands from shaking. I could feel all eyes on me, as if the way I poured the tea or how I spooned sugar into the cups could convey all that was important about me.

After everyone had their tea, I sat down beside my mother.

"No, Samra. Come sit with me," said Fatima's mother. She was patting a spot that she and Fatima had made between them. I looked at my mother. She nodded.

Once I had settled between the two women, Fatima's father started to ask me questions. What was I studying in school now? What did I want to study in the future?

It was a relief to talk about something I truly cared about. But I hadn't got very far in my explanations when Fatima's mother cut me off.

"Enough about school. Tell me, what dishes do you like to cook?"

I had just begun to answer that question, when my mother interrupted me. I could hear the nervous excitement in her voice. "Samra really loves cooking. She made the chicken puffs we had tonight, of course, but she also makes biryani and amazing rotis. And she loves trying new recipes. Just the other day—"

"She also plays cricket and squash," my father cut in.

The room went silent. Fatima's father took a long sip of tea and then put down his cup.

"Oh yes, sports are great for the young, but of course Samra won't be able to do that for very much longer."

Before my father could respond, Fatima's mother had grabbed my hand and pulled it towards her. "Now, let's see what size ring you would wear."

She slipped off her own ring and shoved it onto my finger. It spun around easily. "Hmmm," she said, taking the ring off my hand and putting it back on hers. Next she slid one of her bangles onto my wrist and then lifted my elbow. The bangle dropped off. "She's very thin," she exclaimed, "but that's a good thing. Women always put on weight after they have children."

Everyone chuckled politely.

"And it's good she's so fair. Of course, we have been meeting other girls, but we are looking for a fair and tall daughter-in-law."

In the weeks leading up to Eid, the local markets were always filled with live sheep and goats. My family and other faithful would purchase an animal, bring it home to fatten it up for a while, and then slaughter it on Eid to honour Allah and prepare a feast. I had never thought much about the activity in the market, the way that people inspected a goat's teeth or ran their hands through the thick fleece on a sheep. But now I thought I had a sense of what those poor animals must feel like—being poked and prodded and judged. Fatima's parents didn't appear to be the least bit interested in getting to know me. What they seemed to be looking for was an attractive, well-mannered broodmare.

Fatima's mother still had her hand in my hair and was murmuring about its softness when her husband cleared his throat and said, "Time for the adults to talk now."

I stood up with relief, said my goodbyes and escaped to my bedroom. I tried to calm myself as I sat at my desk, my homework spread in front of me. But the math questions seemed to be floating above the page—impossible to read. I could hear the muted sound of quiet talk in the living room.

I realized, as I strained to make out the words, that although I had hated every second of the inspection, I wanted Fatima's parents to like me. And while part of me was hoping they would reject me so that I could return to my old life, part of me, perhaps the bigger part, yearned for their approval. I had not willingly entered this contest, but now that I was in it I wanted to win.

I couldn't tell what was being said, but not long after I'd gone to my room, Fatima was in the doorway, telling me to come say goodbye to her parents.

I returned to the living room, where Fatima's father patted my head with fatherly approval. "Okay, beta," he said, "goodbye. Take care."

Once Fatima and her parents were out the door, my mother let out a big sigh.

"I don't care what they think," my father said. "Our daughter is one in a million. What's the rush? She'll get plenty of proposals."

"None like this," my mother replied testily.

"That is *not* the purpose of her life!" my father snapped. But my mother wasn't listening. She had disappeared into the kitchen with the tea tray.

※　※　※

A few hours later, the phone rang. My mother picked it up in her room. I could hear her voice clearly through the open door.

"That's wonderful," she said. Her tone was exuberant. I knew she was talking with Fatima. I felt a little flutter of excitement and then my chest grew tight.

When my mother got off the phone, she came into my room, where I was sitting frozen in anticipation. "Congratulations! They like you! They want to set a date for the engagement."

Fatima's parents liked me. I had won the prize. A husband *and* a Canadian education. But the frisson of delight I felt when I first heard my mother on the phone had disappeared in a crest of panic and dread. I didn't really want this. But how could I say no now?

We went into the living room to tell my father. He was not as quiet as I was at the news. "No," he said to my mother. "This is not the right time. Samra is too young. She needs to go to university first."

"Zafar," my mother shot back, "Samra has agreed to this already."

"Really?" he asked, turning to me. "Samra, are you really sure?"

"Yes, she's sure," my mother insisted. "We've talked about this. She knows this is the best thing for her."

As my parents continued—my father's voice increasingly loud and laden with swear words, my mother's quiet but nasty—I retreated to my room. Suddenly, I was exhausted. I crawled under the covers of my bed, falling asleep to the familiar sound of my parents' fighting.

I woke up the next morning to my mother's voice. She was on the phone again. She sounded apologetic. "I'm sorry, but she's really too young. And she needs to go to university." She was parroting my father's arguments.

I threw the covers off and scrambled out of bed. I was at once flooded with relief and overcome with concern that I might be missing out on a great opportunity.

When I got to my mother, she was just hanging up the phone. "I've turned down the offer for now," she said to me. Her face was shadowed with conflicting concerns. I could sense that she felt guilty about the pressure she had exerted on me, worried about sending me so far away, but fearful too that we might be throwing away a golden opportunity.

"Fatima's parents want to come to the house again tonight to talk with us some more," she said. "Perhaps your father is right, but if you think you want to go through with the engagement, you need to talk to him."

The truth was I didn't know what I wanted. But I also knew that I no longer trusted my father wholeheartedly, the way I once had. My teen years had created some distance between us. I didn't like the way he treated my mother, and I knew his decisions were often flawed. I wasn't prepared to let him make this one for me.

When my father came home from work, I cornered him.

"Papa," I said pleadingly, "I want to meet Fatima's parents again. I'm afraid that I might be throwing away my best chance to go to school abroad. What if I never get another offer this good?"

That evening, my aunt also called to talk with my father. By the time the sun set, it had been agreed that we would once again host Fatima's parents and listen to what they had to say about my possible future.

᠅ ᠅ ᠅

The tenor of this evening was entirely different from the first. That earlier meeting had been about Fatima's parents choosing a future bahu, a daughter-in-law. (It seemed clear, in retrospect, that it was more important they liked me than that their son did.) But now they needed to show that they would be a good family for me.

I was in the living room with everyone right from the start, as were my sisters. This time no one examined me or asked me about cooking or other domestic accomplishments. Fatima's mother looked at me instead with great warmth and affection. And she was eager to talk about school—in particular, my university education.

"Of course she will go to school in Canada. If it's important to her, it's important to us," Fatima's mother insisted, while Fatima's father nodded in agreement.

"We have always been strong proponents of education for women." She went on to talk about several of the women in their extended family and the education they had completed. "And Ahmed is very progressive on this issue," she added.

It was what I needed to hear. Even my father looked a little more comfortable.

Fatima's mother continued to charm us all. "Don't worry," she said to my parents. "You know, she would be our daughter. We would love her even more than you do, because she is the one who will continue our family. She will be so important to us."

Fatima appealed directly to me. "Samra, you know I already consider you a sister. But am I not also your good friend? I only want what is best for you. This match will be such a good thing for you—marriage and a wonderful education! Two birds with one stone!"

My mother looked over at me as if to say, "Isn't this great?"

By the time the evening was drawing to a close, Fatima and her parents had made a powerful case for the bright life I might lead if I joined their son in Canada. And my mother and I were swept away by their kind words and warm reassurances. My mother told Fatima and her parents that we would be happy to set an engagement date.

The following evening, Fatima's parents came back for a third visit. This time, Fatima's beaming mother asked me to sit beside her once again. When I was settled, she took my head in her hands and pulled me towards her. She kissed me gently on the forehead.

"You are my daughter now," she said, with great emotion in her voice. Then she took my hand and slipped a huge gold and zirconium ring on my ring finger. "Isn't it beautiful?" she asked.

In truth, I had never seen such an ugly ring. But I nodded politely.

The conversation soon turned to the wedding itself. As we nibbled on mithai and sipped tea, Fatima and her mother talked enthusiastically about the plans. I was startled to hear that the nikah would happen in July, just six months away. That ceremony, to be held in Karachi where both sides had extended family, involved the signing of wedding contracts and would be preceded by the two mehndi parties. But the rukhsati—the part of the wedding in which the bride leaves her family to join her husband—would not be held on the same day, as it traditionally was. Instead, I would stay behind to finish my final year of high school, living with my family, and Ahmed would return to Canada while my immigration paperwork was approved. Once that was done, we'd set a date for the rukhsati, likely a year after the nikah. Hearing that I would have all that time at home, I felt my pulse slow slightly.

Then the conversation shifted to the details of the nikah. All of our family celebrations, even the weddings, tended to be relatively modest and low-key. But despite the fact that my parents would be paying the bills, the nikah plans Fatima and her mother were proposing were splashy and extravagant. My mother's smiles became more anxious as the evening wore on. My father looked increasingly sober. My sisters were simply restless, wanting to get away from the adult conversation and back to their play.

I sat stiffly, unable to tear my eyes away from the ring on my finger. What had I done?

❀　❀　❀

I walked to school slowly the next day, embarrassment and uncertainty weighting my steps. I wished I had left the ring at home, but Fatima had told me I must never take it off—that would be bad luck. I was hoping that somehow the teachers and students wouldn't notice the large, sparkly bauble on my finger. But of course that was impossible.

As soon as I stepped into the schoolyard, a friend approached, took one look at my hand and burst out with, "You're so lucky!" And then I was surrounded by a cluster of girls, all twittering with excitement.

There was no hope that I might keep my new status from the school population at large. Fatima's daughter spotted me during the lunch break that first day and ran up to me, shouting, "Samra-mumani!" She was identifying me in that one honorific as her uncle's new wife. Before the week was out the whole school knew that I was soon to be someone's bride.

And then my world began to shift.

A few days after my engagement I walked outside into the school-yard at recess, looking for my friends. Standing in a huddle at the side of the yard, they started to giggle as soon as they noticed my approach.

"What's up?" I asked them.

"Samra, you know you really shouldn't be hanging out with us anymore," said one of them. "You're going to be married."

"What's that got to do with it? I'm still me," I said.

"Not really," piped in another friend. "You belong to someone else now."

I was both stunned and angry at her words. But my old friends seemed to feel solidarity on this subject, and I began to stay in at recess to avoid their laughter and whispers.

Even in class, I could feel the difference. Boys who had spoken with me calmly and casually in the hallways or the student lounge now avoided me. My old study partner, a Bangladeshi girl who could always match me in the intensity of her work, told me she thought we should part ways. She couldn't be convinced that I was still commit-ted to my studies.

"Why do you care about school, now that you're going to be married?"

The news quickly reached all of the teachers, too. My principal, an Arabic man, congratulated me, but he was the only one. The rest of the largely British and European faculty were clearly shocked. Ms. Harr's dismay was tempered with kindness. It was her room in which I sought refuge during the lonely recesses and lunches. Other teachers, who knew my parents socially, telephoned the house to talk with them. I could hear my mother defending the decision and explaining the significant educational advantages I would have in Canada.

By the time the school year finished in May, I had become a little island, my friends and former social life now far offshore. My only visitor was Fatima, who took to her role of future sister-in-law with relish. During her regular visits to our house, she talked to me about the wedding plans—about the colour of dress she thought I would look good in or the way I might do my hair.

She also began to give me instructions on how to behave as an engaged woman. I needed to leave my childish fashions behind— jeans and T-shirts were no longer appropriate. When I wasn't in my school uniform, I should always wear a shalwar kameez. I would have to stop playing tennis, squash and cricket. A married woman should have no interest in sports.

And the boys at school were right—they were strictly off limits. Even the most casual encounters, like studying together in the library, would raise eyebrows now, Fatima advised.

I bristled at all these instructions, but I followed them. For months, I had been basking in the attention Fatima lavished on me. I didn't want to disappoint her. What's more, while I didn't care about the bridal dress or the wedding buffet, I did care about my future. I filled my now-empty hours imagining myself walking through a cool, green campus, my arms loaded with books, my mind thrumming with new ideas. Sometimes I placed myself at the front of a classroom, lecturing to a room of medical students. This was what lay at the end of the wedding plans. This was where marriage would lead me. Yet Fatima hinted repeatedly that this opportunity was mine to lose.

"There were so many candidates for Ahmed. You have no idea how many girls we had to disappoint when we chose you. He is such a good catch. You are so fortunate."

Even now that we had set a wedding date, failure was apparently still quite possible.

※　※　※

Fatima's attention became more disconcerting in another way as well.

She had invited me over to her house for a sleepover. It was late; Fatima's own children were in bed, fast asleep. Fatima had hauled two mattresses onto the living room floor so we could chat together before shutting our eyes. We were curled up under the covers, talking about my future move to Canada. I was, of course, talking about university.

"Yes, I'm sure it will happen," Fatima said quietly, "but on the off chance that it doesn't, what then?" There was a hint of impatience in her voice.

"What do you mean?" I said. "That's what everyone has promised."

"You just have to realize that the *real* importance of a woman's life is the care of the home and to be a wife," Fatima said. "You should be excited you are getting there sooner than some. That's what you should be happy about."

As I lay in the unfamiliar bed that night, doubt kept me from drifting off. By the time I rose in the morning, I was exhausted and nervous.

To Fatima, the wedding was all-important. One day, as I was cycling past her house, my front wheel caught a jagged piece of asphalt, wrenching the bike from underneath me. As I picked myself off the road, I felt a stab of pain in my shoulder and saw blood seeping through my blouse. I pushed my bike over to Fatima's front door.

When Fatima saw me, she let out a little shriek. "What has happened to your face?" she said with alarm.

"It's my shoulder," I said. "I think I really hurt it."

"You've got a big scrape on your cheek!" she continued. "What if it leaves a scar? How are we going to cover that up for the wedding?"

She agreed to drive me to a clinic so a doctor could look at my shoulder, but she couldn't stop fussing about my face. For days after the accident, she came by the house to consult with my mother about the various creams and ointments I should be using to make sure the scrape healed as quickly as possible.

※　※　※

I was becoming more anxious day by day. And it wasn't only the fear that my educational dreams might not come true.

My social isolation was making me realize that I would be giving up other hopes and expectations. I had had brief crushes on boys and had always assumed that I would meet someone special in one of my university classes. I had, like any teenager, imagined what it would be like to feel my heart beat faster, to give myself over to romance, to fall in love. I imagined myself choosing my future love, and him choosing me. Now this would never happen. I began to see loss after loss in my future. Why had I allowed myself to be so easily convinced that this marriage was my best chance for happiness? Was it just because I wanted to succeed so badly?

I started sleeping poorly, lying in bed awake for hours and hours, only to succumb to nightmares once I drifted off. One night I had an especially vivid dream. I was standing in front of an imposing old build-ing surrounded by a tall wrought-iron fence. I knew it was a university building. I put my hand on the gate and tugged, but it held fast. As I pulled at the locked, unbudging metal, I noticed that I was wearing red-and-gold wedding clothes. I pulled harder and harder as I began to sob.

My tears woke me up and I called out to my mother. When she came into the room, I was still crying. "I'm so scared," I told her. "I don't know Ahmed at all. What if he isn't who he says he is? What if he's mean?"

My mother tried to calm me, but I could not be consoled. Finally she said, "Why don't you talk to him and ask him yourself?"

My mother left my room and came back with the phone. She dialled Ahmed's number in Canada and asked if I could speak with him for a few minutes.

When she handed me the phone, I didn't wait to hear anything from Ahmed. Instead I blurted out my questions. "You won't stop me, will you? You'll let me go to school when I get to Canada?"

Ahmed responded immediately. "Of course I will, Samra. You have every right to make your own decisions."

It was the first time I had heard Ahmed's voice. It was soft and gentle. Reassuring. "Whichever university you want to go to, we'll go. I can get a job anywhere. If we have to move, we'll move."

"Thank you," I said, and then handed the phone back to my mother. I could hear Ahmed reassuring my mother as well before she hung up the phone.

"See?" she said to me. "Everything is going to be fine. Now go back to sleep."

When I got up the next morning, I felt better than I had in days, but my nervousness had been replaced with a certain sad wistfulness. My gaze fanned around the room—the desk with my books, the bookshelf with my awards, the dresser with my squash racket leaning against it. The familiar landscape suddenly looked precious and ephemeral. Soon it would no longer be mine. It belonged to a schoolgirl.

I was about to become a married woman.

CHAPTER 4

RUKHSATI

I moved through the entirety of my long wedding day like an automaton. The morning was a blur of small preparations. In the early afternoon, at my grandfather's house, the men crowded into the living room with Ahmed, and the women accompanied me upstairs to one of the bedrooms. I was led to a bed, where I sat in a stupor. Every corner of the house was filled with fresh roses—the perfume that I had enjoyed so much at other weddings now seemed cloyingly surreal.

I was barely aware of what was being said by the women who hovered around me, but then they parted like a cloud, and my father's younger brother and the imam stood before me. Uncle Ali put the marriage papers in my lap.

His deep voice rolled towards me. "I, Mohammed Ali, as your representative, ask you, Samra Zafar, for your permission to give you away in marriage to Ahmed Khan, with 50,000 rupees in mahr. Do you accept?"

I was supposed to say *yes*, and then the exchange would be repeated two more times.

But my tongue was frozen. I sat looking at the documents in my lap, my blurred vision framed by the red veil that shaded the sides of my face.

My uncle repeated the words, and a chorus of small *yeses* grew from the women around me, as if they were showing me how to pronounce the word. Still unable to make a sound, I nodded instead. An audible sigh of relief fluttered through the room.

Uncle Ali put a pen in my hand. My hand was shaking so hard that the pen bounced out of it and onto the floor. When he put it in my hand the next time, I closed my trembling fingers around it as quickly as I could. I held it over the papers, over the spot my uncle was pointing to, but it was as if my hand were some sort of tool I had no idea how to operate. *Write my name* I told it. *Write Samra Zafar.* In jerking motions I applied ink to the paper, and when I was done, the women in the room started applauding.

"Good girl," said my mother.

The women were now embracing and congratulating each other. Then an arm came around my shoulders. Ahmed's mother was pulling me to her side in a hug that felt more like an act of possession than an expression of affection.

"She's officially ours," she crowed to my mother.

An icy chill ran through me.

❧ ❧ ❧

An hour later, Aunt Nasreen and I stepped through the beauty salon doors into a busy hum. A dozen brides were already seated in the chairs that dotted the place; excited conversation filled the air. The other women were getting their hair put up in elaborate arrangements or their makeup painstakingly applied. Everyone was busy, but I could see the brides and stylists glance over at me, their faces full of curiosity. As soon as I took a seat in the nail section of the salon, I understood why.

"But she's too young!" The manicurist actually gasped. "Is everything okay?" she said to my aunt.

My aunt bristled a bit. "Yes, yes. Everything is fine. This is only the nikah. She is not leaving her family yet. She and her husband signed the papers today, but her husband lives in Canada. He is going home after this."

The manicurist had taken one of my hands and was slowly filing the nail.

"They won't have the rukhsati for a whole year yet." My aunt made it sound as if a year were a decade, that I would somehow no longer be a teenager but a full-fledged adult by then.

The manicurist's alarm had clearly rattled my aunt, as did the questions the other brides and stylists fired at me as I took my seat in the outer salon.

"How old are you?"

"Why are you getting married *now*?"

All the other brides seemed to be in their mid-twenties.

I trotted out the lines I had been offering since my engagement: the chance to go to Canada, the educational opportunities, Ahmed's good job.

All the while, Aunt Nasreen hovered over the makeup artist, giving her instructions. "Make that eyeliner darker," she insisted, "and a bit more blush. Her cheeks should look higher." It was clear that my aunt wanted the makeup to add a few years to my face.

When I finally stood up to leave, I couldn't believe the person who looked back at me from the mirror. The Samra I knew was gone; my youth had indeed been erased by layers of rouge and eyeliner.

From the beauty parlour, I was whisked to Ahmed's family's house for a photo shoot. It was important that the wedding pictures be taken while I still looked doll-like and perfect, before my carefully crafted facade wore off. I was led into the living room by Aunt Nasreen, and then the photographer took charge.

"Look up. Look down. Look to the left. Now to the right. Close your eyelids halfway. Smile—but shyly."

The directions went on and on, through sitting and standing positions, through dozens of solo shots and then more with Ahmed by my side. I responded with the mute obedience of a puppet.

Then the endless snapping of the camera was done, and I was being ushered into the banquet hall where the nikah celebration was to be held. At one end of the room was a raised dais with a sofa in the middle. This is where I was put, on display, while everyone took pictures and occasionally came up to say congratulations. Looking down on the crowded room, I was overwhelmed by the number of people I didn't know—the vast network of my husband's family, now my family too.

Suddenly a familiar face appeared in the crowd. My school friend Zenab had flown in from Ruwais for the wedding. She came running up to the platform, and I leapt from the couch. We flung our arms around each other.

We both started talking at once. I peppered her with questions, wanting to know everything that had happened in the time I had been gone. As we chatted excitedly, I noticed that Ahmed's mother was frowning at us.

Then Fatima was at my side. "Sit down, Samra," she said. "You're not supposed to be acting like this."

"I guess I should go," said Zenab. She slunk away.

All the effervescence I had just felt was gone. I had no problem staying quiet for the rest of the evening. I sat on the dais without a word. When I moved from the sofa to the dining table, beside Ahmed, his very presence kept me mute and unable to concentrate on anything that was happening around me. Dishes of curry and tandoori delicacies came from the kitchen. A plate was filled and brought to me. I moved a few morsels around with my fork, but I could eat nothing.

Eventually, the evening wound down. As people began to amble out of the hall, Ahmed's mother scooted over to me and took my arm.

"Come now, Samra, we're taking you away," she said.

Behind her I could hear Ahmed's friends teasing him. "Go on, time to take her home, Ahmed! She's yours now."

It was all in jest; everyone knew this was not the rukhsati. But a point was being made, nevertheless. I had started the day as Samra Zafar. Now I was Samra Ahmed, Ahmed's wife. And according to Pakistani Muslim tradition, my place was with his family, not mine.

Just then, my father appeared by my side. "Time to go, Samra," he said, directing his comments to Ahmed's mother rather than to me. I felt relief flood through me as we walked together to the car. I was a married woman now, but I could still go home.

※　※　※

Up until the nikah, I had had only one conversation with Ahmed— that late-night phone call. And our few emails were limited to discussing our favourite colours and foods. Now that we were married, we were of course free to be in contact as much as we liked.

A few days after the signing ceremony, Ahmed asked me to join him for an evening out. He suggested that we go with his older brother, Shahid, and his wife, Angela, to Pizza Hut. I wondered—had he remembered that my favourite food was pizza?

Angela was from Eastern Europe, and theirs had been a love match. I had met her at the various wedding celebrations and post-wedding get-togethers, but we hadn't really talked. Here in the restaurant, however, I felt I was beginning to get to know her and Shahid. I loved the easy camaraderie among the three of them. Now, away from the hubbub of the larger extended family, everyone was relaxed and playful, the mood light and celebratory. Shahid struck me as a gentle person; his wife, kind and generous. Even though they were in their late thirties, they talked to me as if I were an equal, a friend even. For the first time since the wedding festivities, I was hungry. As I helped myself to the pizza, I felt my teenaged, high school self slip away, and a new self—my adult self—begin to take its place.

After we had finished eating, the four of us headed for Ahmed's family's house, where my parents were waiting for me. I joined everyone in the living room, but Ahmed and his brother disappeared. Then Angela was asking me to come upstairs with her. She led me to a bedroom, where Ahmed and Shahid were waiting. Ahmed gestured for me to sit beside him on the bed and produced a box from behind his back. When I opened it, I discovered a Swiss Army watch. Ahmed took it carefully from the box and put it around my wrist. I shivered as his hands brushed my skin. Then he produced another box. A matching watch for himself. He asked me to put it around his wrist. For the first time, it felt as if Ahmed and I were making some kind of small connection.

The next time I saw Ahmed, he took me to the passport office to begin the immigration paperwork for my move to Canada. We had never been alone together before, and the enormity of that had my heart pounding, even as he sipped tea and ate snacks with my family before we left. In the car, he teased me about the reappearance of my paralyzing shyness.

"Don't you have anything to say?"

I struggled for a response.

"Am I really that scary?"

"No, no," I managed to mutter.

"You just don't want to talk?"

"I don't know what to say." That was certainly the truth.

At the Canadian embassy, we filled out the forms together and answered the questions of the immigration officers. I fell silent again as we got in the car. When Ahmed pulled up in front of my parents' apartment, he didn't get out.

"I've got something for you," he said. He grabbed a big manila envelope and handed it to me. Inside were glossy brochures from the University of Toronto, York University, University of British Columbia, University of Calgary.

"I ordered these," he said. "So you could think about where you want to go and what you want to study." He sounded excited. "Like I told you, we could move almost anywhere in Canada. I can always find work."

I looked at Ahmed with a big, unguarded smile. He was smiling too, confident and reassuring. I began to flip through brochures, excitedly reading out the names of the schools.

"Here," Ahmed said, opening one of the booklets. "Let me show you where Calgary is and what the school has to offer."

I had been told we would be living in a condo that his parents had bought for a future move to Canada. I asked Ahmed how long we would be able to stay there—and how long we *had* to stay there. When would his parents be moving to Canada? I imagined they wouldn't want to rent out their new condo to strangers if we decided to relocate.

Ahmed waved my concerns away. "Don't worry about that," he said. "They will move when they move. We aren't going to put our life on hold for them."

Our life. The words made my pulse flutter. We didn't speak for a few moments, both lost in our thoughts about the future. Then he took my hand in his.

"You know," he said quietly. "I really want to be your friend. I want to get to know you and for you to get to know me. We don't have to rush anything."

By the time we walked into my family's apartment, I felt as if the world was becoming a bright, safe place again. Perhaps I wouldn't be flirting with boys on campus, but that didn't mean I might not fall in love.

The rest of the afternoon unfolded with remarkable ease. Ahmed joined my sisters on the couch, taking one of their Sega controllers and challenging them to a vigorous game of video tennis. He asked them about school, while I showed the university brochures to my parents. After several rounds of tennis, Ahmed slipped downstairs to the café on the ground floor of the building, returning with tea, Pepsi and samosas for all of us. By the time he left, my sisters were calling him Ahmed-bhai. Big brother.

※　※　※

During the three weeks following the wedding, Ahmed's extended family held one dinner party after another. Each time, Ahmed and his parents took me with them. I found the evenings tense and exhausting. I hated the way Ahmed's parents seemed to watch every move I made and weigh every word I said. I knew there was some perfect balance between talking enough and not too much—and that I was not getting it right. And I flinched every time they referred to me as their bahu.

But more and more, I loved the quiet moments I could spend alone with Ahmed.

On the days we didn't see each other, and even some when we did, Ahmed would call me in the evenings. We talked about how we had spent our days. I chatted about my friends back in Ruwais, about my school and my teachers. He would tell me about Canada. He explained that once there, I would likely have to wait a year before I could start university. But he assured me that this would be a fun time. We could spend the fall visiting campuses, so I could decide where to apply. We could also hit some of the big cities and attractions within driving distance from where he lived in Mississauga—Montreal, New York, Niagara Falls. He even offered to teach me how to drive once we were together in Canada.

"You have to be your own person," he told me.

Despite his parents' prescriptive attitude to their new daughter-in-law, Ahmed reassured me that he didn't care what others thought. We were going to live our life the way we wanted to.

A few days before Ahmed had to return to Canada, he invited me on a shopping trip with all of his siblings. Ahmed and I wandered around the mall together, popping into one shop or another, not so much shopping as enjoying the opportunity to walk together. But then something caught his eye. It was a taupe crushed-silk shalwar kameez dress embellished with gold embroidery. He asked me if I liked it. How could I not? It was stunning. I nodded. "Try it on," he said. When I came out of the dressing room, Ahmed's face lit up. "I'm buying that for you!"

The next night Ahmed's mother held a big dinner party. As I walked through the front door in my new dress, I felt elegant, and suddenly a little older than my years. When Ahmed saw me, he broke into a huge smile. He told me how pretty I looked, and I felt the heat rise in my cheeks. I couldn't keep a grin from spreading across my face.

For the rest of the evening, Ahmed followed me around, filming me with the camcorder he had been given to record the event. He didn't care that he wasn't capturing any of the guests at the dinner.

"I'm trying to make some memories," he explained. "This way I can take you with me. And I will have something to watch when I'm missing you."

※　※　※

Before I knew it our three weeks "together" had slipped away.

A day before Ahmed was scheduled to fly out, my mother and I took a rickshaw over to his family's home. (My father was already back in Ruwais.) Everyone gathered in the living room to say their goodbyes, but slowly people disappeared until only Ahmed and I were left. I had written him a card saying that I would miss him. Now I gave it to him. When he read it, he smiled. "This is a good idea," he said. "We will write to each other as well as talk."

He was quiet for a moment, and then said, "You won't be alone. I'll be with you. And soon, we will make all our dreams come true."

I couldn't believe how different I felt now than I had three weeks ago—and how much I didn't want him to leave. I started to cry. Ahmed came closer to me, cupped the back of my head gently with his hand and kissed me on the forehead. "We will be together soon," he whispered.

Leaving Ahmed's house that day, I thought I knew what it was to be in love. That terrible night before the nikah felt as if it had happened years ago, my fear then overblown and histrionic. I wished I could go back to that evening and tell my tearful self what I now knew to be true: the right choice had been made.

※ ※ ※

Over the coming months, Ahmed and I kept up a steady stream of correspondence, phone calls and video chats. I would rush home from school to check for messages, obsessively dialling into the Internet every hour to see if anything new had come in. We continued to discuss our life plans. Ahmed assured me that he was in no hurry to have children, that he wanted me to get my degree before we started a family. Even with his encouragement, I recognized that medicine—and the marathon route to becoming a doctor—might not be compatible with marriage. Instead, I started looking at business programs and economics.

During one of those talks, the night before I was to start at my new Karachi school, Ahmed raised the subject of hijabs.

"I know that not many women in Pakistan wear them, but I think a hijab makes a girl look even more beautiful."

I was a bit surprised. His mother did not wear one, nor did any of his sisters or sisters-in-law. But like me, Ahmed had been raised in the Arabic world, where the head coverings were more popular.

"Do you want me to wear one?" I asked.

"It's up to you, of course," Ahmed replied. His tone was gentle and wistful. "I just always imagined my wife wearing one, so that I was the only one who could admire her beauty. So that she was always safe and protected from other men's gazes." Ahmed paused. And then the silky words: "It's just that I love you *so* much."

After we got off the phone, I found my mind moving back in time, to another new school year: grade seven. I had been so excited to return to my studies and to see classmates I hadn't spoken with over the summer. As I entered the grassy schoolyard, two girls had approached me. At first I didn't recognize them. Below their white school-uniform shirts, they were wearing long, dark skirts that brushed their toes. Their hair was hidden under tight hijabs. "Samra!" they called out—and I realized that I was looking at Sadia and Hazeema. The last time we were together, their hair had been uncovered, their school skirts the standard knee length.

"Hey," I said, "what's going on? Why are you wearing that?"

"Oh, you know," said Sadia. "We're growing up. It's time. We want people to know that we're good girls."

What was she talking about? Of course we were good girls. We worked hard at school, we did as we were told, we had never been in any kind of real trouble. Why would people think we were anything other than good girls? And what did our clothes have to do with that? And yet, watching my two friends, covered tip to toe, smiling softly at me as they spoke, sent a tiny, sharp current through my chest. I tried to shrug it off. *This has nothing to do with me*, I thought.

Back in grade seven, I had rejected Sadia and Hazeema's self-censure. I never thought of the hijab as something that made women beautiful. Or as something they wore out of love. Or because they were loved. The next morning, as I got dressed for school, I dug around in my clothes drawer and pulled out a hijab scarf. I stood before my mirror looking at it with ambivalence. I didn't want to wear it, but Ahmed's sweet voice kept rippling through my mind: "It's just that I love you *so* much." I loved him too, and if this made him happy, why not? I draped the scarf over my head, tucked my hair under it and pinned it beneath my chin. As I looked at myself in the mirror, I reassured myself: *He only wants to take care of me*.

※　※　※

I stood at the edge of the yard, watching the boys and girls standing in huddles, talking and laughing. It felt strange not to know a soul. I noticed a bench a short distance away and went to sit down. Just a few minutes later, a girl approached.

"What's your name?" she asked. I told her. And then, "Are you engaged?"

I was startled. "Why?"

"The ring on your finger."

I glanced down at my hand. I had forgotten about the ugly ring. "No," I said. "I'm actually married."

As soon as the words were out of my mouth, I regretted them. I realized that I had wanted a year to pretend that I was a normal high school student again—after my experience in Ruwais, I was sure that wouldn't happen if kids knew I was married. I wished I'd left the ring at home. As this thought crossed my mind, another stampeded after it. *I'm in love with my husband. I should feel happy about this*. The mix of embarrassment and guilt fogged my mind.

"Oh, okay," said the girl, cheerfully. "I'll let all of the guys know you're off limits." Then she turned on her heel and walked briskly across the schoolyard to join her friends.

❋ ❋ ❋

Despite the fact that I was very publicly off limits, my time at the high school in Karachi was not lonely. In fact, perhaps because I was new, my married status didn't seem to create the same discomfort among the other students as it had in Ruwais. Rather, as the new-comer, I drew a certain amount of attention. I was exotic, my fluency in English and my pronounced British accent reinforcing that mystique. By the time I had been at the school for a few weeks, I had a nice circle of friends to hang out with during the lunch break or after school, including a best friend: a boy named Fahad. And as I got to know people, my marital status seemed to fade from their minds—I ceased being the married one and became, once again, simply Samra. With this transformation, my return to teenage life was almost complete, although I turned down some invitations that seemed inappropriate now that I had a husband. (I also had to beat back a little crush I was developing on Fahad.)

To my great surprise, however, while my marital status didn't seem to hinder my success at school, my personality did. I had attended co-ed schools almost my whole life, but for most students in Karachi, high school was their first experience of spending the day with the opposite sex. Even those who were in their final year still seemed to be revelling in the hormonal excitement of it all. When a boy and girl were seen talking or sitting next to each other, a current of electricity ran through the whole place. By comparison, I was positively nonchalant. While some girls envied my comfort in talking with boys, others thought I must be a bit loose, despite my hijab.

I shrugged off their insular, old-fashioned ideas. So it came as a bit of a shock when I discovered why my application to run for head girl had been rejected by the school administration. I was told that I wasn't the type of girl they wanted to lead the school. When I asked what type of girl they thought I was, the teacher who was handling the election made mention of my role in the farewell assembly for the senior class. I had choreographed a dance for it and sung a song with Fahad. This public display of friendship between a boy and a girl was not the kind of thing the school encouraged, I was told. Outraged, I marched to the principal's office to complain. He waved away my objections. "Your parents might be fine with your liberal attitude," he said, "but it is not something we encourage here." And with that, the conversation was over.

(The principal did not mention my uncovered head, but at the urging of friends, I had abandoned my hijab for the assembly. I'd felt a spasm of guilt about this act of small defiance against my husband, but it was such a relief to feel my hair about my shoulders, to be fully myself again, that I didn't put the scarf back on. Besides, as everyone had seen my hair now, it was pointless to cover it. Once Ahmed and I could talk about this in person, he would understand, I hoped.)

My rejected head-girl application just underscored the stifling social environment of Pakistan. My sisters and I missed the freedoms we had enjoyed in Ruwais. We hated the fact that we couldn't go on public transportation alone, and that even the short walk to school had to be done to a chorus of catcalls from the men and boys who shared the sidewalks with us.

During my frequent conversations with Ahmed, I sometimes complained about all of this.

"In only a couple of months, you will be able to go where you want, when you want," Ahmed reassured me. "The streets are very safe here. Even at two in the morning."

I could hardly wait for that modern Canadian life to start.

※ ※ ※

Ahmed and I had submitted my immigration paperwork in August, just after the nikah, and I completed the rest of the process, including a medical exam, in the early winter. After that, all I could do was wait.

One day in the late spring, the mail carrier buzzed the apartment. "There's a package here for Samra," he said.

"Where's it from?" I asked, my hopes rising.

"Citizenship and Immigration Canada," he replied.

With that, I was flying out of the apartment. I didn't stop to put shoes on, and I didn't wait for the elevator. Instead, I raced down three flights of stairs, bursting into the building foyer with my hand outstretched. The mail carrier was waiting for me and stuck the envelope in my hand. I ran back upstairs, ripping open the envelope as soon as I crossed our doorway. When I saw the permanent residency papers, I burst into tears of happiness and relief. After sharing the news with my mother and sisters, I called Ahmed.

"That's fantastic!" he said. The excitement in his voice just added to my own.

※　※　※

Now that I could leave for Canada, my family had another wedding to plan: the rukhsati. Since the nikah had been an elaborate party, this would just be a formal dinner, after which I would leave my family to join Ahmed and his family. But it was to take place in Abu Dhabi, so despite its modesty, it would be a further blow to my parents' budget.

My parents purchased plane tickets for the entire family, and my father brought them to us on one of his visits to Karachi. As I looked at them, a little shiver went through me. All of them were return flights to Karachi—except for my one-way ticket. I would not be returning.

※　※　※

On August 18, 2000, my immediate family and Ahmed's met at a restaurant in an Abu Dhabi hotel for the rukhsati. It was the first time
I had seen Ahmed since he arrived in the country, and while I had
been excited at the prospect of being together again, now that it was
actually happening timidity overcame me. My heart was thumping
and my cheeks burned. I managed to talk a little more than I had at
the nikah, but only to my parents and my sisters. And I couldn't stop
thinking about the fact that at the end of this evening, my marriage
would truly begin. I would be leaving my family forever.

After the rukhsati dinner was over, my mother, father, sisters
and I went up to my parents' room to say our goodbyes. Ahmed, his
parents—and I—would be staying in another hotel in Dubai. My
mother gave me a big hug, but once my father's arms wrapped around
me I began to cry. Any distance between my mother and me, any rifts
between father and daughter, now were as inconsequential as a grain
of dust. Somehow, we managed to get back downstairs, through the
lobby and out to the minivan that Ahmed's family had rented. My
family hovered around me as I went from one set of arms to another.
I could only let go to move to another family member.

Behind me I could hear Ahmed's parents sighing and clearing
their throats. Eventually, they gave voice to their impatience. "Come
on, come on, let's go," said his mother.

I stumbled through the door of the minivan, creeping my way to the
back seat. Ahmed followed me, sitting beside me and taking my hand.

As the van pulled out into traffic, Ahmed and Fatima and the
rest of the family began to talk. They reviewed every item that had
been served at dinner. They chatted about the phone calls they had
received from Ahmed's brothers and sisters who could not attend
the rukhsati. They discussed what was new with other family members and people I didn't know.

During the ninety-minute drive, no one addressed me in
any way. I could have interjected with a question or a topic we all

could discuss, but I felt too frightened and disoriented to make the effort.

Sitting next to Ahmed in the back of the van, it struck me that despite our emails and conversations, I really had no idea who he was. His family and his very world were as foreign to me as the people we passed on the street.

When we finally got to the hotel, I followed Ahmed's family into the lobby and up the elevator. Once we reached his parents' room, someone pulled out a camera, and I was instructed to stand with Ahmed and with various configurations of his family. The haze that had enveloped me in the van refused to clear—I moved around as if someone else were controlling my body.

Eventually, Fatima came to my side and took my elbow. "It's time to go to Ahmed's room now," she whispered in my ear.

My gaze dropped to the floor. I couldn't look at Ahmed or anyone else in the room. Silently, I followed her down the corridor. Fatima let us into the room and sat me down on the bed. Her tone was teasing and playful as she broached the topic of my first night with my husband. She told me about her first sexual experience and then began to rattle off her sex tips.

"Never stop your husband if he wants to do something. That will just upset him. And don't start anything yourself. Men don't like it when women are too forward. Always act shy." And finally, "Never use contraception. Birth control pills can interfere with your fertility."

I sat frozen in place, wishing I was anywhere but there.

Finally, she sighed and said, "Well, let's get you ready."

She told me to sit in the middle of the bed, with my feet tucked under me. Then she took the lehnga, my skirt, and spread it around me in a circle. My dupatta was removed and rearranged so it fell over my face, hiding it from view.

"Okay," she said. "I'm going to leave now. You wait like that until Ahmed gets here. He shouldn't see your face until he lifts the dupatta."

As soon as I heard the hotel door click, I began to cry. I had had a year to prepare for this. It was not enough time.

※　※　※

I have no idea how long I sat there. It was an interval that seemed like an eternity but was at the same time terrifyingly short.

I was staring at my lap when I heard the door open. Soft footsteps approached the bed. Then the mattress sagged beneath me. Ahmed was sitting at my side. He took the dupatta from my head.

"Why are you covered up like that?" He was laughing.

Then he bent towards me and gave me a light kiss on the forehead. He handed me a small box. When I opened it, a diamond ring winked at me.

"I love you so much," he said gently. "And I don't want you to be scared. I won't do anything you don't want me to."

Ahmed was true to his word. By the time I fell asleep that night, all we had done was cuddle and kiss, and I drifted off reminded of why I had fallen for him.

※　※　※

Ahmed and I had a week to spend in Dubai before our flight to Canada. During that time, we stayed at the hotel with his parents and extended family. My family had one final morning with me—at the traditional breakfast hosted by the groom's family after the rukhsati. But we had no time alone. When my sisters wanted to take me up to our hotel room after the meal so we could talk a little in private, I shook my head. My mother-in-law had reminded me the evening before that I was a woman now, not a girl. Whatever childish fun I might have had with my younger sisters was no longer appropriate. I knew that she also considered it my duty to remain with the group.

I tried to tell myself that turning down my sisters was the best way to get used to my new reality and to my new family. But when my mother, father and sisters left the hotel, it was all I could do not to run after them and beg them to take me with them.

The following day, my family flew back to Pakistan while I sat with Ahmed's parents in their hotel room. I had to concentrate as hard as I could to keep myself from crying. But my distress was evident to everyone in the room.

Ahmed's mother was offended. "You should be happy," she said sharply. "Happy about your new life and your new family. You know, there is really something wrong with you if you aren't."

I tried to smile and respond with some measure of cheerfulness in my voice, but my mother-in-law was not fooled. She pressed her lips together before she spoke again. "Being so unhappy to join your husband's family means that you are not being a good wife. Or a good daughter-in-law." It seemed from the emphasis she put on the second statement that it was the most important.

Just then, Fatima's husband entered the room. He turned to me and chuckled. "So your parents have finished the chore of marrying you off and left as soon they could, huh?" he said.

"They had to get back so my sister could write her exams," I said defensively.

"Sure, sure," he responded. "They couldn't get out of here fast enough now that they've unloaded their burden."

Everyone in the room was laughing, as if he had just cracked a joke, but I knew they all truly believed it. My parents, whatever their faults, never felt weighed down by having four daughters. My new family clearly didn't share this attitude. If I'd been persuaded earlier that Ahmed's family was progressive, that illusion had now been swept away.

I was just grateful that Ahmed thought this was all nonsense.

❋ ❋ ❋

The week in Dubai crawled by, each day slower and more enervating than the previous one. I spent hours and hours sitting in my in-laws' hotel room, listening to my mother-in-law and other family members gossip about friends and relations. Ahmed often joined us, but sometimes he went out on his own or with his brothers. He would always address his mother when he made this announcement—never meeting my eyes or inviting me to go with him. In the evenings, Ahmed and I sat with his parents in their room, my eyes often drooping shut as the minutes dragged on. When I nudged Ahmed or tried to silently signal that we should leave, he would give his head a quick shake and then turn his attention back to his parents until they told us that they were ready for bed and we could leave.

My only break from the stale air and claustrophobic atmosphere of the hotel room came on the almost daily trips to the Dubai malls. These were done en masse, the entire family trailing after Ahmed's mother—his amma—as she went from shop to shop, looking at almost everything but never making a purchase. Ahmed and his brother sometimes hived off to go for coffee, but it was clear that I was to remain with Amma.

One night after Ahmed and I had been dismissed from his parents' room, I asked him why we couldn't be alone now and then.

"Abba and Amma would be hurt if we didn't spend this time with them, Samra," he said. "Be patient. It is only five or six more days, and then we will have all the time alone we want."

Ahmed was right, but I couldn't help it—I felt trapped.

❈ ❈ ❈

The morning of our departure, I had my bags packed and ready to go. We were taking an overnight flight, and the day stretched out in front of me like a desert. *Just this one more day*, I reminded myself. I pulled on one of my best new outfits and adorned myself with my gold wedding jewellery. Then, I reluctantly joined Ahmed as he headed to his parents' hotel room.

Ahmed's mother was making tea when we arrived; his sister Fatima and her husband were sitting on the couch, chatting about their plans for the day. I sat down next to Fatima without saying a word, quickly losing myself in thought. I was so relieved to be leaving these people, but the plane I really wanted to get on was flying to Pakistan. As much as Karachi had been difficult, anywhere my parents and sisters were was home. And the truth was, I wanted to go home.

My daydreaming was broken by a shriek. It was Fatima. She was looking at the doorway. I heard my father's voice calling out my name. There, standing just inside the room, were my parents, their gentle faces beaming at me. They had flown back to see me before I left! I sprinted to them and threw myself into my father's open arms. My mother wrapped her arms around me too, and the three of us stood in a tight huddle, my parents stroking my hair while I sobbed. All the tears I had been pressing down for the week were now bubbling to the surface.

"Thank you, thank you for coming," I whispered between weepy hiccups, now grateful for my father's financial extravagance.

"What's the matter, beta?" my father said.

"Did you come to take me home?" I asked. I knew that couldn't be true, but I couldn't help hoping.

"We've come to see you off," said my father.

I was too happy to be with them in that moment to be disappointed. After a week of feeling invisible, I was suddenly strong again, both seen and loved.

"Please, come in." I heard Amma's voice call to my parents. She didn't sound pleased.

"No, thank you," said my father. "We are just here to take Samra out shopping for the day."

I turned to Ahmed. "Is that okay?" I didn't ask him if he wanted to join us.

His expression was hard to read, but his words surprised me. "Don't ask me. Ask Amma."

His mother was standing in the middle of the room, a sour look on her face. "Of course," she said tightly. "Why would I stop her?"

I knew that she was incensed, but I was past caring. As I turned to leave, Ahmed pressed a few bills into my hand. My father took them from me and handed them back to Ahmed. "No, she doesn't need that."

And then we were out the door.

※　※　※

In the car, my mother and father wanted to know why I had asked to go home with them. I explained that I hadn't been allowed to leave Amma's side, that Ahmed, despite his kindness when we were alone, paid no attention to me when we were with his family.

"He seems like a very nice man, Samra," my mother said. "He is only acting this way because he is feeling pressure from his family."

"Yes," my father assured me. "When you get to Canada, everything will be different."

At the shopping mall, I was overcome by a giddy sense of freedom. I had been shopping almost every day with Ahmed's mother, but that had always seemed like some kind of forced march. Now I was able to roam wherever I wanted and look at anything that interested me. *This must be what it's like to get out of jail*, I thought.

My parents suggested that I pick up some things for the plane ride. After several hours, I left the mall with a bag of snacks and several of my favourite types of books.

When we got back to the hotel, it was already time to drive to the airport. I told Ahmed I wanted to go in the same car as my parents. I made sure there was nothing of a question in my statement.

※　※　※

The drive was not a long one, but it seemed to be over with uncanny speed. I sat next to my mother, holding her hand and hugging her between short bursts of weeping. Try as I might to think about my love for Ahmed, the impending separation from my family was a heartache I could not beat back.

Once in the airport terminal, I hung on tight to both of my parents. Eventually, Ahmed took my arm and led me into the security lineup. But when I looked back and saw my parents waving at me, I bolted out of the line and ran back into their arms. By the third or fourth time, Ahmed was understandably losing patience.

"Come on, Samra. We're going to miss our flight," he said as he took my arm again. "We *have* to go."

Tears continued to course down my cheeks as we found our way to the gate and then boarded the plane. By the time we had settled into our seats, however, I was finally wrung dry. Ahmed put his arm around my shoulders and pulled me to him.

"It's okay," he said. "I understand. But just think, no more shopping trips with Amma!" His laughter and good humour made me feel better. He took my hand, and I leaned into him. I closed my eyes.

After all my nerves and tears, all my worries and sleepless nights, I was at last with my husband, a man who truly loved me. And I was on my way to a bright future. At my feet was my school knapsack stuffed with presents from my parents—chocolate bars and Nancy Drew mysteries.

PART
TWO

CHAPTER 5

SAMRA-BEGUM

Wake up. Come see!"

Ahmed's voice broke through my deep blanket of sleep. I wanted to drift away again, but his tone was urgent—and excited. I stumbled out of bed, pulling a housecoat around my shoulders. The bedroom was cold, colder than I would have thought possible before I moved to Canada. Ahmed was at the window, pointing out. As I moved towards him, I was startled by the light coming from outside. And then I saw it. A dazzling white world spread out below our condo window. *Snow*.

Ahmed and I stood side by side, staring out—Ahmed chuckling at my slack-jawed amazement. Then he gave my arm a pat.

"Go on, get dressed. Let's go outside."

I put on as many layers as I could, and we went out onto the lawns around the condo. Ahmed showed me how to scoop up the snow in my hands and pack it into a snowball. He was surprised at what a good arm I had. All my cricket playing had paid off.

After receiving a few hits, Ahmed decided we should switch activities—making a snowman and then a snow angel. Finally, cold and wet and thoroughly delighted, we returned to the warmth of the apartment.

After changing into dry clothes, I stationed myself once more in front of the windows, with a cup of steaming tea. My cheeks stung pleasantly from the cold. My future was not quite following the path I had expected, but I was married to a man I loved. And I was excited and hopeful about everything that lay before me. If someone had told me this happiness could melt away as quickly as a November snow, I wouldn't have believed them.

※ ※ ※

We had arrived in Canada in the last weeks of August. Abu Dhabi had sent us off under waves of heat reaching 50 degrees Celsius. Getting out of the cab in front of the condo building in Mississauga, I took a deep breath of the fresh air. The skies were blue, the sun was shining and the air was deliciously warm instead of blazingly hot. My new home was delightful, too. The lobby, with its sparkling marble and gleaming glass, looked like a palace. Ahmed proudly showed me through the condo unit. I was almost skipping as I walked, thrilled with the big windows, the soft-carpeted floors, the spacious master bedroom with its brightly tiled en suite bathroom. I knew we wouldn't be living here long—as soon as Ahmed's parents moved to Canada, we would find an apartment of our own—but for now I revelled in the modern elegance of the place.

The only real furniture in the condo, however, was a futon bed. Ahmed said we could scrape together a few things, but his parents were going to use the cargo permit that came along with my permanent residency status to ship extra furniture they didn't need to set up the apartment for themselves. I was happy to make do.

Ahmed had arranged to take a few weeks of holiday upon his return to Canada so that we could spend some time together and he could show me around. He took me shopping for new clothes and out for dinner. We drove his ancient black Thunderbird up to Wasaga

Beach, where we walked on the sand, ate ice cream and kissed on a park bench in the breezy sunshine. As he had promised all those months ago, Ahmed also took me to the Niagara Falls, where we stood in the mist and marvelled at the roar of the blue water.

But my favourite times were the quiet evenings at home. Ahmed and I would stand side by side at the kitchen counter, making home-made pizza or burgers for dinner. Then we would cuddle up in front of the TV to watch *Who Wants to Be a Millionaire* or old reruns of *All in the Family* as the light faded outside.

Once Ahmed went back to work, I spent my days in the condo, chatting with my family and friends on MSN Messenger and talking with Ahmed on the telephone. I went out for walks by myself a couple of times, but I found the landscape strange and intimidating. The huge mall nearby and other obvious landmarks did nothing to dispel my certainty that I would get lost. Despite my father's encouragement, and my past intrepid solo journeys into Abu Dhabi, I was really a small-town girl. And here, in a foreign land, I felt I had no anchor to keep me from drifting off into dangerous territory.

At the end of August, before Ahmed returned to work, I had begun phoning universities to find out about the application process. I was somewhat deflated to learn that my completed grade twelve would not be sufficient to get me into an Ontario university. At the time, the province still had grade thirteen; I needed six credits at this level to be accepted.

Ahmed told me not to worry. There was a high school nearby that I could attend for the year. But before I could register, I ended up at the doctor's office.

※　※　※

About two weeks into September, barely a month after arriving in Canada, I realized that I hadn't gotten my period. I told Ahmed I was worried. Could this mean I was pregnant? He assured me I wasn't. "We've been careful," he reminded me.

Was that true? Despite Fatima's advice that avoiding sex on days thirteen to seventeen of my cycle would prevent pregnancy, we had used condoms as well—but not consistently. Perhaps avoiding conception was trickier than I understood. After a few more days passed without the arrival of my period, Ahmed agreed that it would be a good idea for me to get checked out by a doctor.

The female doctor at the medical centre next to our building was kind and reassuring. Her first question, however, was how old I was. When I told her I was eighteen, a look of concern crossed her face, but she told me not to worry. "I'll do a blood test, but it could just be the big changes and the move."

A few days later Ahmed and I went back to her office to get the results. Ahmed wanted to go into the examination room with me. "No, no," said the doctor. "I'd like to talk to Samra alone."

Once I'd settled onto the chair, the doctor looked at me with sympathy. "Samra," she said, "the results are positive. You're pregnant."

I felt as if the earth had dissolved beneath my feet. How could this be? I had been married such a short time. And I was starting school in a couple of weeks.

"Samra?" The doctor's voice sounded as if it were coming from a great distance. I looked up at her. She seemed to be waiting for an answer. I hadn't heard her question.

"I asked if you wanted to go through with the pregnancy."

I had no idea what she was talking about. Slowly and patiently she explained my options. I had never heard of abortion before. She told me that it was my choice whether or not to stay pregnant. It was up to me.

Finally, I responded. "I don't think that would be allowed in my religion."

She nodded. "Well, you think about it. You can come back to me."

I walked out of the office in shocked silence. When Ahmed asked what had happened, I said I would tell him once we got to the condo. I couldn't bring myself to say the words in a public space—perhaps if I didn't speak them out in the open they might be less real.

Back at home, I watched Ahmed's face as I gave him the news. He smiled a small smile and said, "Congratulations," but he looked as stunned as I felt.

I didn't want his congratulations; I wanted answers. "How will I go to school?" I asked. "How will I go to university?"

At my panicked words, he put his arms around me and held me tight.

"Don't worry about that, Samra. We'll work it out."

※　※　※

When I broke the news to my parents, they both sounded shocked. My mother tried to adopt a happy tone, but concern laced her words. My father was blunt.

"Don't give up on school," he insisted.

The call to Ahmed's parents went quite differently. His mother was ecstatic. And much to my surprise, she was reassuring too. "Don't worry about school," she said. "We will be there soon, and I will take care of the baby for you."

I hadn't thought of that. Ahmed had already filed the paperwork to sponsor his parents. It was possible they would be in Canada even before the baby was born.

The support of the high school administration took a different direction. The principal was worried about bullying and recommended that I finish my high school requirements at an adult learning centre nearby and through correspondence courses.

Ahmed thought she was right. And he pointed out that going to school full time might be too taxing for me while I was pregnant.

And so I enrolled in an English literature class at the centre and two math classes by correspondence. Everyone in my English class was a lot older than I was, but that didn't stop me from engaging in the discussions. I loved many of the books on the reading list and always looked forward to Monday evenings, when I could share my thoughts.

Before Ahmed drove me over to the first class, however, he made a request. I was in our bedroom, packing up my school bag. "Samra, would you mind wearing a hijab to class?"

I was startled.

"It's just that I don't like other men looking at your hair," Ahmed explained tenderly. "You don't have to do this, but I hope you will—out of love for me."

I hadn't enjoyed my brief flirtation with the hijab in Karachi. I'd realized that even while I was getting to know people and making new friends, the hijab made me feel as if some essential part of myself were hidden. And even if this were not true, I was reluctant to undergo anymore changes now. After all, although it was still early in my pregnancy, the baby was already transforming me into someone new—from the inside out. In a hijab, the old me might disappear a little bit more.

I was also thinking about what this request from Ahmed implied. When he mentioned the hijab to me the first time, he had claimed that it would protect me and also make me look more beautiful to him. He was no longer talking about beauty, however, only about the attention I might receive from other men if my hair was visible.

A memory pushed itself into the light. Before I left Karachi, I had to have a full medical exam as part of my application to the Canadian immigration ministry. When I told Ahmed about the upcoming appointment, he asked the name of the doctor, becoming alarmed when he realized I would be seeing a male physician. He insisted that I call the embassy and demand a female replacement. I balked. "He's a doctor, Ahmed," I said over and over, trying to convince him that my modesty would not be imperilled. When this did not persuade him, I changed tack. "If I request a new doctor, it could really delay my application."

In the end, Ahmed acquiesced. But he did look up the doctor on the Internet and read his reviews. He also insisted that my mother go into the examination room with me—and he gave me some instructions about what to allow and not allow during the examination.

The exchange had left me a little exasperated, but Ahmed's kind and gentle words made me believe that the combination of love and distance had made him overprotective. I hadn't given it another thought until now.

With this second hijab request, I was forced to recognize that Ahmed was not quite as comfortable with my independence as he had originally led me to believe. But did that matter? If he thought I was beautiful, wasn't it natural that he would succumb to jealousy now and again? *I should feel flattered by this*, I thought. And besides, as young as I was, I recognized that marriage was about small compromises. I did love him. I could do this for him.

"Of course," I said to Ahmed. "I'll wear the hijab."

❧ ❧ ❧

When I arrived in my first English class, the teacher told me that since I was so young, missing out on a full-time high school experience was a mistake—and she suggested I switch back. But Ahmed had been right; daily attendance at school no longer seemed like a good idea. By October, I was experiencing terrible morning sickness that lasted all day. The nausea and vomiting were often accompanied by faintness. One day in early October, I collapsed in the checkout line at a grocery store. I came to with Ahmed bent over me, splashing water on my face and calling my name.

After that, my nervousness about being out alone intensified. What would I do if I got sick while I was out? I had no cellphone, no way to call Ahmed for help. I was much more comfortable staying at home during the day, working on my homework and on my correspondence courses. I still talked regularly with my parents in the afternoons, but I began to chat on MSN with friends in Ruwais and Karachi less often. While talking to my family sometimes made me homesick, listening to my friends' tales of life at school provoked not only homesickness but also a great longing for my former teenage social life.

Yet I was happy with Ahmed—I didn't want that happiness dulled by envy.

❊ ❊ ❊

As autumn folded into winter, our married life settled into a pleasing rhythm. Ahmed's parents' furniture arrived in December, and with it another layer of comfort. Because my pregnancy had me sleeping fitfully and I was often tired, Ahmed would get up quietly in the mornings so I could sleep in. Once up, I busied myself with school work. Sometimes Ahmed came home for lunch. But even if he didn't, he would call several times a day to ask how I was doing and to find out what he might pick up for dinner, as my nausea made cooking difficult. As each afternoon progressed, I found myself excited by the growing darkness, knowing that it meant Ahmed would be walking through the door at any moment. In the evenings, once we were finished eating, we would curl up on the couch and watch TV or rented movies. Sometimes we talked dreamily about the future—the baby's arrival, university for me, probably part time at first. We imagined our two-income lives, our family holidays and our future house, with a pretty backyard and plenty of space for our children.

On the weekends, we sometimes packed up the car and headed out on the road. We stayed three nights in Montreal one time; overnight in

Niagara Falls another. We also received numerous dinner party invitations. Ahmed, of course, had a number of friends, some who were married as well. And his family had a network of old friends who had immigrated to the Toronto area. Many of these people hosted us from time to time. Before most parties, Ahmed's mother would call to fill me in on everyone who might be there—and on how to dress appropriately for each occasion. Despite her insistent direction I enjoyed the chance to get out, although the evenings were never as easy as I would have liked. I was so much younger than most of the others, as well as being the only newcomer to their circle. I didn't know the people they spoke of and could share none of their memories.

※　※　※

Then, at the end of February, Ahmed got a call from his parents. Their papers had come through, and they would be flying to Mississauga in a few weeks' time. I was startled. I hadn't expected things to move this quickly.

"Should we start looking for an apartment?" I asked Ahmed. When he first explained that we would be living in his parents' condo, he had told me that we would relocate when they arrived.

"We will need our privacy," he had said, "and besides, every woman wants her own home."

But now he seemed reluctant to move too quickly. "We need to live with Amma and Abba for a bit. It would be rude to rush right out of the condo the moment they arrive."

Remembering my time with Amma in Dubai, I was of course worried. But I tried to remember how disoriented I had felt on the streets of Mississauga when I first arrived. Ahmed's parents were older and surely less adventuresome than I was. It seemed only kind to help them acclimate before we left them on their own. And perhaps with a new baby to bring them joy, Amma and Abba would be a bit more affectionate with their bahu, would behave like the parents I missed so much. At the very least, with a baby to focus on, Amma might be less insistent on my being by her side at all times.

I was disappointed to realize that before they arrived we needed to move out of the master bedroom and into the smaller room. My pregnancy had me up many times in the night, and I'd come to rely on that convenient en suite bathroom. And the other bedroom had no furniture. Reluctant to buy anything before we had our own place, Ahmed arranged to fill it with cast-offs from a friend.

As I watched him set up a lumpy mattress on the battered bed frame, my heart sank. It was just a bed and a bedroom now, but change seemed to hang over us like a dark cloud. I remembered how intimidated I had been by Amma, as she called the shots the entire week in Dubai.

"Ahmed," I said as he wrestled with the furniture, "will we still be able to have time to ourselves when your parents get here? Will we be able to go out on our own?"

Ahmed shoved the mattress into place and then stood up. "Of course we will," he said. "Things aren't going to change."

With all my heart, I wanted to believe him.

✿ ✿ ✿

I awoke to the sound of banging and crashing. It was so early that the sky outside our bedroom window was still an inky grey. I got out of bed, pulled a housecoat over my swollen stomach and went into the kitchen.

Amma was standing before the open refrigerator. All of the kitchen cupboards were open. I could tell that she had been up for a while already. The cabinet where I had put all the spices now contained glasses. The cupboard where I had put the glasses now contained spices. Everywhere I looked, something had been moved or rearranged in some way.

She turned to me, a look of disapproval tightening her face. "Why don't you have fresh chili peppers?" she asked. And then before I could respond, "I don't know why you don't have some meat in the freezer."

I didn't have an answer.

"Never mind." She sighed. "You've clearly never been taught to run a household. I will teach you now that I am here."

She turned back to the fridge and began moving things around again. "I have no idea how my son has been managing without me."

I wanted to tell her how happy we'd been, how happy *he'd* been. But I had already been dismissed.

Our first day all together in the condo continued like that—a strange medley of kinetic activity and dull tension. After Amma finished in the kitchen, she began to unpack the boxes of her personal belongings that had arrived in December along with the furniture. Abba sat in the living room flicking through the TV channels, his expression, as always, unreadable. Ahmed moved between the two of them, oddly quiet and grim faced. Amma didn't seem to want my help, so I escaped to our bedroom, exhausted from my early morning.

As soon as I got comfortable on the bed, Ahmed appeared in the doorway. *Oh good*, I thought. We hadn't talked at all since we picked his parents up at the airport the night before. I was hoping he was coming in to cuddle with me while I rested. He probably wanted to ask if there was anything I wanted or needed, the way he usually did.

Instead, he remained in the doorway. "Samra," he said. His tone was stern. "Come back into the living room. It's rude to be in here when everyone is out there."

"I just wanted to rest a bit," I said. "My back hurts, and I'm tired."

I looked over at him. His arms were crossed and his expression dark. "You're not the first woman to be pregnant you know."

My stomach dropped. He had never been upset like this with me before. As he turned his back, I scrambled out of bed and followed him into the living room, still tired but now worried that I had angered him.

I joined him on the sofa, hoping he might give me a sign of reassurance—perhaps put his arm around me or reach for my hand. Instead he stared intently at the television. As I turned my attention to the screen, I wondered if he too was unsettled by his mother's criticism and all her efforts to underline that this home was hers, not ours. Perhaps we would talk about this when we got to bed that night, and then Ahmed's mood would pass.

But we didn't speak. Not that night or in the many nights to come.

Instead, our life immediately shifted into a gloomy new routine. Each morning I rose at about 6:00 a.m. to make Ahmed's lunch. Amma had chastised me for sleeping in. "It's shameful for you to be sleeping when your husband leaves for work," she said heatedly.

After Ahmed took the lunch I had prepared and left for work, I would help Amma in the kitchen or sit with her and Abba in the living room, watching TV or listening to Amma talk about family and friends. In the afternoon, Amma and Abba would nap, and as much as I would have liked to do my homework then or even talk on the phone with my parents, I was often too exhausted and would sleep as well. Once Ahmed came home, we'd have dinner and then return once again to the living room couch to watch more TV. If Amma went into the kitchen, Ahmed would shoot me a look that made it clear I should accompany her. Just like in Dubai, Amma was never to be unattended by her bahu. When Ahmed's parents were finally ready for bed, we would be allowed to retire as well. Ahmed would crawl silently into bed and immediately roll over to go to sleep. If I tried to chat or engage him in any way, he would mutter that he was tired and then refuse to respond further.

Sometimes, Ahmed came into our room only to leave it once his parents were settled in their bed. Once when I tried to join him, he shooed me back. "It looks bad if you and I are by ourselves in the living room."

I retreated to our room feeling wounded and alone. From then on, I used that time to finish my homework or do my readings for school. But I couldn't stop thinking of Ahmed sitting by himself, just on the other side of the wall but remarkably far away.

Any time I tried to speak to him about the dramatic change in his behaviour towards me, he would glower and wave me off. I was both hurt and confused. All I knew was that there was something about living with his parents that made Ahmed put a great distance between us. But it was bound to disappear, I reasoned, once the baby arrived, and would certainly be gone once we had moved into a place of our own.

For now, however, our former happy life together seemed to have blown away as if by a mighty typhoon.

※　※　※

Perhaps because Ahmed found those evenings on the sofa with his parents almost as tedious as I did, he began to go out with his friends quite often. I was expected to stay home and keep Amma company. One night, I decided to call him, curious about where he was and hoping that he might come home soon. He was furious. "I'll come home when I come home. You have Amma and Abba. Stop bothering me and go to them," he barked, before hanging up on me.

While I found his mute chilliness deeply unsettling, this anger shattered me. I was still shaking from it the next day. Ahmed was at work, Abba was watching TV and Amma was in her bedroom, preoccupied with something. I slipped into my room and shut the door. I sat down on the bed, thinking about the phone call and about how my world seemed to be getting smaller and sadder by the day. I began to cry. The next thing I knew, Amma was standing before me near the bed, her face softened with concern.

"Samra, what's the matter?" she said gently. She sat down on the bed next to me. "Tell me what's wrong. You're my daughter now. You can tell me everything."

Her voice was soft and inviting. It felt like an embrace—and made me ache for my own parents. Perhaps, I thought, Amma had not realized how difficult things had been between Ahmed and me since she arrived. Perhaps she really didn't know how much I loved him and how much I wanted to make him happy. Perhaps she could help me reach him.

"Ahmed has been acting so differently since you and Abba got here." I looked up at her pleadingly. "He doesn't take me out. He doesn't want to spent time with me. He doesn't give me love or attention anymore."

"Oh dear, that's not right," Amma said with concern. She was patting my hand. "Don't you worry. I will talk with Ahmed. I will let him know that he needs to pay more attention to you."

Amma's warm reassurance was exactly what I wanted to hear. I gave her a tiny, grateful smile.

"But right now, go dry your tears and brush your hair. Perk yourself up for when he gets home. And don't worry—everything will be okay." At the sound of this unfamiliar compassion in her tone, a wave of relief washed over me.

I was in my room, putting on makeup and tidying myself up, when I heard Ahmed walk through the front door. The next sound that reached my ears was a high-pitched scream followed by a burst of sobbing.

Amma.

As I came out of the room Ahmed was running to his mother, who was standing, hunched over and gripping the edge of the dining room table as if for support. Abba had got to her before Ahmed did. He was gripping her shoulders as she sagged.

"What's wrong?" asked Ahmed, alarm sharpening his voice.

"I thought of Samra as a daughter," she wailed. "I thought she loved me. But she says I've ruined her marriage. She says I've turned you against her." She was looking at Ahmed, tears racing down her cheeks. "I want to go back," she continued. "I can't live here anymore with this pain." And then, "Just kill me now."

"Amma, what are you talking about?" I said. I moved towards her with my arms outstretched, but she struggled up and pushed me away.

"Go away. Just go away. You've broken my heart."

I glanced over at Ahmed. His face was contorted in fury.

"Look what you've done to her!" Ahmed's father was now spitting at me. "What if she has a heart attack from this stress? You know we have no health insurance yet!"

Then the three voices united in a chorus, all telling me to leave the room.

I sat on my bed in shocked silence. What had just happened? I was trying to catch my breath and clear my head, when Ahmed burst into the room. "What did you do?" he shouted.

I tried to explain what I had said to Amma. I told him that she had been fine when we spoke and for the several hours since. She'd even brought me a glass of juice and said more soothing words. Then we had stood shoulder to shoulder in the kitchen, cooking the evening meal together, joking and laughing.

Ahmed didn't believe me. "You bitch!" he said. "You're trying to create problems between me and my parents." With that, he stormed out of the bedroom and slammed the door.

I slumped down in bed, Ahmed's words coming back at me like a knife. *You bitch*.

I couldn't understand any of it. Ahmed was now further away than ever, and while I didn't enjoy Amma's company, I hadn't meant to hurt her. I certainly didn't want to be on bad terms with her. Guilt and sadness and anxiety churned through me. I felt as if a storm were tearing apart my little world, and somehow I had brought it into being all by myself.

An hour or so later, Ahmed came back into the room. "Go apologize to Amma," he said.

When I went into her room, Amma was sitting up in bed, a wad of Kleenex in her hands. She refused to look at me. "I'm so sorry if I hurt you," I said. "I really didn't mean to."

"I came here with so many hopes," said Amma, now sounding sorrowfully resigned. "I loved you more than I love my own daughters. But you have hurt me so much."

※ ※ ※

For the following days and weeks, I moved around the condo as if I were walking on a thin sheet of ice that might give way at any moment. Ahmed refused to talk to me. Abba fussed about health insurance and Amma's heart (although she had never had a problem with her heart). And Amma treated me with icy disdain. I tried to be as helpful as I could, working in the kitchen, bringing her food and tea, listening to her stories with greater attention. All the while, I watched her carefully, looking for signs of forgiveness, waiting for the silent treatment to end. I knew that Ahmed would never forgive me until Amma did.

Instead Amma became more overt with her criticism of me and my family. Since she had arrived, she'd been muttering about my failings—I had not been taught the proper way to cook a meal, or scrub a floor, or treat my elders. Now she began to complain about my parents, too. In particular about what they had given for my dowry.

My parents had never thought much about dowries, focusing instead on saving for their daughters' education. Despite their feeling that dowry giving was an outdated practice, during the original arrangements for my wedding they had asked Ahmed's parents about their expectations.

Amma had been vague. "We don't want anything. You should just give your daughter whatever you would like," she told my father.

Amma may have expected something, but she wasn't going to admit it. My parents were unsure how to proceed. They decided to talk with Ahmed. Shipping furniture and other household goods would be expensive and impractical. They offered him money instead.

Ahmed, however, refused. He told them that he too thought dowries were a thing of the past. He wanted nothing from them. My parents, already financially strained by the wedding celebrations, had taken Ahmed at his word. They did insist that he and I accept a small amount of cash, nevertheless.

Now, almost a year after the rukhsati, Amma expressed her shock at their frugality. "I don't understand your parents sending you here with nothing." She waved her hand around the room. "Everything here belongs to me."

She began to list all the items she had purchased for both her daughters' dowries. "No fewer than one hundred shalwar kameezes for each of them! So many lovely bangle sets. Thousands of dollars in gold jewellery. And, of course, for their homes—everything! The fancy LG washing machine, the stainless Whirlpool dishwasher. So many shopping trips I made. Dishes, pots and pans, a microwave . . ."

I tried to challenge her. "You said that you weren't interested in a dowry."

Amma snorted. "If you love your daughters," she said, "this is what you do. You give a good dowry."

※　※　※

As April began, my stomach ballooned, and my May due date loomed ever larger in my mind. The arrival of a baby was becoming more real with each passing day. I hadn't gone to any prenatal classes and was aware I had no idea what lay ahead. What's more, the crisis with Amma had proven that I was on my own. The thought of going through childbirth with my kind, loving husband now buried somewhere deep inside Ahmed, and with no other family or friends whom I could trust or rely on, had me lying awake at night, sweating and terrified.

Since Amma and Abba had arrived, I had managed to share some of what was going on in the condo with my parents. I could not, however, talk freely to them on the phone. For one thing, Ahmed's mother spent enormous amounts of time on the home line, so it wasn't often free. But more important, the condo was just too small to give me the privacy to discuss anything other than my school work and the weather. In the early months of my pregnancy, it had been decided that my mother would travel to Mississauga for the birth. But when my father heard about the strain in the condo, he thought my mother's presence might heighten it, so had discouraged the idea. Now I knew I couldn't manage without her. I wrote an email to my mother begging her to come. She immediately booked a flight that would have her arrive on my nineteenth birthday—April 19th.

I had hoped that with my mother's arrival, Ahmed and his parents might allow all our misunderstandings and the lingering resentments to be swept aside. But Amma's obsession with the dowry and my lack of wifely training should have taught me better. My mother was immediately caught up in the domestic turmoil.

Mama was tired and hungry after her long flight, but Amma, after greeting her with an icy hello, retreated to the living room without offering any refreshments. I peered into the fridge, hunting for something to serve, but everything seemed designated for a dinner party Amma was hosting the following night. I eventually scrounged up some cookies, a glass of milk and a mug of tea. As I set this paltry supper down in front of my mother, Amma sniffed.

"Until today, I do everything around the house, and you don't even lift a finger. Now your mother wants to be waited on, and you suddenly have the energy? Doesn't she care about you?"

The chill did not disappear, and during the dinner party the next evening, Amma interrupted anyone who tried to draw my mother into the conversation. The next day, when my mother suggested she could make me one of my favourite dishes, Amma told her that she didn't want another woman cooking in her kitchen. During the afternoons and evenings, sitting in the living room, any time my mother and I actually addressed one another, the exchange was met with sighs and frowns from Amma and Abba.

Eventually, Mama and I retreated to the bedroom when we wanted to talk.

❋ ❋ ❋

Ahmed had set up the solarium as his sleeping area, so Mom could sleep with me. This at least had the advantage of allowing us to chat at night before we went to sleep, and for a few evenings, we retired before Amma and Abba had left the living room. We sat on the bed together and talked in hushed tones about the tension in the condo and the strained relationship between Ahmed and me. My mother suggested that I push a little harder for some private time with him— the occasional evening out, she felt, could set things right. She told me that she was worried about me, that I needed to start taking care of myself, resting a little more, sleeping when I needed to.

And she talked about how difficult marriage could sometimes be. Two or three years into her own marriage, she had caught my father involved with another woman. She was certain he had either been unfaithful or was hoping to be. At her brother's wedding a short time later, she found time to talk with her mother and brothers. She wanted a divorce. She explained that with her teaching certificate she could manage financially with two children, but she was look-ing for the family's moral support. Her mother, her brothers and their wives were beside themselves. My mother's own parents had separated when she and her siblings were fairly young. Rather than make another divorce more palatable, my grandparents' split made it unthinkable. My mother's brothers and their wives reminded my mother that everyone considered my grandmother an enormous failure. And if my mother were to follow her lead, people would think that the entire family carried a deep flaw. They insisted she not bring this dishonour to them.

"Even if your husband has sex with another woman right in front of you, you must stay," insisted one of the sisters-in-law.

Mama still bristled at these memories, at the lack of support from her family. She intended to be there for me, but she also felt my situation was different. Things had started out so well that my plight was bound to be only temporary. She assured me that once we moved out on our own, Ahmed would become loving and companionable again.

Even these tiny bits of mother–daughter time ruffled Amma's feathers. A few days after my mother arrived, Ahmed took me aside. "Why are you neglecting Amma? You know a good wife's mother-in-law takes priority over her mother. You need to stay up to talk with Amma."

I was confounded. My mother knew no one in Canada. She was homesick and lonely. Yet fearing Ahmed's anger, I started to remain in the living room with his parents while my mother retired to the bedroom.

One morning Mama and I did not leave the room the instant we heard Ahmed and his parents. I was fully nine months pregnant and so round and swollen that I could find almost no position in which to sleep comfortably for more than a few minutes. My mother had heard me moaning softly when she woke and told me to stay in bed while she worked some of the stiffness out of my neck and shoulders. As she gently massaged my aching body, we heard Amma's voice in the hallway.

"Samra and her mother are ignoring me."

The next minute the door flew open, and Ahmed marched in. He looked at us with disgust. "Your daughter is so disrespectful," he snapped at my mother. "She is so spoilt. Haven't you taught her anything?"

My mother's mouth fell open, and then her eyes began to fill. "Why did I come?" she said, as tears wet her cheeks. "I shouldn't have come. I will go home."

At that, I started to sob.

Then Amma was scurrying into the room, Abba at her heels. "What's going on?" she said, pushing past Ahmed.

"I'm going home," said my mother, sniffling.

"No, no, you're not going home. You need to be with us."

"I'm not trying to ignore you, Amma," I said desperately. I couldn't bear the thought of my mother leaving before the baby was born.

Amma had nudged herself onto the bed next to me. She put her arms around me and gave me a big theatrical hug. She kissed me on the cheek and patted my mother's hand. She continued to produce a flurry of soothing sounds and comforting gestures. Then she looked over at Ahmed, as if to to make sure he had witnessed her acts of "kindness."

He had. "You are so ungrateful, Samra," Ahmed yelled before turning on his heels and stomping out of the room. A few seconds later the condo door slammed.

The next few days had all the calculated calm of a recovery room. Ahmed avoided my mother and me, but Amma smiled at us and asked how we were, even offering the occasional cup of tea. It was as if she had suddenly imagined what my mother might say to friends and neighbours once back in Karachi and Ruwais. She seemed intent on re-establishing some sort of amicable relationship before my mother left. But one afternoon, when Amma was out of earshot, Ahmed's father leaned towards my mother. His grey face was etched with bitterness. "It's because of *you* there is all this tension in my house."

❋ ❋ ❋

A few days later, I went into labour. As the contractions rolled over me, my mother and Amma made excited phone calls to the doctor and to Ahmed at work. Eventually I was bundled into Ahmed's car, along with Amma and my mother, and taken to the hospital. When we got to the hospital doors, Ahmed pulled up but would not get out of the car.

"You don't need me," he said.

Amma and my mother helped me into the hospital and stayed with me through the afternoon as the contractions grew stronger and stronger. I was tense and frightened, but even with all the pain, I tried to remember not to talk to my mother more than I talked to Amma. At one point during the long afternoon, I managed to whisper into the nurse's ear, "If my husband comes, can you tell him to stay. Tell him that only husbands can stay during the birth." I looked over at Amma to make sure the nurse understood my meaning.

As the evening approached, Ahmed reappeared. "I just came to check in," he said to the three of us.

He wasn't happy to discover that the attending doctor was a man and immediately asked if I could be treated by a female physician. The nurse declined, adding that Ahmed should stay with me but my mom and Amma should wait outside.

I was sad to see my mother go, but there was no way to ask her to stay without asking Amma. I was cheered when Ahmed pulled up a chair to sit beside me. As a wave of pain crashed through me, he took my hand in his. When the next contraction struck, he started to stroke my hair. As I struggled to breathe, he leaned over to kiss my forehead. I began to cry—not from the pain, but from happiness and relief. I had been right. The baby would bring gentle, loving Ahmed back. I had missed his tenderness so much.

A few hours later, the nurse was placing a beautiful baby girl on my chest. I felt her warmth spread through me. Lifting her tiny hand in mine, I gazed at her long lashes, her pink lips, her glossy, smooth cheeks. My heart ached with love. And a feeling I hadn't experienced in months. Serenity. This small, precious person was my daughter. And her simple existence meant that I would never feel alone.

Then, when I closed my eyes, I had another thought.

Now that I am the mother of his child, how can Ahmed not love me again?

CHAPTER 6

A GOOD WIFE

Those hours I spent with Ahmed, in the throes of labour, were riven with physical pain but filled with warmth, too. That warmth glowed like a little ember in my mind long after we were separated again.

The baby's arrival had brought something of the old Ahmed back. I noticed tears in his eyes when he first gazed at his daughter lying on my chest. And when he picked her up, his nervous gentleness made my heart swell.

But within only a few minutes, the reality of our lives began to reassert itself. My mother, Amma and Abba rushed into the labour room as soon as they were allowed. Amma scooped the baby from Ahmed's arms, and Abba bent over her to whisper the Azaan, the Muslim prayer call, into her ear. Then the tiny bundle was passed from one person to another. Ahmed and I both got our turn during the rounds, but we didn't get a say in how long we held her or where she went next.

And Ahmed's strange sense of modesty returned. Once I had been moved to the ward, he refused to be in the room alone with me when I attempted to nurse the baby for the first time.

What's more, fatherhood didn't quell Ahmed's irascibility. When the nurse pricked our daughter's heel to draw blood for a test and the baby let out a wail, Ahmed was beside himself. He grabbed her from the nurse's arms, then kicked a nearby cart, berating the startled nurse as he did. I begged him to calm down, but that only made him angrier.

"Be quiet," he said peevishly. "You don't know anything."

I was embarrassed—and oddly conflicted. It was good to know that Ahmed felt a deep connection to our daughter already, but it was frightening to think it could lead to such volatility.

❀　❀　❀

The morning after the baby was born people began to arrive in my hospital room. Amma brought me gond—a sweet mix of semolina, nuts and condensed milk—a traditional Pakistani dish thought to restore a new mother's energy. Family friends came through the door with their hands filled with flowers or stuffed animals for the baby. As I sat in bed in my starchy hospital gown, trying to smile and express gratitude, I found myself wishing the other bed in the room was occupied, so we'd have some excuse to turn people away. The chatter and commotion prodded me to keep my eyes open hour after hour, until it was finally late enough for my mother to shoo everyone out. When the last person disappeared into the corridor, my mother settled on the empty bed to spend the night with me. The second day was a copy of the first. And then, after forty-eight hours in the hospital, I was told I could go home. *Home.* That felt like a cruel joke. As I settled the baby into the car seat for the short drive, I couldn't help thinking that the last place I wanted to be was back at the condo.

Once there, two things happened almost immediately.

First, Amma named my daughter. While I was still in the hospital, Ahmed, his parents and I had talked about names. Amma had suggested "Kinza." I had my heart set on "Saarah." When we got home, however, it became clear that the decision wasn't up to anyone but Amma.

"This is Amma's first grandchild. She didn't get a chance to name any of her own children, so she should get to do this. You can't take that happiness away from her," said Ahmed.

I knew full well that a happy Amma was better than an unhappy one. Besides, I was too bone-weary for a debate.

Next, my mother left the following morning. She hadn't booked her return flight originally, thinking she might be needed for a while after the baby was born. But three weeks with Ahmed and his parents had wrung her out, and she wanted to escape their barely concealed hostility as soon as she could. I was sad to see her go but did not protest her decision. Once she was gone, I thought, Amma and Abba might be a little less on edge and a little less unhappy with me.

After my mother had finished packing up her things, we lingered in the bedroom to say our goodbyes. As we hugged, Mother reassured me that things would get better.

"Just try to find ways to make him happy," she advised. "Ask him to give you a bit more time. Try to enjoy your life together."

"I'll miss you so much," I told her, "but I'm glad I won't have to see you disrespected by this family anymore."

We embraced one last time, and then she was disappearing out the door with Ahmed.

By the time Ahmed came back from the airport, I had returned to bed and was lying quietly, listening to Kinza's whisper-soft breathing as she dozed in her crib. The lumpy mattress felt like a cloud compared to the stiff, vinyl-encased hospital bed. I could feel sleep beginning to take me off. But a voice jolted me awake—Ahmed's, telling me that I needed to be out in the living room, sitting with his parents. If I had thought having a baby would change any of the rules, I was wrong.

I sat bleary-eyed on the sofa, not even aware of what was being said or what was playing on the TV. Eventually, however, Kinza's mewls broke through my haze. I stood up shakily and walked into the bedroom.

Once I had fed Kinza and got her settled again I crawled back into bed, so tired that I was sure I wouldn't make it back to the living room even if I tried. When the bedroom door opened, I expected to hear Ahmed once again telling me to get up. But it must have been late. He got undressed and lay down in bed next to me. It had been weeks since we'd been alone together in our room. I reached out and put my arms around him.

Ahmed stiffened. He put his hands on my shoulders and pushed me back. "Get away," he said. "I'm trying to sleep." He rolled away from me.

As tired as I was, I knew I wouldn't fall asleep now. For the next few hours, I sat in the rocking chair next to Kinza's crib, awash with tears. I thought back to the first eight months we had spent together—all the times Ahmed had made me feel beautiful and loved. Where had I gone wrong? How could I change things back? How could I make him love me again?

Eventually Kinza let out a cry. Before I could get her out of her crib and nursing, Ahmed was awake. "You can't even keep a baby quiet," he muttered angrily. Continuing to grumble, he got out of bed and left the room. From then on, he slept in the solarium.

※ ※ ※

The first few weeks at home with Kinza were a dark blur. I had no experience with babies and was overwhelmed by the enormous responsibility of having a new life in my hands. In a year of change, this was the most seismic shift yet. And I was a physical wreck.

By the third or fourth day, I was bleeding and cramping, some-times so badly that I doubled over with the pain. Kinza had eventually taken to breast feeding, but I had not—my nipples were raw and cracked. And my episiotomy stitches were beginning to get infected.

Ahmed was impatient with my obvious suffering. "Stop creating so much drama" was his response to any expression I gave to my pain or discomfort.

His mother didn't provide any support either. "I gave birth to six children, and I never had any of these problems," she scoffed. Nor did my relative youth evoke any sympathy. She had married at fourteen and had her first child at fifteen, after all. She didn't hesitate to remind me that by the time she was my age, she was an experienced mother.

Despite Amma's earlier assurances that she would help me with the baby if I wanted to go to school, it was now evident that the care she intended to provide was not what I had imagined.

She did love to play with Kinza, it was true. Early one morning, my bedroom door swung open. I was just drifting off to sleep after a long night with Kinza, who had been fussy and wanting to nurse almost constantly. I had managed to doze for only a few minutes at a time. (I couldn't let more than a peep come out of her or Ahmed would appear in the room, furious that he had been woken.) As the sun began to rise, she seemed to finally slip into a deep sleep, and I fell back into bed with relief. But now Amma was scooping Kinza out of the bed and cooing in her face to wake her up.

"Amma, she just fell asleep," I begged.

"I have a right to my granddaughter," Amma said with a smirk. She turned her back and waltzed out the room with Kinza in her arms.

I closed my eyes and drifted into slumber.

Fifteen minutes later, Amma was back. She was holding Kinza out to me. "She's fussing. I think she's hungry. And her diaper needs changing." There would be no sleep for me for the rest of the day.

☀ ☀ ☀

That became the routine. If Ahmed was around, Amma would occasionally change a diaper or give Kinza a bath, commenting all the while about the need to teach me how to do things properly. But most of the time, Abba and Amma cuddled and played with Kinza until she needed something, and then she would be handed back to me. The one time I tried to enlist Ahmed in some child care—changing Kinza's diaper—Amma was indignant.

"That is a job for a mother. It's shameful to ask your husband for help," she said to me. And then to Ahmed, who was holding Kinza, "If your wife can't do it, I will."

I took Kinza back and changed the diaper myself.

But I wasn't left to myself when Ahmed's parents were entertaining the baby. I sat in the living room with them, sometimes falling asleep sitting up. When my dropping head woke me, I would open my eyes to see Ahmed or his parents glaring at me.

The only time I was allowed to stay in my bedroom during the day was when I was nursing. Often, sitting in bed with Kinza at my breast, I would nod off. But Ahmed and his parents quickly put a stop to that.

One evening, as Kinza and I dozed after she had finished eating, Ahmed came into the room and demanded that I get back out into the living room. I was desperate with fatigue and tried to convince him to let me stay for a while longer.

"You are so disrespectful!" Ahmed exploded. "You're not the first woman to have a baby!"

When I got into the living room, Abba was smirking at me. "Ah, the princess has finally come back," he said.

"Abba," I said, pleadingly, "I've been up all night."

"Well, of course you have," he said. "We brought you here to take care of our grandchild, but that doesn't absolve you of your duties towards us."

Ahmed was nodding in agreement.

I felt as if my heart had been dragged to my feet. It wasn't because Abba was taunting me or that he insisted I sit with them. It was the implication of his words. *Kinza was not my daughter. She was their grandchild.*

❀ ❀ ❀

A week after Kinza was born, Amma and Abba held a party to introduce her to their friends. Amma was excited but also annoyed that my mother hadn't waited for this big event.

"She clearly doesn't know her duty." She sniffed. "Like mother, like daughter, I guess."

We all gathered in the party room of the condo the afternoon of the celebration. Tables had been piled high with sweets and snacks, and the ceiling dripped with balloons and streamers. Music was playing on the sound system. Amma, Abba and Ahmed were positioned by the door, Amma with Kinza in her arms. I stood a little to the side, watching people's faces brighten as soon as they saw the baby. Amma and Abba looked as happy as I had ever seen them. Ahmed was glowing with pride.

I was wearing one of the fancy shalwar kameezes I had been given for my wedding celebrations, but as people filed into the room I thought how little it mattered that I had dressed with such care. No one seemed to notice I was there. When Abba made a speech, thanking everyone for coming, he talked proudly of the new addition to the family but made no mention of me, even though I was as much a newcomer as Kinza to many of the people there. *Kinza was Amma and Abba's grandchild. Not my daughter.*

When Kinza eventually began to cry with hunger, I was relieved. It was a chance to stop smiling, ease my aching breasts and be upstairs alone for a while. I bundled Kinza up and took the elevator to the condo.

I was still nursing Kinza when Ahmed burst through the door. His temper was raging. How, he demanded, could I disappear without anyone's permission? "You are so rude! So shameless! You should have fed her before the party!" His voice was louder than I had ever heard it before.

"But I did, Ahmed," I protested. "You know that she feeds every two hours. And I don't want to leak and stain my clothes."

"You have breast pads!" He was still yelling. "You should have made do and stayed. Amma is so embarrassed and insulted that her guests are all downstairs and you and the baby are up here."

This felt like a bad dream. Nothing I did was right. I began to cry.

"Stop being such a drama queen," Ahmed snapped. "Just give her a bottle."

"But the doctor said to only do that in emergencies."

The moment the words were out of my mouth, I knew I should have stopped talking. Ahmed's face twisted in anger. His words came out like gunfire: "What kind of useless woman are you that you can't take care of a baby?"

I had no response to give.

Kinza had finished nursing. There was nothing to do but wipe my face with trembling hands and follow Ahmed downstairs. Back in the party room, I forced myself to stay steady, to smile, to chat cheerfully to anyone who spoke to me. The only thing more unforgivable than disappearing from the party, I knew, was letting anyone know that I wasn't blissfully happy.

※　※　※

During the days of preparation leading up to my wedding, I had seen my marriage as a huge, rushing river that was about to sweep me away. Once Ahmed and I actually started our life together, I came to see that river differently. It seemed to have turned into a gentle stream, and I had been happy to float along, curious to see where it might take me. With the arrival of Ahmed's parents, the river changed once more. In those three eternal months, I had been dragged under again and again. First Ahmed's new behaviour left me gasping for air. But now, after his outbursts with my mother, his rage at the hospital nurse and the explosion at the party, I felt in danger of drowning. While he had not laid a hand on me, I was truly afraid. My father and mother had fought, and certainly my father had said and done unkind, even violent, things. But Ahmed's fits of temper seemed to be something else altogether—a loss of control that wiped out who he was or had been, that turned him into someone truly threatening. I began to feel relieved when he walked out the door to work.

As the weeks passed, I stayed trapped in the condo with Amma and Abba. Ahmed had stopped talking to me and, fearful that any exchange might turn fiery, I started to communicate with him through his mother. Mostly I asked for things Kinza needed. I couldn't shop for anything myself: I was told it would be unseemly for me to be seen walking out on my own. And Amma and Abba weren't interested in accompanying me. If we needed something, like diapers, I would ask Amma to ask Ahmed to pick them up on his way home.

My weekly forays past the condo doors—my Monday English literature classes—were also a thing of the past. I had finished that course before Kinza was born, and as I was breastfeeding, there would be no more courses that required attendance in a public place. Instead, I ordered the next calculus course through a distance-learning centre.

When the package came in the mail, I felt a shiver of excitement. The simple act of starting a new course, even if taking care of Kinza meant that the work would have to be done slowly, made me feel lighter.

In my room, talking to my parents on the phone shortly after the package arrived, I mentioned the new course. They were encouraging.

"Yes, yes," my father said. "Don't give up on your education."

My mother was a little more circumspect. "Yes," she said, "that's good. But remember, you are now in a country where you can go back to school at any point. Right now, you need time to care for yourself and your daughter. You can always take more than one course when things settle down a bit."

When I got off the phone, Amma wanted to know what we had talked about. When I told her, she looked thoughtful. Then she said, "Do you know what the problem is, Samra? The problem is that you have not been raised properly. It's my job to train you now. To undo all of the damage."

I felt my stomach begin to churn.

"If you were in medical school and we made you stop, well, that might be unjust. But you don't even have high school yet. If we stop your education now, there's nothing wrong with that because you haven't achieved anything. We gave you the opportunity to marry early, to get to the real purpose of a woman's life—without having to waste so many years on this school nonsense. You should be grateful to us that we've saved you all this time. So just forget about school."

I sat down on my bed, unable to speak. I couldn't believe what I was hearing. The whole reason I had agreed to get married in the first place was to further my education. The very terms of our agreement were being denied. I knew by now that what Fatima had told my mom wasn't true: Amma hadn't gone to school even after she was married. But I hadn't imagined that all the promises Ahmed's family had made were pure fabrications.

I looked up at Amma for some hint of hesitation or accommodation. But her expression was smug and satisfied. She had duped me, and we both knew it. We also both knew that no one in the family would contradict her.

I stared at Amma's broad back as it disappeared into the hallway. I was numb with the shock, too stunned even to cry. And then my stupor gave way to a volley of emotions: defeat, helplessness, panic. I was only nineteen, but already doors were closing.

I remembered the nightmare I had had two years ago in Ruwais—and the late-night phone call to Ahmed that had set my mind at rest. Had he been lying then? Was he lying when he brought me all those university brochures? And what about when he told me we'd find a way to continue my education once I got pregnant?

❋ ❋ ❋

I had scarcely come to grips with Amma's announcement when another flew at me.

I was in the kitchen one afternoon, helping Amma prepare dinner. As I chopped onions at the counter, she began to talk about looking for a bigger house. I didn't want to ask what this meant for Ahmed and me.

"It's so sad," she said wistfully. "All my other children have gone away. My daughters have married and gone. And my sons. So far away. They have all abandoned me."

I continued to chop the onions, but I felt the ground shift under my feet.

"But as I always tell my friends, at least I know that Ahmed will not leave me. He wouldn't do that to me. He will always live with his Amma."

I stared at the lifting and lowering knife before me, hardly aware that I was the one moving it. Amma had said it with such conviction that I knew it was the truth.

Amma didn't want to leave me in any doubt about our living arrangements. The next night at dinner, she raised the topic again. "Ahmed, you would never move out, would you?" she asked sweetly.

There was a brief silence. Ahmed's head was bent over his plate. "Of course not, Amma," he finally said in a quiet voice. "How could I ever leave you?"

I looked over at him, hoping against hope—but he would not meet my eyes. There could be no doubt now. Everything Ahmed had ever said to me about our future together had turned out to be untrue.

※　※　※

As the humid days of July settled on us and my shock started to dull, I tried to let myself be buoyed by positive things. Kinza was, I now realize, a wonderfully easy baby. At six weeks, she was sleeping through the night. Freed from constant sleep deprivation, I could enjoy playing with her. Bath time was soothing for both of us, and I adored the peaceful spell as she drifted off to sleep in my arms after nursing. And with each passing week, I began to feel more confident in my ability to take care of her and give her what she needed.

The summer also provided renewed opportunities to get out of the house. Family friends issued a steady stream of invitations to backyard barbecues. Sitting on lawn chairs in the warm evening air was a welcome break from the claustrophobic condo, with its ever-present TV. Sometimes, however, the hot weather got too much, and we would be herded indoors. This always presented me with a dilemma. There was no mixing of the sexes at these parties, so I had two choices. Did I go into the living room, where all the "aunties" congregated? Here women decades older than I was chatted about people I didn't know or boasted about their latest designer hand-bags and shoes. Or did I go into the basement with the "girls," who were the daughters of all the aunties? The girls were much closer to my age, but most were unmarried and childless. Their conversation about summer days spent at amusement parks or plans for univer-sity in the fall filled me with envy—and put me on my guard. Once, shortly before Ahmed's parents arrived in the country, I had dis-cussed my own plans for university with one of these girls. Word had gotten back to Amma.

She had been annoyed. "It's not good to discuss your personal life with others. People talk. Don't give them anything to talk about."

So I tried to spend most of these visits playing with Kinza and lingering as long as I could outside, with the grass under my feet and the sun on my face.

Early July also saw us on the road—the first time I had been out of the city since Amma and Abba arrived. One of Ahmed's brothers had started a master's degree in Indianapolis. Amma and Abba rented a minivan, and Amma packed a cooler of snacks for the nine-hour drive. The morning of our departure, everyone piled into the van—Ahmed behind the driver's wheel, his father beside him, Amma in the middle seat, and me in the very back with Kinza. I knew that Amma and Abba didn't like music in the car, so there would be no radio. I had brought a Walkman and headphones. As soon as Ahmed spied me in the rear-view mirror, he barked, "Take those off, Samra. It's rude not to be listening to the conversation."

I couldn't imagine what his parents might be saying that I hadn't heard a million times already. But I did what I was told, keeping quiet, looking out the window as the seemingly endless miles of asphalt flew under our wheels.

After a few hours, Kinza began to wiggle and squirm, her mouth opening and closing like a baby bird's. Knowing that any request of Ahmed was likely to be met with annoyance, I tried to postpone the inevitable. I gave the baby a pacifier, but she would have none of it. I got a bottle of formula out of the cooler and tried to warm it between my hands. But Kinza moved her little head every time I tried to get the nipple between her lips. It wasn't what she wanted. I suspected she was wet too, and even if she hadn't been hungry, she needed to be taken out of her car seat. Finally, I gathered up my courage and told Ahmed that we needed to stop so I could feed and change her.

Ahmed refused. It was going to be a long enough journey. He wasn't about to make it any longer.

A needle of panic pricked my heart. Kinza started to wail.

Amma and Abba both turned in their seats to glare at me. By now, both Kinza and I were desperate. I attempted to distract her with a rattle, tried to squeeze droplets of formula out of the bottle into her twisting mouth. Fighting to keep my voice from shaking, I hummed lullabies to her and kissed her on the head—anything I could think of that might calm her down. But she continued to convulse with sobs, her little brow beaded in sweat.

"Why is she crying so much?" snapped Ahmed.

"I told you," I whispered helplessly. My heart was hammering. "She's hungry. I'm trying to settle her, but she's hungry."

"What kind of useless bitch can't keep her own baby quiet?" Ahmed spat out.

By now both Kinza and I were in tears. And we were *both* long overdue for her feeding. As Ahmed drove on, his foot heavy on the gas pedal, I tried not to think about her empty stomach and my engorged breasts.

Eventually, I heard tires squeal and felt the car swerve hard into the right lane and then onto an exit ramp. Ahmed was pulling into a roadside gas station. But he was clearly in a rage.

"Do what you have to do—quickly!" he said as he threw the car into park.

I got Kinza out of the car seat and scuttled into the gas station washroom. I went into a stall, lowered the toilet lid and sat down. Kinza latched on and began to nurse with desperate energy. When she finally slowed down and took a breath, I pulled her away. It had been six hours since she last ate instead of the usual two, but I couldn't risk staying any longer. Holding her in one arm, I squeezed milk from my other breast into the toilet. Then I closed my blouse and ran back, sweating and breathless, to the car.

By the time we pulled into the parking lot of the apartment building, I had to pull my dupatta across my chest to cover my soaking-wet blouse and my excruciatingly swollen breasts.

For the next few days, Ahmed and his brother went off on their own more often than not, while I accompanied Amma and Abba to shopping malls or helped Amma cook. In the tiny one-bedroom apartment, I would retreat to the bedroom or the bathroom to nurse Kinza, but when we were out no one wanted to wait while I disappeared. So I brought bottles of formula. After a bit of struggle, Kinza submitted to this new routine. But I was worried. I knew that once she got used to the bottle, she might not want to nurse. The doctor and nurses at the hospital had impressed on me the health benefits of breast milk for babies, insisting that a minimum of six months was necessary. I tried to nurse Kinza as often as I could when we were back at the apartment, but as each day passed she became less and less interested. By the fourth or fifth day, I could tell I wasn't producing as much milk.

By the time we got into the van to go back to Mississauga at the end of the week, Kinza's breastfeeding was over. It made the trip home less traumatic, but I was bereft that she would no longer get the nutritional advantages of nursing, and that this wonderful connection with my baby had been needlessly severed.

I also felt a stab of loss at the thought that now I had no excuse to retreat to my bedroom several times a day.

※　※　※

The week in Indianapolis, sleeping on the living-room floor, traipsing through shopping malls, sitting in the hot, stifling apartment with Ahmed and his family, had been a trial—save for one all-too-brief afternoon. On our last day, Ahmed asked me if there was anything else to see in the city, as I had been reading up on it on the Internet. I mentioned a military museum. That caught his attention, but no one else in the family was interested. To my surprise and delight, Amma said she would take care of Kinza if we wanted to go. I was up and out the door before anyone could think twice about it.

I don't remember a thing about the museum.

What I do remember is Ahmed's transformation once we were out on our own. As he walked through the museum displays his stride was leisurely, his shoulders loose, his whole demeanour relaxed and natural. For the first time in months, I saw his easy smile and heard his round laugh as he chatted and cracked jokes. Outside the museum, he waved down another tourist to ask if he would take our picture. Posing for the camera, Ahmed put his arm around me. I leaned into him, happy to feel the warmth of his body and his tender touch. Just like old times. My smile for the camera was wide and genuine. After the museum, we stopped off for a hamburger, lingering happily over the last few French fries before making our way back to the van. If there can be moments like these, I thought, Ahmed is not gone for good.

※　※　※

The house hunting began in earnest on our return to Mississauga. In August, Ahmed, Amma and Abba made an offer on a house and put the condo up for sale. And then there was another, truly exciting change.

Ahmed's brother Shahid and his wife, Angela, were expecting a baby. In September, Amma flew to join them for the birth and to help with the baby. She would be gone for three months.

As Amma's huge suitcase rolled out the door, a fresh breeze blew through the condo.

One of the first things I did was rearrange the kitchen cupboards. It was a small act of defiance, but in an odd way it made my world feel a little bigger. And I began a new routine of my own. In the afternoons, I would put Kinza into her car seat and set her on the kitchen floor before putting on the radio. As music filled the kitchen, I began to cook our evening meal, moving in time to the music, revelling in the freedom to work without constant critiques. I cooked only the kind of food I enjoyed, avoiding the too-spicy dishes that were Amma's staples. I searched online for recipes to try, and I allowed myself to enjoy the praise Ahmed and his father offered about the meals I set out on the table.

Abba was now working as a security guard, which meant that he often had evening or night shifts. On those days, Ahmed, Kinza and I would sit at the dinner table together—like a happy family. Ahmed started talking to me again, and we began to plan our evening meals together, discussing which new dishes we would like to try and the ingredients Ahmed would need to pick up on his way home from work. He started joining me in the kitchen each evening to make dinner.

Even when Abba was at home, he often disappeared into his room to pray, giving Ahmed and I stretches of quiet time together. I still tiptoed around Abba, but angry, frightening Ahmed faded from my mind. I didn't let myself dwell on the hurtful things he had said or the callous way he had treated me.

Now we had this precious time alone, intimacy returned to our relationship. Ahmed had had a car accident in August, and the rear-end collision had hurt his back. With Amma away, he seemed happy to let me give him massages or rub analgesic cream into his muscles. While he didn't move back into the bedroom, I often brought him water in the night, and he would visit me, too. It wasn't quite the same as our early months of marriage, but it felt like a fairy tale compared to the previous weeks.

I suppose I could have used this time to confront Ahmed about what Amma had said about my education and about where we would live. It was certainly the route my mother would have liked me to take. During her visit and our later phone calls, she encouraged me to raise my concerns with Ahmed, to demand that he stand up to his parents, to tell him what I wanted and needed. But after months of feeling as if I were being rubbed raw, the peace that was returning to my life was like a cool, soothing balm. I didn't want to give that up. Besides, Ahmed had had to sign on to the mortgage so that Amma and Abba could qualify for a bigger loan, so for the time being our future was locked into that house. As for school, well, Ahmed's actions seemed to be challenging my assumptions about that. In the evenings, I would pull out the calculus workbook. He didn't say a thing. Instead, he often came to sit beside me and patiently help me with the questions. He never discouraged my work or asked why I kept at it. And when I did well on a test or assignment, he responded with enthusiastic encouragement and what seemed to be a measure of pride.

Ah, I thought. *Perhaps he wasn't lying to me after all. This is how we will do it. I will work quietly at night until I have finished my high school courses. Then I will apply to university. Once I am accepted, we will tell Amma and Abba about our plans.*

But in the meantime, we would have to be careful not to show our cards.

CHAPTER 7

TURBULENT WATERS

Amma was, of course, still present in our lives that fall. She called every day, and although she had packed up her personal belongings before she left, she supervised the rest of the packing by phone. Eventually, with her guidance, Ahmed, Abba and I had the whole condo in boxes.

At the beginning of November, we moved into the new house.

When Ahmed pulled the car into the driveway, I felt my heart beat a little faster. It was a large, salmon-coloured two-storey brick house at the end of a cul-de-sac. When we walked through the front door, space opened up before me. On the ground floor was a living room and a den, as well as a family room adjoining the kitchen. Upstairs was a pretty little bedroom where I could have a desk for my late-night school work, with a bathroom across the hall. Next to it, a bedroom that would be Kinza's. And out back, a yard where Kinza and I could play in the open air, maybe even putter in the garden when she was a little older, the way I used to do with my father.

But as we moved our furniture in, it became clear that Ahmed did not quite see the new house as the fresh start that I did. I watched sadly as he moved his computer and the sofa bed into the den. We would not be sharing a room. I was disappointed but had to think we had a better chance at a nice life together now that there was more room for privacy.

The first month or so in the house was almost as relaxed as the previous weeks in the condo. I tried to set up the house as best I could. I unpacked the glassware and spices and put them in the cupboards, knowing full well that this was only their temporary home. Amma would come back and change everything.

As the days got shorter and darker, I found myself increasingly overwhelmed with dread at the thought of her return. And then it was mid-December and Amma was striding into the house, clearly happy to be back—but not so happy that she didn't comment with disapproval on the arrangement of the furniture and the contents of the fridge.

A pervading tension returned to the house with my mother-in-law. Almost as soon as Amma had unpacked her bags, Ahmed stopped talking to me. He no longer wanted back rubs in the evening. And while he was still positive and encouraging when I occasionally showed him a test I did well on, he quit helping me with my homework. I tried to see this as temporary, as simply a bend in the river. *Just keep your head above water*, I told myself. Our course will change again.

When it did, however, the waters became more turbulent. Ahmed lost his job.

❀   ❀   ❀

As soon as we took possession of the house, Ahmed had come under financial strain. Amma and Abba had used the equity in the condo as a down payment, but even with Abba's job they couldn't afford to carry the house on their own. Ahmed had joined Abba in taking out the mortgage, and it had been agreed that the payments would be made by one person: Ahmed. Amma and Abba would pay for groceries, but most of the bills for the house, as well as all the things Kinza needed, were Ahmed's responsibility—a burden that had resulted in maxed-out credit cards. And now Ahmed was without a steady income to cover even the minimum payments.

Of course, he explained none of this to me. Whenever I asked about money, he dismissed me. But I overheard his conversations with his parents—and I could put two and two together.

After a few weeks, Ahmed managed to find a couple of part-time, under-the-table jobs. This helped, but the new jobs didn't generate enough money to pay the bills.

This new stress unleashed an anger in Ahmed that was almost constant. And it was focused in my direction. The very sight of me seemed to agitate him. He took to calling me names: useless, worthless, bitch. One evening I went into the den to ask him if he wanted a cup of tea. He was sitting at his computer. Instead of answering, he picked up a pen from the desk and threw it at me.

"Get out of here, bitch!"

Another time, I told him Kinza needed diaper cream. He picked up a water bottle and pitched it in my direction. "Get lost. I don't have money to waste."

This happened more and more often—this throwing of things as a way to respond to me. And no matter how affectionate or supportive I tried to be, I simply couldn't seem to reach him.

It was bizarre and utterly deflating. I remembered my mother's advice about confronting Ahmed about his behaviour. There was no peace to disrupt now, nothing to lose, so I began to question him.

"What's wrong?"

"Stop bothering me."

"What could I do to make things better?"

"You don't deserve anything better."

"Why don't you love me anymore?"

"You don't deserve to be loved."

Each time I was rebuffed, I retreated until desperation pushed me to beg him once again for answers.

※ ※ ※

One evening his parents went to a dinner party without us. We finally had a night alone. If we could just spend a few hours together, I thought—as we had in Indianapolis, as we had when Amma was away—we might build a little bridge back to our happy marriage.

Ahmed was in the den. I picked up Kinza and walked into the room. He didn't move. "Ahmed, maybe after I put Kinza to bed, we could watch a movie together. Or maybe just have a cup of tea and talk?"

"Leave me alone, haramzadi." He had called me "bastard woman."

I wasn't going to hide my distress this time. "Why are you doing this, Ahmed?" I was trying not to cry. "You never used to be like this. Don't you remember our good times together?"

I put Kinza on the floor, crossed the room and knelt at his feet. I wasn't able to stop my tears.

"Stop being so dramatic," he snarled.

I reached out and took his hand. "Please talk to me," I pleaded. "Don't do this."

He turned to look at me, his face a picture of hostility. Then he shifted his body towards me. "I told you to get lost!" he shouted. "Get out of my life."

With that he kicked me in the chest, knocking me over.

I screamed out, not from pain but from shock. I scrambled up, grabbed Kinza, and raced up to my bedroom. Once there, I put her on the bed, then dropped down myself. Through my sobs, I heard the front door slam. Ahmed had left the house. He would not be coming to see if I was hurt; he would not be apologizing.

Kinza crawled over to me and put her chubby little hand on my face. She was trying to get me to play with her. I was too absorbed in my own grief to lift my head. I imagined packing up a few things for Kinza and me, calling a cab and escaping—but to where? The only people I knew in Canada were friends of Ahmed or his parents. Certainly none of them would take me in. I imagined a hotel and plane tickets to Pakistan. But who was I kidding? I didn't even have enough money to pay for the imaginary cab.

There was no way out. My eyes were closed, but I could see walls closing in on me, my life narrowing to a small dark space. Everything was draining from me—hope, joy, light itself.

I had to do something. I sat up, pulled Kinza into my arms and moved off the bed. Placing her on the floor, I got my prayer mat from the cupboard, unrolled it and knelt to pray. But instead of asking for Allah's forgiveness, I asked for his mercy. *Please end my life, Allah*, I prayed. *That* would be a mercy. No one needed me in the world. Amma, Abba and Ahmed would give Kinza all the love she needed. They could hire someone to help them take care of her.

I wanted to be released. I didn't want anymore heartache or disappointment or despair. I didn't want the future that lay before me.

Holding my hands in front of me, lowering my forehead to the floor, I continued to beseech Allah as Kinza crawled around me. Whenever I lifted my head, she nudged herself under my praying hands. When I lowered it again, she wrapped her little arms around my neck. She touched my hair and stroked my cheeks. As she did, I began to realize that she wasn't asking me to play with her anymore.

She was comforting me.

I sat up and looked at her. "Mamamama," she burbled, crawling into my lap.

I pulled her to my chest, rocking her and kissing her soft curls as my tears dried. Then I got up and carried her to the bed.

With Kinza lying quietly in my arms, I thanked Allah—and I thanked Kinza. She had reminded me that I was not alone. And that *she* was my reason to live.

Before I knew it, sleep had stolen over both of us. We didn't wake until dawn.

※　※　※

I had imagined the move to the big house might give Ahmed and me the privacy we needed. I had imagined if we could take advantage of time alone, we might find ourselves again. But I had been shown the folly of these small hopes. *Perhaps*, I thought now, *if I could just manage to be a better wife, the kind of wife Amma expects me to be, I could bring my happy marriage back*. And so, to be a good wife, I gave myself over to the world that Amma fashioned for me. I got up early to make Ahmed his lunch and then went back to bed for several hours. Amma didn't approve, but she allowed me this small indulgence. During the day, I took care of Kinza and did housework or helped Amma with the cooking. When the chores were done, Amma and I would play endless rounds of cards, watch her favourite Indian soap operas or play with Kinza.

Ahmed would come home for supper and then most evenings go out again with his friends until the early morning hours. I would clean the kitchen and then put Kinza to bed. As soon as she was asleep and Amma had retired for the night, I'd go into my room, pull out my math books and turn on a small CD player I'd convinced Ahmed to buy me. Listening to music, I escaped into the safety of homework, just as I had in Ruwais. Sometimes, I took a little break by standing in front of my mirror, imagining myself on a stage. I would hold my hand out in front me, smiling as some gowned phantom placed a university diploma in my outstretched palm. Often I embellished this wistful pantomime with a little acceptance speech, smiling at myself in the mirror as I practised it. I knew it might be easier not to entertain this kind of fanciful hope, but other than the intervals I spent playing with Kinza, this time of homework and daydreaming was the best part of my day. And then the whole routine would start again in the morning.

※　※　※

For days and days, the only adult I talked with was Amma. Mostly I listened to her chat about her friends or nodded at her observations about dinner party menus or home decor. The soap operas gave us something we could both talk about—we dissected the plot lines and characters endlessly. But every once in a while, Amma led the conversation into more personal territory—like my obvious unhappiness.

One evening, we sat playing rummy at the kitchen table. Midway through the game, she put her cards on the table and looked at me kindly. "Why are you so sad, Samra?"

Ahmed had thundered out of the house, enraged once again by my offer to bring him tea after supper.

Her gentle tone was seductive. I had not forgotten what had happened the first time we'd had a heart-to-heart talk, but somehow I felt this time I might be able to trust her. The balance of power had shifted so definitively that it was hard to imagine why she would want to betray me now.

I told her that I didn't know why Ahmed was always so mad at me. I told her all the names he called me—the ones he hadn't yet said in her presence. I hinted at some of his physical actions.

She leaned over to give me a hug.

"Just be patient," she said. "Husbands get nicer as they get older."

She told me how difficult it had been for her in the early days of her arranged marriage. She had been just fourteen and had immediately moved in with Abba's mother and sisters. Apparently, all these women delighted in picking on her. And her husband never said a word when they pushed and slapped her. She also told me of Abba's slavish devotion to his mother. Once they moved to Kuwait, he had spent all his money buying things to send back to his family in Pakistan, leaving nothing for his own wife and children. I felt for her, but in those two tales I saw a truth that Amma never acknowledged. The time with her in-laws had been brief; she and Abba had spent the bulk of their marriage living on their own.

While Amma seemed to be genuinely sympathetic, she also took the opportunity to remind me of my place. "It's a woman's duty to stay quiet," she told me. "You mustn't tell anyone, not even your parents or sisters, about what goes on in your marriage. This is our business, not theirs. I will talk to Ahmed. His father will talk to him."

I nodded, hoping that this might happen—and that it might help.

"But don't forget," Amma continued, "it is perfectly permissible in Islam for a man to hit his wife. It's written in the Koran. And other women have it much worse than you do, but they still stay. It is a good wife's duty to make things better. After all, you need to keep your family together. If you were ever to leave, the government would give Kinza to Ahmed since you have no education and no money."

Amma's words made me feel queasy. Ever since Ahmed kicked me, I had been fantasizing about making a daring escape: tying my bedsheets together and shinnying down from my bedroom window. Rapunzel with a baby strapped to her back. Amma's words reminded me how silly those thoughts were. And dangerous. Ahmed was sponsoring me, and although Kinza was a citizen I was not. If I left the country, he could come and get Kinza, and I would never get her back. And even if I stayed in Canada, Amma was telling me, I might lose my daughter. She was right. I needed to focus on keeping my family together. After all, the kick had hardly hurt. It was like the occasional slaps my father gave my mother. These small smacks didn't mean we were being beaten.

As I took our teacups to the sink, I reminded myself that this family life was not entirely miserable. It meant I was raising Kinza in a comfortable home, with people who loved her.

And they did adore her. As Kinza's personality began to blossom, Amma and Ahmed became more and more attentive. Amma spent hours knitting and sewing little outfits for her granddaughter, and loved to bounce Kinza on her lap, chatting with her and singing songs. Ahmed would sit on the floor and play games with Kinza. And he took hundreds and hundreds of photos. I was enormously comforted that at least everyone was intent on making my little girl happy.

✼ ✼ ✼

When the warm weather of spring arrived, I started to take Kinza into the backyard to play. After months of confinement, this small patch of grass was a veritable oasis. Neighbours' yards bounded two sides of ours, but on the third side was a public walkway, separated from our lawn only by a chain-link fence. The occasional sight of people walking back and forth made me feel a little more involved in the world again. I often found myself thinking about where they might be going and how they might be spending their day.

But if Ahmed was home, I had to be careful how much time I spent outside. He seemed to hate the idea that people might see me. Before his parents arrived, he had wanted me to wear the hijab just to English class, the only time I wasn't in his company. Now he insisted I wear it wherever I went, including the backyard. He was clearly bothered that our next-door neighbours or people on the walkway might catch a glimpse of my uncovered hair. (Ahmed and his parents occasionally exchanged snippets of conversation with the people next door but I had never been introduced, and Ahmed made it clear he didn't want me to talk with them, ever.)

And then one day the full force of his new possessiveness hit me.

Amma, Ahmed and I had gone to the mall to look for party decorations and loot-bag items for Kinza's first birthday—invitations had already gone out to Amma and Abba's friends and their children and grandchildren, along with a few of Ahmed's friends and their families. As I pushed a shopping cart down the aisle of the dollar store, Ahmed's hand suddenly gripped my elbow. I stopped and turned to him. His mouth twisted with rage.

"Bitch, what's the point of wearing a hijab if you can't keep your hair covered properly?"

I reached up and touched my face. A tendril of hair had escaped my scarf.

"If you want to be a randi, why not sit out on the street?"

I knew the term *randi*—whore—but in Urdu it is a swear word of such ferocity and condemnation that I had never before heard anyone actually apply it to another person. Tears welled up in my eyes.

"Don't you dare do your drama here," Ahmed said. His tone was threatening.

I shoved the hair back under my scarf and walked shakily to the next aisle, where his mother, her hair uncovered as always, was lifting up a glittery multicoloured banner: *Happy Birthday*.

"We should get this," Amma said to me.

"Yes," I replied, trying to keep the tremor from my voice. All I wanted to do was go home.

There was something shattering about this public censure. Ahmed had been speaking in Urdu, assuming he couldn't be understood by those around us. But there was no mistaking the look on his face or the quiet violence in his voice. It was both an upbraiding and a humiliation. Here, out in the open, Ahmed was telling the rest of the world that I was his property. If I had had any doubt about what the hijab meant to him, I now knew the truth of it.

❄   ❄   ❄

By the time Kinza reached her first birthday, I was talking to my parents less and less often. Ahmed no longer provided me with calling cards, and we certainly couldn't afford long-distance calls without them. But even when my parents called me, I got off the phone quickly. I had begun to find their hopeful chatter irritating. I knew they hadn't imagined that my marriage would be so bleak. They had no idea Amma expected us to live with her. And they wouldn't have believed Ahmed's cold and cruel transformation. But their naïveté had helped lead me here. And now they could do nothing for me.

As I thought about all the freedom and encouragement I was given growing up, I started to feel increasingly bitter. Not towards Ahmed and his family but towards my own parents.

The endless talks of school and careers. My father cheering on our street cricket games, signing me up for squash lessons, driving me to the tennis club. My parents waving goodbye to me as I wheeled off on my bike or got on a bus bound for the Abu Dhabi shopping malls. What good was all of that if it made the business of "real life" so torturous? Why lead my sisters and me to believe we could make our own decisions and follow our own path when, in the end, we would have to leave our colourful little home and enter a tight, grey, box-like world? My parents had created a shimmery veil that obscured the truth of a woman's life. Yet that truth had been revealed every time my father shoved my mother or shut down a disagreement with one of his bullying tirades. Why did I think things would be different for us? I began to resent my parents for setting me up, for failing to help me understand how I would have to behave and think in order to survive.

Once, Amma had caught me watching cricket on TV. "You like cricket?" she asked. When I told her how much I loved the game, she clicked her tongue in disapproval. "As soon as I have rid you of all of these hobbies, I will have done the job of making you a proper woman."

Maybe Amma was right. Maybe life would be better for me now if I hadn't been allowed so many "hobbies."

※　※　※

And so I let myself disappear into days that came and went with the relentless monotony of rain. Occasionally there would be a small break. Perhaps it was a simple smile and thank you from Ahmed when I brought him his breakfast. Or a question from him about Kinza's day. Or he might show up late at night after his parents had gone to bed, holding a Burger King bag out to me, saying, "I thought you might be a bit hungry." At those times, a happy calmness washed over me. But then, like a clap of thunder or a flash of lightning, some sharp and unpredictable interaction would have my heart pounding. Sometimes it was just a slamming door or a volley of hurtful words. Sometimes it was more.

One of those lightning flashes came out of what looked for all the world like blue skies. My mother had told me that her sister's son was planning to move to Canada. I was excited at the prospect of family close by. When my cousin called to say that he had finally arrived, I was ecstatic. We talked for well over an hour, catching up on my family's exploits back in Pakistan and the UAE. Near the end of the conversation, he asked if Ahmed and I would like to come for dinner. I told him I would talk to my husband and get back to him.

But when I hung up the receiver, I could see Ahmed sulking at the other end of the room. "That was so disrespectful," he said. "Your cousin should have spoken to me first. Asked permission. You're *my* wife."

I didn't have the courage to mention the dinner invitation.

The next day, when my mother called, I told her about the phone call and my exchange with Ahmed. I was upset that this new opportunity for family and companionship had gotten off to such a bad start.

"Don't worry," said my mother. "I will call my nephew and explain. He can smooth things over with Ahmed."

The next time the phone rang, it was my cousin asking to talk to Ahmed. But when Ahmed said goodbye, he was angrier than before.

"So you thought you'd get him to phone me to ask again, did you?" He was standing very close to me. He punched two of his fingers into the centre of my forehead.

"No," I protested, "I just talked to my mom."

He continued to stab my forehead with his fingers. "You show me no respect," he spat. "We aren't going to your damn cousin's for dinner." With that he lowered his hand and pushed me onto the sofa before charging out of the house.

The next time my mother called, I told her to tell my cousin never to call us again.

Years later I discovered that my cousin, worried about me, had driven over to the house to speak with Ahmed. He had been put into the living room, but when it became clear that no one—especially not me—would be coming to talk with him, he left. I had no idea that he'd been there, and I wouldn't have any contact with him for another eight years.

❊   ❊   ❊

Other tempests compounded my desperation and had me returning to dark, sometimes even suicidal, thoughts.

One afternoon, I was helping Amma get ready to host a dinner party. She was at the counter, working on a curry; Abba was sitting at the kitchen table with a cup of tea.

"I need the cilantro, Samra," she said to me. "It's on the bottom shelf of the fridge."

I opened the refrigerator and squatted down to look for it. I could see the green leaves peeking up behind a large Tupperware container of Amma's gulab jamun—small fried sweets that sat soaking in a sugary syrup. I pulled the box from the shelf. But I had grabbed the lip of the lid to do so, assuming that it was on tight. As I lifted, the bottom of the container pulled away from the top, spilling the sweets onto my lap and sending a great wave of syrup all over me and the kitchen floor.

Amma let out a shriek. "What did you do? That was the dessert for everyone!"

"This is what she is learning from her parents," Abba fumed. "She talks to them and learns all these tricks to annoy us!"

Under Amma and Abba's shouts, I could hear the terrifying sound of running footsteps. Within seconds, Ahmed was in the room. As I sat hunched on the floor in a puddle of syrup, he turned to his parents, his voice savage.

"Why don't you grab her by her braid and give her a few slaps? Then maybe she'd learn some sense."

My eyes flicked up to Amma. She had never said a word of protest about any of Ahmed's name-calling or pushing. But would she actually join in?

Her face was hard as she looked at the mess on the floor and her ruined dessert. For a moment, I was truly afraid. But then I heard her sigh. "Just get up and go upstairs. Clean yourself up for the party," she said in disgust. "The guests will be here soon."

With relief, I scooped the sweets back into the container and wiped the syrup from the floor and fridge before escaping to the bathroom.

Perhaps Amma had remembered her own suffering at the hands of her mother-in-law, or perhaps there was just a line she was not willing to cross. But as I stood in the shower, trying to shampoo the last bits of sugar out of my hair, I didn't feel any comfort in that. How could I, knowing what Ahmed wanted done to me?

※　※　※

Amma may have refused to put her hands on me, but as my third autumn in Canada bore down on me I felt close to breaking. It was a grey evening. Amma and Abba had already eaten dinner and disappeared into their room to watch television. I was waiting for Ahmed to come home from work so we could eat together. (As Amma had told me many times, it was inappropriate for a woman to eat before her husband.)

As I put some small pieces of banana on Kinza's high-chair tray, I heard Ahmed's footsteps thudding from the entrance towards the kitchen. He appeared in the doorway and moved past me without saying a word. After patting Kinza's dark curls, he seated himself at the kitchen table.

I took covered containers from the fridge and began to put together our plates. I set Ahmed's dinner on the table and sat down beside him. My whole body felt tight with apprehension. I needed to ask him to spend a little more money that we didn't have.

"Ahmed," I said, hesitating slightly. If only I could leave the house to buy groceries and other necessities, instead of being trapped inside all day with my in-laws. This daily ritual of begging for the things we needed was humiliating. "We are out of diapers."

Ahmed didn't say anything for a moment, but then his fork cracked down on the plate. "We can't afford diapers," he snapped. There was a pause. And then an explosion: "You think I have money to throw around? You're such a useless whore! Why haven't you toilet-trained her already?"

I had expected him to grumble or perhaps even to ignore my request, but his anger knocked me back like a blast of hot air.

"She's only a year and a half."

But it was no use defending myself, I knew. I had done it. I had provoked him, and every word I said next would be met with another flare of rage. I needed to get away. I stood up.

"Sit down, bitch!" Ahmed roared. "Finish eating."

"I can't," I said. Suddenly, there was not enough air in the room.

Ahmed reached out and grabbed my wrist. He yanked me closer to him and began twisting my arm. His grip was so tight it felt as if he were trying to take my hand right off. Then, with his other hand, he reached for his glass. A wave of ice water hit my face.

I gasped. And then I heard, "Mommy!"

I looked over at Kinza, strapped into her high chair. Her arms were lifted into the air, reaching out to me. Her pink lips were trembling, her eyes filling with tears. Ahmed's grip loosened, and I broke away.

Behind me, the tiled floor was wet from the water Ahmed had thrown. As I stepped back, my feet slid out from under me, and I crashed to the floor. As I scrambled up, I saw the phone lying on the kitchen table. I grabbed it and ran upstairs to the bathroom.

Slamming the door behind me and quickly locking it, I sank onto the edge of the bathtub. My heart was pounding and my back was screaming in pain. I looked at the phone in my trembling hand and tapped 9-1-1. But before I hit the talk button I stopped, my finger hovering in mid-air.

What would happen if I made that call? Where could I go? How could I support myself? Amma had told me that in Canada the government would not let someone with no money keep her child. If I left, I would lose my baby. Now my whole body was shaking, my cheeks slick with tears.

The door handle rattled. Then Ahmed's voice was coming from the other side. "Please open the door, Samra." His tone was calm now, gentle.

"Go away," I choked out. "Just go away."

Ahmed continued a soft patter, his smooth words sliding through the cracks in the door frame. "Come on, Samra. I'm sorry. I didn't mean it."

I sat and sat. And then in the break between Ahmed's supplications, I heard Kinza's tiny cries. I gulped in air, trying to calm myself, trying to prepare myself.

Then I stood up and opened the door. I walked past Ahmed and went down to the kitchen. Taking Kinza into my arms, I returned to the stairs. In my room, I put her on the bed and curled up beside her. I held on to my child, letting my tears fall into her soft hair, waiting for the escape of sleep.

The next morning I woke in agony. The muscles in my back were locked in a fiery knot; on my wrist was a bracelet of dark bruises. Downstairs in the kitchen, Ahmed took in my wincing movements but said nothing. We both knew that he would not take me to a doctor. I might be able to provide an innocuous explanation for an injured back, but the purple shadow above my wrist and the sadness in my eyes would tell the real story.

This seemed to chasten Ahmed. In the days that followed, he refrained from calling me names or berating me, and I kept my bruises hidden under my clothes. He occasionally smiled at me and made small talk. Then, about three days after my fall, he suggested that he, Kinza and I spend the afternoon at the park. This was the first time the three of us had gone out without Amma and Abba. We left without telling his parents what we were doing.

Kinza had started to walk during the summer, so now we could watch her toddle through the park, cooing at the pigeons and squirrels that darted before her. We stood together pushing her on the swing, and Ahmed held her in his lap as we rode the see-saw up and down. Finally, the sun getting low in the sky, Ahmed smiled warmly at me and suggested we go for pizza before returning to the house. My eyes widened in surprise. Since Amma had arrived, we never went out to eat. It would be rude, Ahmed said, not to eat her cooking.

By the time we got home, I felt so cheerful and light that I almost floated through the door. But Amma was clearly upset. "Where did you go?" She cast a wounded look at Ahmed. She didn't actually care where we'd gone—just that we had gone without her.

Ahmed looked down guiltily and muttered about the park and the pizza.

Amma's grumpiness did nothing to dampen my mood. When my parents called the next day, I was bubbling with renewed hope.

I'd come to suspect that some of Ahmed's anger might be caused by guilt and regret. During one of his explosive rants he had said that marrying me was the biggest mistake of his life. Of course, after all his other hurtful comments, I took this to mean that I was a great disappointment to him. And while he may have wanted to make me feel that way, another idea eventually took hold. Perhaps it was marriage itself that was so problematic for him. He was stuck between his wife and his mother. He knew that he couldn't make us both happy, so he had chosen his mother. But perhaps he mourned what he had lost by doing so, just as much as I did.

Now, with this small gesture, this afternoon at the park, he had for the first time risked his mother's displeasure to spend time with me. I couldn't stop myself from inflating the occasion into a portent of great significance. This was certainly the initial step towards a new phase in our marriage, I thought. And given that Ahmed had finally got another good, full-time job, everything was bound to get easier.

My parents were happy. Like me, they were unrepentant optimists.

※　※　※

Of course, the harmony did not last. The second winter in the house was as cold and grey and lonely as the first. Ahmed's anger roared back repeatedly, chilling me with the knowledge that each explosion now held the possibility of more than verbal barbs. And the more frightened I became, the more ridiculously happy I was whenever Ahmed talked to me in a calm voice, or smiled in my presence, or laughed at something our daughter was doing.

Kinza was a delightful distraction for all of us. She was a happy, energetic toddler, with a burgeoning vocabulary and a calm, easy-going disposition. Ahmed doted on her.

Parents often tell you that their greatest joy is their children. For me, during these years, that was true. But it was also true that Kinza was my *only* joy, the only way I found real happiness. As she got older, I spent hours and hours playing her favourite game of make-believe— "Dora the Explorer." Kinza was of course Dora. And I would be her sidekick, Boots, following her every lead. Sometimes, I'd take the role of her nemesis, Swiper, stealing things out of her backpack until she stopped me by saying "Swiper, no swiping" the requisite three times. Sometimes, she'd instruct me to be "The Grumpy Old Troll," a role I took to with relish. At birthday celebrations and dinner parties, I could play the cheerful wife, smiling and laughing, by watching Kinza or thinking about one of our wonderful Dora adventures. And even on the most difficult days, Kinza gave me a reason to keep going. But the spring that she turned two, she gave me something else. My first small taste of freedom.

᭟ ᭟ ᭟

As the days began to warm again, I could feel my "hobbies" begging to be indulged. At the very least, I wanted to be outside, to walk in the sunshine, to be among people. At one of Amma's dinner parties, another new mother had mentioned to me that she was going to a parent–child drop-in centre with her baby. The program offered storytime, singing, crafts for the kids and companionship for the moms. I came home and phoned Ontario Early Years. There was a drop-in centre an easy walk from our house.

I had mentioned the idea to Ahmed and got no response, so I pushed it to the back of my mind. But after a week or two of relative tranquility in the house, I decided to try again. This time, much to my surprise, Ahmed told me to ask Amma and Abba to make sure they were okay with the idea.

A few mornings later, over breakfast, I mustered the courage to speak to them. "Amma, I was thinking of taking Kinza to a parent—child drop-in program, like the one Beenish goes to."

Amma was at the sink; Abba was at the table, having his morning meal—digestive biscuits and tea.

"It would be good for her to hear English." We spoke mostly Urdu in the house. I thought that if I suggested the program had some practical value, Amma and Abba might be more receptive.

Amma turned from the sink and swatted the idea away. "She will learn English anyway. There's no need to worry about that now."

I wasn't going to give up yet. "But it would be good for her to be around other children and to get out of the house." And then before I could stop myself, "It would be good for me, too."

Amma raised an eyebrow.

This was maddening. I wasn't asking for much. Why did I need to ask them at all? My irritation made me incautious. "I feel like I'm in jail sometimes!" I blurted out.

Abba exhaled loudly. "You get food and clothes and everything you could want," he blustered. "Everyone should be so lucky to be in this kind of jail."

I ran my hand down the front of my faded and tired shalwar kameez. Most of my clothes were now hand-me-downs from Amma.

I wanted to say that you get food and clothes in jail, too, but what you don't get is freedom. But I knew what kind of response I'd get to that. Freedom for a woman was never a good thing as far Amma, Abba and their friends were concerned. Women with freedom were "shameless": immoral and promiscuous.

I let the conversation drop. But I didn't let the idea go. I knew that the one weak point in Amma and Ahmed's fortress was their adoration of Kinza. Later in the week, I once more made mention of how beneficial the program might be for her. How could they deny their granddaughter this opportunity? Reluctantly, they agreed that Kinza and I could try it out.

※　※　※

Ahmed drove me over to the centre my first time. He escorted me into the room and looked about. It was a large space filled with tiny chairs, plastic toys and a cluster of mothers and toddlers. There were no men in sight. What's more, the head of the program was a Pakistani woman named Nuzah. Ahmed deemed it all harmless enough.

Yet as soon as he left the room, I was seized by uncertainty. I felt self-conscious and conspicuous. Surely everyone could see what Ahmed saw—a useless mother and a worthless girl. But Kinza was clearly delighted by the sight of so many new toys and so many other children. I had to work to keep up with her as she moved about the room. Before long, I was sitting at the crafts table with her, playing with poster paint instead of thinking about myself.

A few days later, I made my second visit. Amma and Abba were chilly as I packed up the stroller. This time, I would be walking over by myself.

It had been almost three years since I had ventured out on my own. I'd felt overwhelmed by the foreignness of my new home back then. Now it was familiar and yet, strangely, even more frightening. For the last few years, whenever I asked about going anywhere, Ahmed had shut down my suggestions with grim warnings. The safe haven he described to me when I was in Pakistan had vanished. No Western man could ever be trusted by a woman. Men were only interested in sex. And most of the white people who filled the streets hated Muslims—especially Muslim women. All alone, a Muslim woman might be a target for violence, and no one would come to help. By keeping me indoors, he was both protecting me and safeguarding my honour from Western corruption.

None of our family trips to the shopping malls or grocery stores had ever given me evidence of this kind of danger, and for the most part I suspected that Ahmed's rhetoric was just an attempt to curb my interest in going out. But now that I was finally on my own, I realized his words had burrowed deep in my mind.

As I left our quiet, dead-end street, the world seemed so much bigger than when it was rushing past our car windows. Once I got onto the busier roads, I was unnerved by the people and the traffic. Each time a vehicle passed me, the drum of its engine and the gust of air had me quickening my pace. Each time another person approached me on the sidewalk, I cast my eyes down and held my breath until they were past. At any moment, I thought, I might be run over by a car, or kidnapped and raped. I had found the catcalling and harassment by Karachi men upsetting and stressful, but the quiet streets of Mississauga were positively terrifying.

Even at the drop-in centre, I couldn't shake the feeling that I wasn't safe. Why would any of the women want to talk to me? And what would I talk to them about, even if they were willing? I didn't trust myself to keep my misery in check. If word got back to Ahmed and Amma that I had been talking with strangers about my life or making non-Muslim, non-Pakistani friends, I would never be allowed to return.

So, during my hours at the centre, I focused tightly on Kinza, joining the circle of moms and caregivers to sing songs or listen to stories but rarely exchanging words or looks with anyone other than my daughter.

One afternoon Nuzah introduced a craft that was taking longer to complete than usual. I was sitting at a low table with Kinza, nervously watching the clock as the usual end time of the program came and went. Getting increasingly agitated, I tried to hurry Kinza along.

Nuzah came up to the table. "Do you need to be somewhere soon?" she asked.

"I have to get home," I said—and then noticing her questioning look—"or my family will be angry."

"Why would they be angry if you spend a little extra time here with your daughter?"

I couldn't answer that.

Kinza had finished gluing pompoms on her picture. I helped her get off the chair and was about to gather our things when Nuzah pulled me aside.

"Is everything okay, Samra?" Her voice was softened with such care and concern that I felt tears filling my eyes. But I couldn't say a word. What if she told my husband? What if she called the police? I simply nodded at her and moved off quickly to get the stroller.

Nuzah began to approach me every time I came to the drop-in. She would chat casually, asking how I was, offering opportunities to talk. But I resisted.

One afternoon, however, I was even more silent than usual. I had awoken in the morning with a headache, which made me subdued with Amma. Ahmed was angry, accusing me of being rude and thoughtless. I had been feeling fragile already, so Ahmed's yelling shook me more than usual. I cried the whole walk over to the drop-in centre. When Nuzah tried to talk or smiled at me during an activity, I had a hard time responding.

After the program was over, Nuzah asked me to stay behind for a minute. She took me over to the carpet where we had circle time and sat down beside me.

"What's going on?" she asked. "You can trust me, Samra. You can tell me."

I still wasn't sure this was true, but before I could stop myself the words were spilling out. I told her that Ahmed wouldn't let me out of the house save for my hours at the centre. I told her that he wouldn't allow me to make friends. I told her about the yelling and shouting. I rattled off all the bad words he called me. I said that I had no idea how to change things, how to make him happy.

"Do you want to leave?" Nuzah asked me.

I started. "No, no, I can't," I said. "I don't want to lose my daughter."

"You won't," Nuzah said. She was holding my hand. "Next time you come, I'll give you some numbers to call, places that can help. You can use my phone."

The next afternoon at the drop-in, Nuzah took Kinza from my arms. "Don't worry about her," she said. "I'll look after her. You go into my office and make some calls."

She handed me her phone and a list of numbers. The Assaulted Women's Helpline was on top.

My hands were shaking as I dialled. A female counsellor came on the line, and I began to tell her what I had told Nuzah. The counsellor asked if I had children. When I told her about Kinza, she asked if Ahmed swore or yelled at her.

"No, no," I said.

"Okay," she said, "but does he call you bitch, slut, whore in front of your daughter?" I could hear the change in her voice, the shift from gentle support to sharp concern.

"Yes," I said.

"That's a real problem," she said. "We have to report that."

A chill ran through me. I snapped the phone shut. As Amma had often reminded me, I was a penniless woman without resources. I knew that if someone came to check on Kinza's well-being, they would snatch her away from both Ahmed—and *me*. What had I done? In my self-centred desperation for some comfort I had nearly lost my daughter. I went back into the play room, grabbed Kinza and started to pack up the stroller.

Nuzah noticed my frenzied actions and rushed over to me. I told her about the phone call. She reassured me that nothing would happen. I hadn't put my daughter in peril. I should call again another day, gather information, get some words of advice. But in the future, perhaps I shouldn't mention that Kinza had witnessed Ahmed's tirades.

I let some time pass before I had the courage to call again. The next time I called, the counsellor listened with compassion and empathy and let me know that what was happening in my home life was not okay. She suggested I consider leaving Ahmed and mentioned that there were shelters and resources for women like me. She assured me the authorities would not take Kinza away.

And while it was a relief to know that I wasn't crazy, that others found my distress and unhappiness completely understandable, I wasn't able to shake the feeling that the counsellors didn't quite understand. They were both white people (or at least I assumed they were). They didn't know my culture. They didn't believe that the fact Ahmed was not hitting me or cheating on me meant I was a lucky woman. Nor did his occasional flashes of tenderness and generosity—like bringing me fast food while I was studying at night—strike them as hopeful signs. Their words, while soothing, could not banish from my mind the message I was getting from Ahmed, Amma, Abba and even, sometimes, my parents: *You are making a big deal out of nothing*. After all, these counsellors talked about a kind of marriage I had never witnessed and suspected wasn't possible for anyone in my world.

In the end, I came away feeling that Ahmed's words and actions were not acceptable but that it was up to me to find a way to stop them. Perhaps if I worked harder around the house, did my chores more quickly, wasn't so gloomy, or made Amma and Abba happier Ahmed would relax and return to his old self. Outsiders couldn't help me do any of that. They would only put my family at risk.

※ ※ ※

While Nuzah provided much-needed support, she also helped me with my parenting skills. Kinza had plenty of toys at home, but English-language storybooks were in short supply. Nuzah suggested

I check out the library. There was a branch near the strip mall that housed the drop-in centre, so I began to pop in after the drop-in program was over.

Amma and Abba noticed my late arrival home. "Where were you roaming?" demanded Abba.

I explained about the library and the benefit of reading to Kinza. "Just another excuse to roam around shamelessly."

He was not entirely wrong. I was still a little nervous about being out on my own, but I was always reluctant to rush the walk home. The thought of what awaited me in that salmon-coloured house weighed upon me and slowed my steps. One afternoon, as I was crossing the bridge over the Credit River, I stopped. A small path leading from the road to the water had been beaten into the grass at the end of the bridge. It was a little steep, but I thought I could manage to get the stroller down and up again. I made up my mind. I hadn't gone to the library that afternoon, so I could steal a few more minutes and sit with Kinza on the riverbank.

Lying back on the cool grass, surrounded by trees and bushes that I had no names for, I felt as if I had been transported to a tiny corner of paradise. The roof peaks edging the horizon were easy to ignore. The sound of water burbling at my feet was all I heard; the cars and trucks barrelling over the bridge had been silenced. Kinza was cooing and chattering, her round legs kicking as she watched the dragonflies dart through the air. The air smelled aquatic and alive.

Tension seemed to flow out of my neck and shoulders into the earth below. My outstretched limbs felt lean and powerful. With my eyes closed, I imagined what it would feel like to be standing on soft ground, maybe on a cricket pitch, and then kicking out, running and running across the grass.

Kinza's gentle burbling brought me back.

It is so lovely lying in the fresh air, I thought. *What would happen if I just stayed here? If I refused to go back?*

I let fifteen, twenty, thirty minutes slip by. But then I could feel my heart beginning to beat a little faster. Would they miss me now? Had I lingered too long? What would they say? Reluctantly I sat up, brushed the grass from my tunic and trousers and turned Kinza's stroller towards the path.

But I knew I would be back.

CHAPTER 8

SHOPGIRL

t was another short delay in my return home from the drop-in centre. A quick stop at Tim Hortons to get a donut with sprinkles for Kinza. I stood at the counter after ordering and dug into my coat pocket to retrieve the toonie I was sure was there. But I couldn't find it. I stepped back from the counter, searching all of my other pockets and then turning my attention to the diaper bag. My embarrassment was ratcheting into panic.

Even as I anxiously worked my way through the bag, I knew my search was fruitless.

I never had any money on me. I had a bank account, which I'd been required to open when we got the mortgage, but it sat empty. The only deposit had been a thousand dollars that my father wired to me for my birthday the spring that Kinza turned one. I'd managed to buy myself only a few toiletries with that money before Ahmed transferred everything into his own account.

And Ahmed gave me no spending money of my own. If we were out shopping and I needed to buy something for Kinza or for the house, he might hand me a few dollars. "Why do you need money?" he once said. "It's not like you go anywhere without me."

He had been right, of course, but every once in a while I tried to squirrel away a few coins, like the one I thought was resting in my coat pocket.

I had moved the stroller away from the counter and was getting ready to slink out of the store when I heard a voice.

"Excuse me, can I buy you a coffee?"

I looked up. A white man in his early thirties was standing before me. He was pointing to the counter.

"No, thank you," I said, mortified. "I don't want coffee."

All the things Ahmed had told me about men were beating through my mind. Why was the man doing this? Was this some way to get me alone? To attack me?

"What did you order, then?" the man asked. I glanced quickly at his face. His eyes were kind and soft. And his tone was sympathetic—not seductive, not coercive. He felt sorry for me.

"A donut," I said weakly, glancing down at the stroller.

The man smiled at Kinza. "Let me get that for her."

I protested, but he put the money down on the counter and handed me the bag with the donut. "Have a nice afternoon," he said, as he headed out the door. I watched him get in his car and exit the parking lot. Then I pushed the stroller outside.

Sitting on a dusty bench, feeding small pieces of donut to Kinza, tears overtook me. I wanted to be grateful for the man's generosity, but all I felt was stinging humiliation. What kind of life was I living that I didn't even have two dollars on me? And what kind of person was I that people took such pity on me?

The answer was obvious. I was poor. I was powerless. I was pathetic.

By the time Kinza had finished eating, I came to another conclusion. My father had thought that money didn't matter. I always suspected he was a bit misguided, but now I was convinced he was wrong. Money mattered. Or at least, not having it did. Just like in my parents' marriage, a lack of money was making my bad marriage worse. It was certainly fuelling Ahmed's surliness. And perhaps most important—it was trapping me.

None of that was actually going through my thoughts, however, when a few months later, Ahmed made an unusual demand.

Despite his new job, he simply couldn't keep up with the costs of running the house, keeping the family car on the road and providing for Kinza and me. He often had to resort to payday loans, and he even began to talk of selling my wedding jewellery, just as my mother had done with hers.

One day, he came away from his computer with a look of misery on his face. "You need to get a job," he said to me. "It's impossible to pay for this place with only one salary."

He got his jacket and left the house for the evening, slamming the door behind him.

I knew he must have his back to the wall to have said this, and that he would hate it if I actually did start working, but nevertheless I was elated. A job! Another way to be out of the house and away from Amma and Abba. Time on my own. Responsibility. Things to learn. A chance to be with people.

That night, after I got Kinza to sleep, I went to the computer to type up my resumé. While I hadn't quite finished my Canadian high school credits, I wrote that I had completed my British O-levels. But I had no work experience at all. I dug deep into my past to fill the page.

When I told Ahmed I was ready to apply for jobs, he was grim. He didn't offer to drive me to the malls so I could start the process. A few days later, he was muttering again about the need for more money—and about my lack of contribution to the financial health of the family.

"Ahmed," I reminded him. "I can't leave the house to apply for jobs. You have to take me!" The logic of this annoyed him. Ambivalence, frustration, suspicion, humiliation—I could see the emotions roiling through him.

Eventually, however, he hustled me into the car, driving me from store to store as I dropped off my CV.

Much to my surprise, I quickly got two interviews, and then an offer from a discount department store called Zellers. And then another surprise—Ahmed actually let me accept the job.

※ ※ ※

Amma and Abba were deeply unhappy—with both Ahmed and me. They couldn't understand how he could even contemplate having a working wife.

"What does he want you to do?" Amma asked when I told her the plan. "Sit on the roadside naked so people will pay you?" Any sort of work outside the home, no matter how ordinary, was a sort of prostitution as far as her family was concerned.

The shame of having a working daughter-in-law was compounded by the inconvenience. I would not be around as much to help with the house or chat with them. And in my absence, they would have to take care of Kinza.

Ahmed was working the day I had my first shift. There was nothing for me to do but take the bus, all by myself, to the store. I had travelled by bus once or twice with Amma, but this would be my first solo journey—and the first time I had left the house without Kinza. As I stood beside the bus stop with the warm breeze ruffling my clothes, I was filled with a giddy awe. I couldn't believe I was here, alone. I had seen other hijab-wearing women working at dollar stores and Walmart. They always seemed as exotic as peacocks to me. How did they get there? How did they achieve such responsibility and independence? How was it possible to do something as daring and extraordinary as work at a checkout counter?

Now I would be one of them—a woman with a paid job. I could barely wait to slip into my uniform and take my place on the floor.

❈ ❈ ❈

The manager at the store was charmed by my British-accented English and decided that the ideal spot for me would be on the switchboard, making store announcements. In truth, the switchboard was just a phone, set up outside of the women's changing rooms. I would also be in charge of those—letting customers in, checking their merchandise and cleaning up the stalls after.

It was the perfect job.

My chief concern about working had been how to manage my interactions with the customers—especially the male ones.

Once I started going to the drop-in centre, I had begun to feel a bit braver about reconnecting with my old acquaintances. The profiles of a couple of friends popped up whenever I chatted with my parents over MSN, and I decided to renew contact with both of them. My old friend from Karachi, Fahad, was delighted to hear from me, and we started to exchange messages. In one I told him something hurtful Ahmed had just said to me. Fahad offered the comforting words I needed.

The next day, I noticed that the temperature in the whole house had dropped several degrees. No one was talking to me. As I helped Amma get dinner prepared, she broke her silence. "Why do you talk shit about your husband behind his back?"

I asked her what she meant. She quoted a line or two from my message to Fahad. Then she said, "Are you having an affair?"

I sputtered something about just being friends, but I couldn't concentrate on my defence. The question of how she knew about Fahad was fogging my mind.

It turned out that spyware had been put on the computer, and my MSN chats were being monitored. I didn't know exactly how it had come to be there, but Amma could not have been the one to install it. I stopped corresponding with my friends again, but Ahmed's growing possessiveness now became jet fuelled. Any contact I had with any man, no matter how casual, could be suspect.

Recently, while out shopping with Ahmed, I had asked a male sales associate where the baby shampoo was. The young fellow directed me to another aisle and I thanked him. But before I could move off, I felt Ahmed's hand around my forearm, his fingers pinching deep into my flesh.

"You really enjoy talking to other men, don't you?" I protested that I couldn't find the shampoo. "You could have found a woman to ask, if that was the real reason," he snarled.

As soon as I was offered the job at Zellers, I'd realized that men might soon be approaching *me* to ask about shampoo. And I knew that any career in retail would be short-lived if you couldn't smile or talk to male customers. As I walked into the manager's office that first day, I had tried hard not to think about what would happen if Ahmed witnessed such an exchange.

The ladies' change room area, therefore, was about as safe a place as I could be in the store. Here, I worked chiefly alone but was constantly with people. And I could talk. At the drop-in centre, the familiarity and intimacy of the group was a minefield. How to talk every day and not become friends? But at the store, my interactions could be friendly but brief. I could talk to the customers about fashions or the weather, or just about anything, without ever worrying that our conversations would veer into dangerous territory. Even if a customer wanted to reveal some aspect of her life—or ask about something in mine—she would be gone in five minutes, and the chances were good that I would never see her again. Nothing in this work, I thought, could upset Ahmed.

I was wrong, of course.

Since I was only part time, I worked primarily late afternoons and evenings. Ahmed would pick me up in the car at the end of my shift. Knowing better than to keep him waiting, I always hustled out of the store. One day, I couldn't wait until we got home to go to the washroom. I ducked into the toilets and got back out as soon as I could, but this tiny delay meant that other employees were already exiting into the parking lot.

Ahmed had a friend in the front seat, so I climbed into the back. Before I could even shut the door, however, Ahmed was interrogating me. "Why were others out before you? Where were you?" I tried to say something but he cut me off. "Who were you talking to? What guy were you flirting with?"

"Ahmed, I just stopped to go to the washroom!"

"Stop lying to me," he came back. "You love talking with other men. You're just a shameless whore."

I could see Ahmed's friend sitting in the front seat, silent. Heat rose through my chest and into my face. My throat was tight. This was the first time Ahmed had so openly derided me in front of his friends. It was an act of belligerent humiliation.

It seemed that I might be allowed to keep my new job and the small scraps of freedom it afforded me—but Ahmed would make sure I knew my place.

※　※　※

If Ahmed was ambivalent about my job, Amma and Abba were simply put out. They still had not gotten over my defection to the drop-in centre—my obvious desire to spend time away from the home was an affront to them.

They agreed to look after Kinza because it was what Ahmed wanted. But I knew they weren't happy with me for going along with it, which made me nervous. During my shifts at Zellers, I called home every couple of hours to find out how Kinza was doing. Most of Amma's reports were complaints. Kinza, now three, was curious *and* mobile. Our house was more or less baby proofed, but you still had to keep an eye on her. I knew it was exhausting.

After about two weeks, Amma began her campaign to have me quit work. "I can't take care of your daughter," she said when I called one day. (It didn't escape me that at times like these, Kinza became "your daughter" instead of "my grandchild.")

"If you love working so much, find someone else to take care of her." But Amma knew we couldn't afford that.

"I'd rather give you the money than have you work," she finally said. I knew that wouldn't happen either.

Amma complained to Ahmed when he got home from work, too. "Kinza is too much for me to handle these days, Ahmed. Make Samra stay home."

Ahmed was clearly conflicted. All the money I made was trans-ferred into his bank account, and it was a big help. But he didn't like the fact that my working made his parents unhappy—and me *happy*. Perhaps he worried about the way work might transform me.

The job did bring me both satisfaction and pleasure. At work I felt competent and independent, someone who could take respons-ibility and handle it well. It gave me a little thrill every time I strung the lanyard, with its enormous collection of keys dangling at the end, around my neck—or answered a question, or made an announcement.

At the same time, I missed Kinza. And I worried about her, too. Amma was used to playing with her, not taking care of her daily needs. Was she getting her meals on time? Was Kinza going to bed when she needed to? One day I came home from work to discover that she had been left too long in her pull-up diaper. She was soaked and beginning to get a rash. I felt sick.

Just as the leaves were beginning to turn, Ahmed told me to stop taking shifts. In some ways, I was surprised it had lasted as long as it had. I let my manager know that I wasn't quitting but wouldn't be available to work for a while. I suspected that when the cheques stopped coming Ahmed's mind might change again.

Sure enough, after a few months the budget shortfalls reappeared. It was late November—the Christmas shopping rush was underway—and I had no problem picking up shifts again. But I could feel the strain in the house intensify.

When I came home one evening with shopping bags of things I had bought on my own—some snacks, a few clothes for Kinza—Amma raised her eyebrows and Ahmed frowned.

"Why are you wasting money? You know we need that for the household." His obvious resentment made me feel guilty, as if I had been thinking only of myself.

I knew Ahmed's parents thought that I was selfish—and that my parents were, too. They both began talking about my missing dowry again. "That's the trouble with people who have no sons to support them in their old age," Amma would say. "They think they have to keep all of their money to themselves."

Now, when my parents called and asked to say hi to Amma and Abba, Ahmed's parents either refused to come to the phone or rushed off.

The point was clear: if my parents had cared enough about me and my "new" family to give us a big dowry, Amma and Abba would not now have to live with the shame of having a shopgirl as their bahu.

❀　❀　❀

My Zellers job was, among other things, a much-needed distraction. As well as the excitement of getting my first job, that spring had held a huge disappointment.

Earlier in the winter, I had finished my fifth grade-thirteen credit. I had everything I needed academically to apply for university. But I still had to discuss the process with Ahmed.

It was never easy to know how to broach my school work with him. He had been supportive whenever his parents weren't around, and I had been sharing my results with him as I worked through the courses, always careful not to boast or to telegraph my hope and ambitions in any way. In the early days, he had tried to act pleased for me, but I could tell that it was becoming more of a strain for him. With each credit I earned, we moved closer to the troublesome idea of university—and to the possibility that I might spend more time out of the house and out of the family's control. I just couldn't be sure how Ahmed would react now that I was ready for the next step.

When the grade for my course came in, I sat down with the transcript and tried to figure out what to say. In the end, I decided to focus on the fact that I had earned 100 percent. Wasn't that a great way to finish off?

When I handed Ahmed the transcript a few days later, I was shocked by his unalloyed response. "Wow!" he said, a big smile on his face. "Congratulations! You've really got a knack for this. So, what's next? What are you going to do now that you are finished?"

Of course he knew what I wanted, but I was thrilled he was inviting me to make plans.

"Apply for university!"

"Which schools?" he asked.

We talked for a little while about where I might apply; in the end, I put in my application to just two—York and University of Toronto, Mississauga campus.

Then it was a matter of waiting.

The intervening months were not always easy, but whenever I felt low, I was lightened by the thought of next year. The drop-in centre had been a lifesaver but going to university—that would get me out of the water altogether!

And then, one afternoon in the early spring, two envelopes arrived in the mail for me. I ripped them open before I even got out of the front hall. I had been accepted to both York and U of T. I could hardly wait until Ahmed got home to share the good news.

When I did, in the den, out of earshot of his parents, I could tell he was proud of me. He let me break the news to his parents.

That evening, as we cleaned up the kitchen after dinner, I brought out my acceptance letters to show Amma and Abba. There was a moment of quiet. No one made a move to look at them.

Amma smiled stiffly. "Oh, that's good," she said, but there was a little mocking lilt to her voice.

"Yes, congratulations," said Abba. He did not look up.

Then Amma let the smile drop from her face. "But who will take care of Kinza if you are at school?"

"Well," I said hopefully, "when you first heard I was pregnant, you did say you would be happy to care for the baby if I were in school."

Amma shook her head. "Kinza is too much work for me now," she said.

I had expected this response and had thought of a solution. "Well, then, I'll only go part time," I offered. "I can take night courses, or classes in the afternoon when Kinza is napping."

Amma turned her back to me and began to put the leftovers into the fridge. She clearly didn't want to talk about it anymore.

During the next couple of weeks, I pored over the university websites, looking at courses and professor profiles, imagining what it would be like sitting in a lecture hall or studying in the library. But I started to get a little worried. I could hear hushed conversations between Amma and Ahmed leaking out from under the door to the den. Ahmed was becoming very quiet whenever I mentioned anything about school.

One day, Abba told me to sit with him while he was having his afternoon tea. He occasionally did this—sat me down for talks about the proper role of wives and mothers, or how a Muslim family should behave.

"Samra," he started out earnestly, "tell me, what is your goal in life?"

"Well, university first, and then . . ."

"What do you want, a PhD, a master's?"

"I'm not sure yet."

"So explain to me what is so important about an education if you don't really know what you want to do."

"Abba," I said, a little impatiently—it was frustrating to have to justify something that seemed so obvious to me—"I want to push myself to reach my potential."

"But your potential for what?" Abba said. He was talking to me as if I were a small child. "Why would your potential depend on education? A woman's real potential is in her work as a wife and mother. And you don't need school for that."

"But—"

Abba ignored my interruption. "Look at Amma. She has only an eighth-grade education, and yet she is the most admired woman in our family. In our circle of friends." He looked at me over his cup of tea and raised his eyebrows as if to say, "You understand, don't you?"

I understood. University would only make me unhappy and strain my marriage. It was best to forget about it. I nodded at Abba and then excused myself, taking my tea mug to the sink. I had no intention of forgetting about it.

And then another letter arrived. It was from the Ontario Student Assistance Program, OSAP, and it held bad news. Ahmed's salary combined with his assets, which unfortunately included a brand new car that Abba had bought in Ahmed's name in order to save on insurance, meant that our family income was too high for me to qualify for any grants or loans. I called the office immediately and explained that my husband would not pay for any of the courses, but they were firm. Our family income was high enough that some portion of it could be allocated to my education. We had decided not to do that, and OSAP had to be reserved for those who did not have the means to make that choice. As I hung up the phone, my shoulders sagged. There was no way to explain that I wasn't actually part of my "family" in any meaningful way—at least, I certainly didn't have the power to make any choice about how the family income was spent.

After dinner, I went into the den to speak to Ahmed. I stood nervously with the OSAP letter in my hand. He was sitting in front of his computer. I told him that if I were going to start university in the fall, we would have to come up with the tuition. But I tried to assure him that if I started with only one or two courses, it wouldn't be that expensive.

Ahmed didn't seem concerned about the OSAP decision. But he also wasn't interested in talking about solutions. He waved me away.

"I don't have money for useless things," he said. His tone was as curt and quickly dismissive as if I'd asked for some ridiculous kitchen gadget.

"But Ahmed, I thought—"

Before I could remind him that he had let me apply, before I could argue about the agreement we had made before we were married, he had moved on to another objection. "Besides, Kinza is too young. Who would take care of her?"

Ahmed's question didn't require an answer. He had turned his back to me. I could see his shoulders becoming rigid and his jaw clenching. There would be no more discussion.

I tried to broach the subject again a few days later, but Ahmed's response made it evident that this was about more than finances or daycare. "What do you want me to do?" he shouted. "Fight with my parents?"

The following weeks were heavy with disillusion and despair. I thought back to that afternoon in the condo when Amma had dismissed my hopes for an education. The decision had been made even before then. And it was *Amma and Abba* who made it. Why had I allowed myself to believe Ahmed would stand up for me when the time came? Why had I imagined my life could be any different now?

* * *

I couldn't stop thinking about the opportunity that was being snatched from my hands. Some evenings, I would pull the acceptance letters from my desk drawer and lock myself in the bathroom to cry undisturbed, sitting on the edge of the tub, reading the offers over and over again.

The letters weren't the only reminders of what I had lost. We lived fairly close to the University of Toronto Mississauga campus, UTM, and any time we drove to shopping malls or dinner parties, I would sit in the backseat and peer out the window, trying to spot the signposts that pointed in the direction of the school. Before that OSAP letter, whenever I spied one of the blue graduation-cap icons, I'd smile wistfully. The signs always seemed like a promise—a tiny beacon of my future. *That's where I will be heading soon.* Now I felt foolish for believing in this fairy tale. The little blue caps became a taunting reminder of the cramped, closed world I lived in. Every time one flashed by the car window, I turned my head away and swallowed hard to prevent the tears that threatened to come.

⁂

My university application was not the only one I had made.

I had been asking Ahmed about the possibility of returning home for a visit ever since Kinza was born. Of course, our financial situation effectively ruled it out, but the idea that I would at some point go home to visit was never disputed. After all, my family had never seen Kinza, and even Amma and Abba could not object to a grandparent's desire to meet a new grandchild. But despite their openness to the *idea*, a trip was entirely hypothetical as long as a financial argument could be made to keep me back.

Since going to the drop-in centre, I had begun to talk with my parents more often again. (Nuzah and the counsellors had implied that they had not been as misguided in their hopes for my sisters and me.) During one of our conversations, my father advised me to get my Canadian citizenship as soon as possible.

"As soon as you have it," he said, "apply for passports for both you and Kinza. Once you have those, I'll buy your plane tickets."

My citizenship was important. I had shared with my parents what Amma had told me about the precarious nature of a woman's parental rights in Canada. And while Nuzah and the counsellors told me this wasn't true, my parents and I were nervous. We feared Ahmed, as my sponsor, might be able to prevent me from re-entering Canada if I left. Could he come and get Kinza from my parents' home, bring her back to Mississauga and leave me behind?

The solution was to get Canadian citizenship and a Canadian passport.

When my father first made the offer, I suspect we were both still thinking that the trip would simply be a visit. Yes, during many of the dark days since Amma and Abba had moved in, I fantasized about escaping my marriage and returning to live with my own parents. But whenever the clouds lifted slightly, I'd find myself thinking of another future—one in which I attended university, in which Ahmed and I lived in our own home, in which I had a career that gave us a bright financial future.

And I knew that this was my parents' hope for me as well. But now that I had been forced to abandon my postsecondary education, I found myself looking at the prospect of returning home a little differently. Neither my parents nor I talked about the visit as a way to leave the marriage, but the possibility hung in the air between us.

In August 2004, I had my citizenship test, and in the early days of 2005, my paperwork came through. And then, in March, the passports I'd applied for came. The day the heavy envelope arrived in the mailbox, I felt my spirits lift. I phoned my parents immediately. In whispers, we discussed my visit home. My father said he would book one-way tickets for the following week for Kinza and me.

"No, Papa," I said. "They have to be return tickets. I don't want Ahmed or his parents thinking that I'm not coming back."

I knew that if they guessed there was a chance of that, they might not let me go. My parents and I agreed that my return trip would be booked for August—to get Kinza back in time to start junior kindergarten.

※ ※ ※

The following week was frenetic and emotional.

I was both excited and a little dazed. For four and a half years, I had gone virtually nowhere on my own. My conversations with my family had been conducted in hushed tones. My Internet chats had been monitored. I had lived in a world with no privacy and no autonomy, a world that had stripped my voice and my independence away. Now, I was about to leave that all behind. I could hardly believe it. As I went about collecting the things Kinza and I would need for our trip, I often found myself holding my breath, as if a wrong move or a misguided word might slam the door shut.

No one appeared suspicious that I wouldn't return, but Amma and Abba were skittish and on edge. They didn't seem prepared to stop me from leaving—that would have been a clear indication they weren't the loving family they claimed to be. But they weren't happy about my absence either. Perhaps they worried about what I might tell my parents. And Amma was clearly embarrassed that my father had purchased the plane tickets himself. She phoned my parents after I had told her about the trip.

"Oh, Zafar-bhai, this country is so bad. All our paycheques go to taxes and the mortgage. There is never any money left," she said, to explain why she and Ahmed couldn't pay for the flights.

She then flew into a shopping frenzy, making trip after trip to the mall to purchase gifts that I was to deliver to her relatives in Pakistan and Dubai. Of the four suitcases I would be taking with me, only one held clothes for Kinza and me. The rest were Amma's presents.

While Ahmed's parents were unnerved by my departure, Ahmed seemed somewhat sad. Of course: he would miss Kinza terribly.

❦ ❦ ❦

As I packed my suitcase, I made sure to take every bit of paperwork I had—school report cards, Kinza's birth certificate and vaccination records, bank account information and anything else I thought I might need in the future. Slipping the papers under my folded clothes, I reminded myself not to give Ahmed any hint that I wanted to remain in Ruwais. A week's worth of relative peace had not expelled my thoughts of escape.

The morning of my departure, Ahmed reminded me once again of why I felt so desperate to return to my family. He was sitting at the kitchen table, not talking to me, and I could see that his mood was dark. Something was brewing. I didn't want to find out what it was.

These days I always felt jumpy whenever Ahmed and I interacted, but today, with so much at stake, that mix of uncertainty and fear slowed my steps, had me almost tiptoeing as I moved in his direction. *What words might soften his brow rather than harden his eyes? What can I tell him that will make him speak calmly rather than erupt with invectives?*

When I got to his side, I put my hand gently on his shoulder. "Ahmed," I said as sweetly as I could. "I'm going to miss you. Are you going to miss me?"

He made no response. I paused. *Perhaps I shouldn't push him into emotional territory. Perhaps I should focus on something practical as a way to get through our goodbyes.*

"Do you have ten dollars to give me for the trip? We have a lay-over in Heathrow, and I will probably need to buy us a little something to eat."

Ahmed shrugged my hand away. "Haramzadi! Ask your dad for the ten dollars, too!" His voice was brimming with resentment.

I was taken aback by his anger, but I also felt bad. By asking for money, I had reminded him of his own powerlessness. All his money was going into the house. Even if he had wanted to buy the plane tickets, or to come with us, he didn't have the financial resources. I suspected that since he couldn't take his frustrations out on his parents, he was taking them out on me. Or perhaps he was just sad about Kinza and me being away and didn't know how to express that.

I decided not to press the issue. Besides, despite Ahmed's out-burst, despite the fact that I would be flying across the ocean without a penny—or a credit card—I was buoyant. I just had to be careful not to let my cheerfulness show, in case my good humour provoked Ahmed further and he refused to let me go.

That fear—that my return home would be derailed—kept my heart pounding as the day went on. Once we arrived at the airport, Ahmed stayed close beside me at the check-in counter. As we moved towards the security gate, he put his hand on my arm and stopped me. I felt a stab of panic.

"Not yet," he said. "Let's have a coffee first."

As we sat in the airport Tim Hortons, I felt as if a bird were caught beneath my rib cage. It was hard to concentrate on what Ahmed was saying. He was talking to me as if I were a child, giving me instruc-tions on how I was to behave once we parted. I can only recall one of the many rules.

"Remember," he said, "now you are someone's wife. You must wear your hijab at all times—even at home."

Eventually, there was no more time to delay. Ahmed got up and reluctantly walked Kinza and me to the security gate. I tried to look sombre as I passed through the checkpoint, but as soon as Ahmed was out of sight, I burst into a huge smile.

As I pushed Kinza in her stroller, I was almost skipping. An hour later, safely on the plane, I pulled the hijab from my head. I was going home, and I was going to be myself again.

CHAPTER 9

THE STICKY WEB

The restaurant was filled with my family and friends. All about us were decorations that my mother had put up. In the centre of our long table was a large cake. Gifts for both Kinza and me were piled at one end.

When the group broke out into "Happy Birthday," my throat caught, and I felt the sharp pain that happens when joy washes over an open wound. It had been five years since I celebrated my birthday. In Canada, April 19th came and went with little fanfare. Amma would wish me happy birthday in the morning and give me a present—perhaps a tube of lipstick or a small bottle of perfume. My family would call; a card or two might arrive in the mail. But Ahmed never acknowledged the occasion, and the rest of the day always unfolded like any other. To be here on my twenty-third birthday, surrounded by people who loved me and whom I loved, was the best gift I had ever received. When a slab of cake appeared before me, I dug into it with guiltless pleasure.

A little more than two weeks before the party, I had burst through the arrival gates in Abu Dhabi, propelled by a wave of happiness and relief.

It had been an eighteen-hour journey with a four-year-old child, but the moment I stepped into the terminal my exhaustion fell away. As soon as I saw my family standing by the gate I ran, Kinza's little hand in mine, straight to them. The poor porter who had loaded a cart with Amma's bulging suitcases had to jog along beside me. I threw myself into my father's arms and immediately burst into tears. It was as if a dam had broken and every sorrow and pain that I had felt over the last years was flowing through the breach. Between sobs, I moved into my mother's embrace. She hugged me hard and then pulled back, putting a hand to my face. She looked aghast.

"You're skin and bones, Samra," she said. "I feel like I'm looking at a ghost."

I moved from her to my sisters, as my mother and father fussed over Kinza. We began to walk to the car, but I simply could not let go of my sisters. We moved awkwardly together, our arms locked around each other, like some sort of human crab. At times, I felt as if they were actually carrying me along.

Once we were in the car, I began to tell everyone what had happened in the time I'd been away. All the things I hadn't been able to say on the phone—because of lack of time or lack of privacy—spilled forth in an unbroken stream. The drive from Abu Dhabi to Ruwais was long. For the entire journey, I talked and I talked and I talked.

As we pulled into Ruwais my father was grinning, but there was sadness in his eyes. "Four and a half years of conversation in two and a half hours!" He chuckled ruefully.

Walking through the front door of the house was as disorienting as a dream. This was not the house I grew up in. My parents had been assigned a new address by my father's employer when my mother and sisters moved back from Pakistan. But while the floor plan was different, this house was filled with all the furniture and decorations of my childhood. It was at once familiar and yet distorted. But then, I was changed too—a different person than the one who had packed up all her belongings for the move to Pakistan over five years ago. Now I was a mother, as well as a wife, and lived a life that would have been unimaginable to my sixteen-year-old self. Holding Kinza's hand, I walked through the living room, leading her upstairs to the bedroom my parents had set up for me. My bed. My desk. My bookshelf. I felt a rush of bittersweet nostalgia.

That night, lying beneath the covers with Kinza beside me, I was overcome by echoes of my distant childhood. The bedsheets smelled like home, the quiet rustling sounds that drifted through the windows were soothingly familiar, even the shadows in the room were comforting. I sensed the deep, dark weight of sleep reaching for me, and I let go, feeling safer than I had since I was a tiny child. I was finally back.

※ ※ ※

My first days in Ruwais were spent close to home. My two middle sisters were working in Abu Dhabi, but they had arranged to have some time off with me for the first week, and then they returned on weekends. During the day, I drank tea with my sisters and parents, watched movies, took Kinza out to the park and spent hours happily cooking in the kitchen with my mother.

Even though I was free to go where I pleased and do what I wanted, even though I was safe in the arms of my family, I felt anxious. Every time the phone rang I jumped up to get it.

"Why are you doing that?" asked one of my sisters after I had rushed to the phone only to discover that the call was for someone else.

"Ahmed wouldn't like it if I let it ring for too long," I explained with embarrassment. I could see how ridiculous it must seem to them—that while thousands of miles separated me from my husband, I was still worried about meeting his demanding expectations.

As the days passed, I began to relax, some of the confidence that I'd had in my youth pulsing again through my veins. That confidence took me to the recreation centre with my sisters to play tennis and squash, as my parents watched Kinza. And to the market, where I puttered around the stores and window-shopped, enjoying the breeze through my hair once more. My loose hair and my old jeans made me feel as if my married life were far away.

My father offered to teach me to drive, so we went out together, me behind the wheel, slowly navigating the quiet streets of Ruwais. A couple of times, I left Kinza with my parents and took the bus to Abu Dhabi, where I stayed with my sisters in the apartment they shared with another family. I found it hard at first to venture out of the building on my own when they were at work. It seemed incredible to me that so many women walked freely down the streets, unafraid of strangers. My sisters scoffed at my nervousness. They were right. What had happened to Samra-baji, their intrepid older sister?

I worked at bringing her back.

※　※　※

I was beginning to feel like myself again, but it didn't take much to knock me back down. Ahmed called the house one evening a little over a month after I arrived. This time, I wasn't at home to take the call. My father told Ahmed that my sisters and I were out at the movies. Ahmed said he would call back.

The next evening, Ahmed called again. As soon as I got on the phone, I could tell he was upset.

"What are you doing, going out to the movies with your sisters? Girls don't go out alone!"

"It's okay, Ahmed. I was wearing my hijab," I lied. "And there were four of us together." I felt as if he had reached right across the ocean and grabbed my wrist. I could see his clenched jaw and creased brow hovering in front of me.

Ahmed wasn't interested in my defence. I listened for several minutes while he upbraided me, reminding me of my duty and my role as a wife. I got off the phone as soon as I could. When I hung up the receiver, I looked over at my parents. My mother stared back at me with an expression of sympathy, but my father did not raise his eyes from his teacup. His expression was stormy.

For days to come, the first thing Ahmed asked when he called was "Where have you been?"

Finally, after a half dozen of these phone calls, my father had had enough. "That's it," he said to me. "I'm not sending you back to that man. You are staying here with us."

I wasn't sure how to feel. Relieved, yes. This was what I had hoped for, after all, when I packed my bags in Mississauga. But also sad that my marriage had come to this. And ashamed that I hadn't been able to make it work. But perhaps more than anything frightened—frightened of telling Ahmed.

"Don't worry about it," said my father. "I'll talk with him."

For the next few weeks, back in the safe embrace of my family, I tried to put even more distance between Ahmed and me. I avoided his phone calls when I could. And when we did talk, I challenged him about the way he had treated me, the names he had called me. I made it clear that I had not been happy with him.

I also thought a lot about what it would mean to not return to Canada.

I would be separating Kinza from her doting father, yes, but she would still be surrounded by a loving family. My parents and sisters adored her. I saw how the idea that a wife and her children belonged to a husband's family had robbed my parents of time and connection with their only grandchild. If Kinza could be close to only one set of grandparents, I knew which ones I would choose.

And then there was my own future. My sisters Warda and Saira did not have university educations and yet both had found good jobs. They had had to move to Abu Dhabi to do so, but perhaps I could find something in Ruwais so my parents could help me with Kinza—at least for the short term. And maybe I would take a few university courses through correspondence. I asked my sisters to help me put together my resumé.

By the end of June, my father decided it was time to break the news to my husband. When Ahmed called, Papa gestured for me to hand him the phone. He told Ahmed that come August, Kinza and I would be staying put. He didn't want us to return to Canada. His voice was firm.

※　※　※

Ahmed was too shocked when my father initially spoke to him to say much, but over the next weeks he called frequently to speak to both my father and me. He pleaded with us, crying, apologizing and making promises about the future. And he sent me long, sad emails in which he professed his love for me again and again. He had lost his temper only because he adored me so much, he explained. It caused him pain when I wasn't being modest or when I wasn't my best self. He swore that if I returned, we would get our own apartment and start over. He told me he would work on his professional qualifications so he could get a better job that would allow us to pay for my tuition and to get our own house eventually. He was full of hope and ambition for us.

Amma contacted my parents as well. She tried to distance herself from everything that had happened since her arrival in Canada. She and Abba were shocked by her son's behaviour, she claimed. They had no idea why he acted the way he did. His anger was certainly a problem. They had tried to talk about it with him. When I came back, they would make sure that he changed his ways.

But my parents were not fooled.

"The days when daughters were told that they would leave their married homes only on their deathbeds are gone," my mother told Amma. "Daughters are not burdens anymore."

We all agreed that Amma and Abba were deeply entwined in my marital problems. They had misled my whole family about their attitudes and intentions. And the expectations and pressures they were foisting on Ahmed were clearly beyond his ability to resist—or tolerate. He had become an unkind husband, and I had been turned into a quivering wreck.

Bolstered by my parents' support, I continued to reject Ahmed's weepy pleas to return. One evening, I held the receiver tightly and made myself say the words I had been thinking for so long. "Ahmed, I can't live like this anymore." He heard what I was saying, but I had no idea if he believed me.

While I was trying to push Ahmed away, I couldn't help thinking about the promises he had been making. I was fairly certain that if I returned, nothing would change. It was true that I didn't want to be with the person Ahmed was now. But perhaps there was another way for the old Ahmed to return and for us to have a happy life.

One evening, near the end of July, I took the phone when Ahmed called. "If you want to stay together," I told him, "then you must move back here. Get a job in Ruwais or Abu Dhabi, and we can get a place of our own."

Ahmed didn't say anything in response, but I could tell he was thinking.

It was only a few days after this conversation that I opened my email to see another message from Ahmed, this one with a file attached. The document was a lease on an apartment in Mississauga.

Ahmed's signature was clearly visible at the bottom of the page. I called my father to take a look. We sat side by side, staring at the computer screen, reading every line of the document.

Ahmed had rented a two-bedroom unit not far from his parents' house.

The arrival of the lease seemed to shift the mood in the house. One afternoon, Ahmed phoned to talk with my father. Papa was on the call a long time. After he hung up, he came into my bedroom.

"I need to talk with you," he said as he sat on the edge of my bed, a look of concern clouding his face. "Ahmed is clearly suffering. He misses you and Kinza," Papa said. Evidently some of my husband's pleas had found their mark. After all, my father knew what it was like to be separated from one's wife and children. He had missed us all desperately when we lived in Pakistan and he stayed in Ruwais.

Then Papa continued, "He says that you like to talk with men when you are out. At the mall. He says you let your hair out of your hijab. He says this is why he becomes angry."

I rolled my eyes at my father. He had always encouraged his girls to think of themselves as equals and not to hide from talking with *any-one*. And his wife and daughters had never worn a hijab. But I could see that Papa understood jealousy and could empathize with Ahmed.

"He says he knows it wasn't right to yell at you or hurt you, and he will not do it again."

I took a deep breath. It seemed as my father's resolve to keep me in Ruwais had vanished. Ahmed had managed to convince him that this separation was an awakening for him, that he really was a changed man.

And now my mother as well seemed conflicted about my staying in Ruwais. She was concerned that a separation between Ahmed and me might make my sisters' chances at marriage more difficult. And like my father, she thought the new living arrangements could solve our problems. I should give the marriage another chance. My parents had, after all, stuck it out after my mother's one attempt to leave. They had had two more daughters and had given their four children a relatively happy childhood despite the periods of turmoil. And they had done all that within an arranged marriage that never blossomed into love, the way mine had.

As the date on my return ticket approached, I was a mess of conflicting emotions.

There was guilt. We had our own place to live now. If I didn't return, could I really say I had tried everything to make my marriage a success, to provide a two-parent home for Kinza, to create a happy family?

There was defeat. Without my being fully aware of it, Ahmed's accusations and judgments, his claims that I was worthless and undeserving of respect, had become the rhythm of my life. Sometimes the drumbeat was there for everyone else to hear; sometimes those staccato judgments were silently thumping in my own mind—even in Ruwais. Part of me no longer expected the happy home I thought I had when I first moved to Canada. If it didn't happen, then I didn't deserve it. If only he had *really* hit me, I found myself thinking. Then I might have more justification to leave.

There was fear. If I was perfectly honest with myself, I didn't want to be known as the woman who had left her husband. I remembered what my mother had said about her own mother. Everyone thought she was a failure. Before marriage, I had never failed at a single thing in my whole life. I was the one who got the top marks, won the awards, garnered the praise. A single mom? How could I be proud of that?

And finally, most important, there was hope—I could still imagine a bright future with Ahmed. Those first eight months we had had together were potent. And the three months of harmony we'd had when Amma was in California were reassuring. I still loved him, and I could see myself falling *in love* again. After all, since his anger was not moored to anything real, as far as I could understand, it seemed quite possible it could float away for good if the circumstances were right. Despite everything that had happened, I had a picture in my head—the three of us together, happy in a home of our own. Ahmed and I cooking together, playing with Kinza, curled up on the sofa in front of the TV. Now that he knew I could leave him, things would be different.

On August 4th, after four wonderful months with my family, Kinza and I stepped onto a plane back to Canada. I felt well rested and well fed and more in control of my life than I had before I left— if nothing else, the trip had been restorative. I was not as terrified as I had been at my nikah, and not as nervous as I had been leaving Pakistan five years ago. I was, instead, resigned.

I held Kinza's hand tightly as we walked down the aisle of the aircraft.

Well, I thought. *I have survived the rapids. From here the waters can only get calmer.*

※　※　※

Ahmed managed to get an apartment for us so quickly because he had agreed to pay market-value rent in a geared-to-income building. The place therefore had none of the simple luxury of the condo nor the ample comfort of the house. Its cut-rate finishes were bruised and battered, its windows small and gritty. The basement laundry room was damp, the tiny lobby was always filled with smokers, and the halls echoed with the sounds of squabbling children and blaring TVs. Since it was an older building, however, its rooms were relatively large, which was a bonus even though we only had a few bits and pieces of furniture that Amma and Abba had let us take from the house. But all that mattered to me was that for the first time, Ahmed, Kinza and I had our own home.

Ahmed had met me at the airport alone. He wrapped his arms around Kinza immediately and then stood to face me. "Hi, how are you?" he asked stiffly.

During the drive home we chatted about my time away and about his work, but the awkwardness of our reunion had me doubting my decision to return.

At the apartment, Ahmed and I moved into the master bedroom—the first time we had shared a bed since his parents moved to Canada. But the close quarters did not seem to close the distance between us. Those first few days in the apartment were uneasy for both of us. I was plagued with doubt. I called my parents whenever I could. I confessed to them that I was feeling crippled with homesickness, that I wanted to go back.

"You've got to give it a chance, Samra," my father said.

My mother suggested this might be the time to have a second baby, now that we were away from Ahmed's parents. Kinza was four and a half, she reminded me. It would be good for her to finally have a sibling. She too felt I needed to commit myself to this second opportunity.

I also let Ahmed know I was unsure that coming back had been the right move. He was, of course, frustrated and angry.

"Why did I get this apartment then?" he fumed.

But he did seem to be trying to make the transition easy for me. For the first few weeks, he took Kinza over to his parents to visit, but I wasn't required to accompany them. Eventually, however, I had to make an appearance.

I was not expecting a warm reception. Ahmed's parents knew that while I was home I had talked about their treatment of me and their effect on my marriage. My parents and I had made a short trip to Karachi to see relatives. I'd met Fatima there and told her how unhappy I had been living with her parents. I wanted her, as well as Amma and Abba, to know I thought they were at least in part at fault.

Of course, at the time, I hadn't imagined that I'd be back, sitting at the dining-room table with them.

Amma spent the visit tightly focused on Kinza, addressing me only when it was necessary in order to get food on the table or clean up afterwards. Abba said not a word to me. Neither of them looked me in the eye all evening.

Driving back to our apartment, Ahmed was even quieter than usual.

"Well, that was awkward," I said, to break the silence.

Ahmed frowned. "Well, what did you expect?" he replied. "You took their son away from them."

Yes, I *had* proved Amma wrong. Ahmed had left her. I knew I would not be easily forgiven for that.

※　※　※

By the time summer was drawing to a close, my homesickness had fallen away and Ahmed's easy warmth of old had returned. I was beginning to truly enjoy my new life in the apartment. I loved the fact that I could go out on my own to get groceries or take Kinza to the park when Ahmed was at work. The freedom to cook what I wanted, without criticism or direction, made the kitchen a cheerful place for me again. Ahmed was under considerable stress—both from his parents and from the financial strain of paying their mortgage and our rent—yet his spirits always seemed to lift once he'd spent time with us in the evenings or on the weekend. Our little family had many happy hours together.

What's more, I found myself in the centre of a bustling community. Because many units in the building were subsidized for low-income families, the hallways and elevators held a constant parade of parents and small children.

Once the school year started, these parents and kids would meet every morning in the lobby to wait for the school buses. Some of the other mothers were quiet, like me, but I soon noticed one woman who always seemed to be chatting and laughing. Pretty soon, she noticed me too.

Renu was about ten years older than I was, with two girls in elementary school. We hit it off right away. Ahmed wasn't pleased that while she was Pakistani, she was also Christian. "They have different values than us," he warned me. But he didn't say I couldn't spend time with her.

Renu and I began to get together during the day, after our children had left for school. When she confessed that she didn't like to cook the way I did, I began to bring her leftovers and portions of our evening meals. Delighted, she asked me for recipes, and sometimes to cook for her when she was having guests. When she discovered that my other passion was school, she wanted to know if I was interested in tutoring her two daughters. She would be happy to pay me. And she knew other parents in the building who might be interested in my services.

Before I knew it, I had a little after-school business happening at my kitchen table. The money wasn't much, but I was excited to think I might be able to help with our household expenses.

And then in early October, another development—I discovered I was pregnant.

※ ※ ※

My mother wasn't the only one who thought a second child would be a good idea. Ahmed had brought up the idea during the occasional peaceful periods when we lived with his parents. Like my mother, he thought Kinza should have a sibling. The prevailing wisdom of our family and friends was that a baby always strengthened a marriage. It hadn't quite worked out that way with Kinza, but now we were on our own perhaps a new baby would work its magic. And, I reasoned, with two children it would be much harder for Amma to argue that we should move back in with her.

When I suspected that I might be pregnant, I went to the doctor to have a blood test. Ahmed was home when the doctor's office called with the positive result.

This time, I felt none of the shock or fear I had with my first pregnancy. I was looking forward to having a baby in my arms again, to sharing this special time with Ahmed and Kinza. I was excited.

When I hung up the phone, I looked over to Ahmed. His face barely registered the good news.

"Aren't you happy?" I asked him.

"Yes, I'm happy," he said, without a smile. "What should I do? Dance?"

※   ※   ※

In the days that followed, I could feel tension building in the apartment. Ahmed's smile became rarer and rarer and his words increasingly few. He often seemed anxious and frustrated but never more so than when he returned from a visit with his parents. One night he came back looking especially angry. I asked him what was the matter.

"Leave me alone," he snapped. "What do you want me to do? Do you want me to give up my parents? Or should I give up you?"

I felt sick. Amma and Abba must have been putting pressure on him to move back in. Perhaps they were using the new baby as an excuse.

The next time Ahmed and Kinza came back from visiting his parents he was even more upset. "Samra, you don't know what I have to deal with. If we don't move back, I might as well die. Is that what you want?"

He put his thumb in his mouth and bit down on it. I rushed over and pulled his thumb from his mouth, the deep red indentations giving me a stab of guilt. Because of me, Ahmed was in pain. He didn't look at me.

"I just don't know what to do," he said. "I'm so frustrated."

Ahmed's eyes met mine, and I could see his unfocused anger finding its target. Kinza was hovering between us, looking upset. "Why can't you be a normal woman and just live with your in-laws?" he shouted.

His hands shot out and slammed against my chest. I stumbled and fell back onto the couch. Then he turned on his heel and disappeared out the apartment door.

I lay motionless on the couch for several minutes, Kinza crying and clinging to my side.

It's still hard for me to believe how shocked and surprised I felt every time Ahmed's anger reappeared. Even if I could tell he was agitated, could see the tightness in his face and feel it in his words, when his fury erupted I felt as if all the oxygen had been sucked from my lungs. In the aftermath, with my chest stinging and the blood thumping in my ears, I would resolve never to let my guard down again, never to let hope worm its way back into my heart. But then, while Ahmed was playing with Kinza or telling me how good my cooking was, that amnesic traitor slipped back in. And the next time Ahmed exploded I would be knocked over once again.

Perhaps the shock was especially potent this time because we had shared a little over two months of peace together. And all those weeks of love-filled phone calls in Ruwais. I was not at all prepared for this anger. But as I thought of what had just been erased by Ahmed's outburst, another sad idea formed. Despite his promises, despite having our own space, our marriage had returned to its darkest form in just two short months. It had taken no time at all for Amma and Abba's shadow to overtake us.

I had thought our life together would get better with the advent of another baby, but now I knew I had fooled myself. I wept quietly in my bed that night, but when I rose in the morning, I resolved to do something.

Once Ahmed was off at work and Kinza was at school, I called the Assaulted Women's Helpline and all the other counselling centres I could find online. I was looking for a Muslim woman. I didn't think a white woman would understand my situation or be able to offer a solution that I could actually use.

Eventually, I connected with a Muslim counsellor. I told her my entire story. At the end of it I said, "I want to go home to my parents. But I don't have any money."

"Why don't you explore ways to make money from home?" she suggested.

"I'm already tutoring a number of children, but it doesn't bring in enough."

"No," said the counsellor gently, "it wouldn't. But what about child care? If you could look after a couple of children full time, that would be considerably more money."

I got off the phone quickly. If there was one thing my new neighbourhood had, it was children. That morning, I drew up a flyer and printed copies off at the nearby FedEx office. After I was done, I walked the nearby blocks, sticking my ad to lampposts and grocery store bulletin boards and the laundry rooms of our building and the one next door. I knew that Ahmed wouldn't object if I was able to make more money without working outside the home.

I started to get calls right away. The mother of an eighteen-month-old girl was looking for full-time care. The mother of a two-year-old boy was hoping to find someone for a few days a week. I felt a little guilty, offering to take their children when I was planning to work just long enough to save for plane tickets, but I hoped the parents would understand when the time came.

My days became much busier, with two small children to attend to as well as Kinza at the end of the school day. But both my new charges were adorable, cheerful toddlers, and I could still get out with a stroller on the days when I had only one of them. I was also relieved to find that this second pregnancy was not making me feel ill or exhausted the way the first one had. In fact, I was surprised at how well I felt, how much energy I had now that I had a plan.

With the tutoring and the babysitting, I was now making between eight and nine hundred dollars a week. I paid a few bills with the money, but I tried to save as much as I could. Then I got a call from Ruwais that made building that nest egg even more urgent.

Warda was getting married, and the wedding had been set for early February 2006. I would have wanted to go even if things had been working out with Ahmed, but it was the perfect excuse to return home. I knew, however, that my parents would be strapped for cash. I told them I would find a way to pay for a flight for Kinza and me.

For the next month or so, I siphoned away as much of the babysitting and tutoring money as I possibly could. At the end of November, I called a travel agent and booked two seats back to Abu Dhabi for the end of December.

I had told Ahmed about my sister's wedding as soon as I heard, saying that I would pay for the tickets myself, but I waited until he was in a good mood to let him know that I had actually booked my trip. My return to Canada, I explained to him, would be in late March. But his recent behaviour convinced me I would not be on that flight.

That first physical encounter in October seemed to remove any control Ahmed had been maintaining over his temper. His rages became increasingly frequent, and he now pushed and grabbed me with almost every outburst. Sometimes, he would shove me onto the couch and pin me down, pinching my arms while he yelled at me. By the time I called the travel agent, my upper arms were covered with bruises, the newer ones throbbing each time I moved.

"March?" said Ahmed, when I told him of my journey home. "I'm not paying rent on this place for three months while you're gone. I'll

With my father in Abu Dhabi in 1982. My mother often told me how adventurous I was, even as a baby. Exploring, pushing boundaries and defying norms. I was often chastised for my rebellious streak. Now, I embrace it with pride!

Courtesy of Samra Zafar

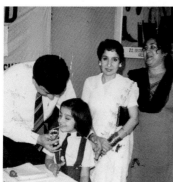

From the very start, I loved school. In grade one I received the award for top student in the class.

Courtesy of Samra Zafar

With my parents in our apartment. Only a few years after this, I would be deemed old enough to venture to the convenience store in the building on my own.

Courtesy of Samra Zafar

One of the many happy childhood memories I have is of this afternoon during a family weekend away in Dubai. Despite the fact that I couldn't swim, I loved being out on the water.

Courtesy of Samra Zafar

This was taken the summer I was fifteen during a family vacation in Pakistan. I remember being called too brash and outspoken, but I loved laughing freely and talking passionately. I wasn't willing to change myself.

Courtesy of Samra Zafar

When famed squash player Jahangir Khan came to Ruwais, my father took me to watch him play. When I approached Mr. Khan to get his autograph, he chatted happily with me and even gave me a few tips about how to hold my racket—squash was one of the sports I loved to play. I couldn't help noticing that I was one of the very few girls at the event.

Courtesy of Samra Zafar

It's not hard to see my fear in this photo taken the morning of my nikah, July 23, 1999. It was all I could do to get through the day without collapsing in tears.

Courtesy of Samra Zafar

After a visit to the beauty salon, my formal wedding photos were taken. I looked older than I had that morning, but no happier.

Courtesy of Samra Zafar

With Kinza and another child. I had just started university at this time. After I left my marriage, a relative asked me, "What's the point of winning awards and scholarships if you failed at the real purpose of being a woman?" But I had learned by then that it was important for me as a woman to define my own purpose. My honour lies in my freedom to be me—unapologetically.
Courtesy of Samra Zafar

A day or two after a violent assault by my then-husband at my uncle's house, I was still playing the good wife at family functions, feeling trapped by the pressures of my culture, too ashamed to tell anyone what had happened and growing ever better at hiding the bruises.
Courtesy of Samra Zafar

Receiving the John H. Moss Scholarship at the University of Toronto in April 2013 was one of the highlights of my academic life. Pictured with me are Dr. David Naylor, then president of U of T; Matthew Chapman, then president of the U of T Alumni Association; and the Honourable Michael Wilson, then chancellor of U of T.

Education gave me wings to fly and allowed me to dream. It opened my mind to the opportunities that exist in this beautiful world. I graduated from the University of Toronto in June 2013, and publication of my personal story in the *Express Tribune* that same day directed my future in a different but no less important way.

Courtesy of Samra Zafar

Telling my personal story can be painful, but it's also healing and cathartic. The best part, however, is the opportunity to meet wonderful, inspiring people who welcome me with open hearts. I'm constantly amazed by everyday heroes who do so much and give so selflessly to create a better world for others.

Courtesy of Samra Zafar

In early 2019, shortly before the release of this book, I went skydiving for the first time. I've heard people say that this experience was life-changing for them. But for me, it was the most powerful validation of the wonderful life I already have—a life that I have created for myself, by myself. The kind of life I could never have dreamed of just a few years before. The life where I can live my dreams, not my fears. The girl who was denied the most basic freedom was flying like a free and fearless badass! That girl is my hero. I am my hero. And I'm just getting started!

Courtesy of Samra Zafar

During my marriage, I never had the chance to travel. After a business trip to Croatia, I seized the opportunity to visit Switzerland, Germany, Holland, the Czech Republic and Austria. The trip was a life-changer—exploring this diverse world and its amazing cultures and people is now a passion. My goal is to visit fifty countries by the time I am forty.

Courtesy of Samra Zafar

Halina von dem Hagen is one of my first and closest mentors. Not only did she introduce me to RBC where I got my first job, but she has become a great friend who has included my daughters and me in her wonderful family circle.

Courtesy of Samra Zafar

Speaking about gender inequality at an International Women's Day event in Toronto. While we often discuss inequality in terms of breaking glass ceilings, I know that many are still struggling for the basic rights of safety and respect in exactly the ways I did. In Canada, over 6,000 women and children are forced to sleep in an emergency shelter every night to escape domestic violence. Every six days, a woman is killed by her intimate partner. Having escaped abuse myself, I'm working to help address these issues by supporting victims and raising awareness.

Courtesy of Samra Zafar

I met John Rothschild at the Moss scholarship interview in my final undergraduate year at the University of Toronto. Since then, he has become my mentor, my dear friend, and the closest person I've ever had to a real parent. Every conversation with John leaves me feeling empowered to go after my dreams and carve my path. He has taught me to pay it forward with the belief that true power lies in empowering others.

Courtesy of Samra Zafar

This is one of the proudest moments of my life—being named among the winners of Canada's Most Powerful Women: Top 100 Awards in 2019 (I won the award again in 2021). For most of my life, my power was taken away from me, my voice was silenced, my agency was stolen. Through a fierce belief in my dreams and the support of many amazing people around me, I was able to discover my power and rewrite my life story. Everything I do today is to pay it forward. True power lies in our freedom to be ourselves—authentically and unapologetically. And real power lies in empowering others.

Courtesy of Samra Zafar

By 2024, another childhood dream of mine came true— to become a doctor, a healer, and to help people see the light they have within themselves. I graduated from medical school at McMaster University in 2024 and am now well into the Psychiatry Residency program at the University of Toronto.

Courtesy of Samra Zafar

move back with my parents as soon as you leave. We'll figure out what to do when you return."

With those words, the second chance was truly over. I would never go back to that salmon-coloured house. There would be no place to return to, even if I were tempted to do so.

As I slipped out of the living room, I thought about what was in store for me. I would have to have the baby on my own. I would be a single mother of two children. Yes, I told myself, I would be a failure. But I would be a failure raising her children with doting grandparents and aunties who spoiled them. I would be a failure surrounded by people who loved and supported her. And I would be a failure without fear in her step or bruises on her arms.

❧ ❧ ❧

Nine months after my first return to Ruwais, I was bounding again towards my family at the Abu Dhabi airport. Back in Mississauga, I had made my apologies to my daycare clients, bid Amma and Abba another chilly goodbye and packed up all of my documents and precious belongings once more.

This time, the reunion with my parents and sisters was not awash with tears. I was no longer mourning my marriage but was looking, instead, to the future. I was here to celebrate my sister's new life and to start one of my own. This time, I really had escaped the sticky web of my Canadian life.

I thought I would never be caught up in it again.

CHAPTER 10

DARK DAYS

My sisters, my mom, Kinza and I were crowded into a hotel room in Abu Dhabi. We had spent a wonderful week together in Ruwais and were staying overnight before leaving for Karachi the following day. There was so much to talk about. But unlike the previous spring, this was an unbroken outpouring of upbeat news—my sisters filling me in on the details of Warda's engagement and their plans for the big celebration in Karachi. We had decided to stay in Abu Dhabi for a day so that my father could visit his doctor and we would be closer to the airport the following morning.

When Papa came through the hotel room door after his appointment, he was gripping a manila envelope, a sober look on his face.

"My results," he said, lifting up the envelope. My father had been suffering from kidney disease for years. About six months previously, frustrated that his treatment was not improving his kidney function, he'd opted for a holistic treatment plan. Recently, he had visited his doctor in Abu Dhabi to follow up. Now he had received the results of his tests.

The room grew quiet. Papa moved to the sofa while the rest of us gathered around him. He tore open the end of the envelope and pulled out a sheet of light-blue paper.

I didn't read the words on the left side of the page. My eyes were instead drawn to the column on the right. It was simply a long string of one word repeated—"critical." For each and every function tested, the result was critical. My eyes turned to my father. The expression on his face gave me another shock. He looked truly terrified.

My mother gasped. Saira stood up and ran over to the closet. She closed herself in, but we could still hear her sobs. I looked over to my mother. She was trying to maintain her composure. I knew I couldn't manage that. Instead, I excused myself and went to the bathroom to cry.

It didn't take long before it was clear we had all given ourselves over to tears. I returned to the room and joined my sisters and my parents. Squeezing together in a circle that spilled from the couch to the floor, we wrapped our arms around each other and wept over the bitter truth: my father was gravely ill.

※　※　※

The weeks that followed were a frenzy of preparations, the wedding activities unfolding under a cloud brought by the unexpected and sad business of my father's medical care.

Papa needed to start dialysis, but Ruwais had no facilities, so several trips to Abu Dhabi would be required every week. That would leave him exhausted—it was hard to imagine that he would be able to keep working or living his life the way he wanted. The other option was to start dialysis but follow it with a transplant. That surgery would be exorbitantly expensive in the UAE and my father's sister Nasreen, who had offered to be his organ donor, was in Pakistan. My parents decided they would stay in Karachi after the wedding—Papa would get his surgery there.

Once we got to Karachi, we moved into Uncle Ali's house and started to arrange for wedding flowers and to review menus, while my father was shuttled back and forth to the hospital for dialysis and pre-op tests. One day he walked into the house looking defeated.

Aunt Nasreen had just finished her donor evaluation. She had been rejected.

"They discovered she has diabetes," he said.

One by one, his siblings were disqualified because of various health concerns. My sisters and I went for tests as well. Only two of us were matches, and I wouldn't be able to donate a kidney until after my baby was born. Papa refused to consider taking a kidney from Warda as she was about to get married. We would have to look beyond the family for a potential donor.

My father's illness was like a powerful narcotic that dulled my memories and made me look at the world through a haze. The confidence I had felt stepping onto the plane alone with Kinza was gone. The world was dark, treacherous and confusing. The only thing I could see clearly was my mother's distress. After years and years of mercurial union, my parents seemed to have come to an understanding and settled into a relatively contented companionship. It was obvious that my mother was petrified at the thought of now being alone. I noticed the gentle way she spoke to my father and the comforting replies he made in return. They were leaning on each other in a way I suspected that they had done even during all those years of fighting. I found my thoughts drifting to Ahmed.

When I left Canada, Ahmed had talked about coming to Karachi for the wedding but eventually decided that he just couldn't afford it. I'd been hugely relieved. Now, however, I really *did* want him with me and my family. It was difficult to go anywhere or do anything in Pakistan without a man. And so many men in the family had been sidelined by my father's medical crisis. Having another man to negotiate with the wedding suppliers or act as an escort would be a big help to everyone. I was also worried my father wouldn't make it. It seemed important for Ahmed to see him one last time.

But more than anything, I hoped that Ahmed would be able to support and comfort me. I knew he had it in him. I remembered how he had shored me up when I first discovered I was pregnant with Kinza, how he had soothed me and helped me stay calm in the midst of the unknown. During one of our phone calls, I raised the possibility of his joining me in Pakistan. A few days later, he agreed to come. I phoned the travel agent immediately and booked him a ticket for the end of February.

The day of Ahmed's flight arrived. I called him a few hours before his plane was scheduled to depart. "Are you headed to the airport now?" I asked.

"Yeah, in a while." He sounded a bit surprised at my question, as if he weren't aware of what time it was.

"Ahmed," I said, "you'll have to leave right now if you want to give yourself enough time."

"Yes, yes," he said. "I've just got a few things to do first."

It made me nervous that he was cutting it so close. I waited anxiously for the next couple of hours. Then, after the departure time had come and gone, I called him again. I knew if he had made the flight, he wouldn't answer.

He picked up after a couple of rings.

"Why aren't you on the plane?" I asked in alarm.

"Amma had to go to the bank," Ahmed said. "I had to take her."

I was dumbstruck. As Ahmed continued to make excuses, it became clear to me that he had never intended to take the flight. No doubt he hadn't wanted to upset Amma with his absence. With the safety of thousands of miles between us, I let my frustration loose. Why had he let me book the ticket in the first place? Did he not care that we had just wasted a huge amount of money we didn't really have?

And why was he still more concerned with how his parents felt than with what his wife needed?

By the time I got off the phone, I realized the only thing that mattered to me was the last idea: Amma and Abba were still pulling the strings.

❋ ❋ ❋

We all tried to put my father's health crisis out of our minds during the celebrations, but it was hard to do with his obvious fatigue and frequent trips to the hospital. By the time the wedding had come and gone, his condition had visibly deteriorated. Dialysis had kept him going for a little over a month, but a transplant appeared to be his only real hope. There was a hospital in Lahore that arranged for independent organ donations. My parents travelled there to begin the process of finding a match, taking my sisters, grandfather and uncle along for support.

With so many people having to be put up by our Lahore relatives, I decided to stay behind in Karachi with Kinza until closer to the surgery. Only able to talk with my sisters and parents by phone, I felt the full weight of the situation descended.

After several weeks in Lahore, however, my father was told that a suitable donor had been located and the surgery was scheduled. As I walked through the doors of the hospital, my spirits sank. I had been in many hospitals in Pakistan, and this one was better than most. But there was still no comparison with hospitals in the UAE or Canada. The hallways and rooms were white, but the paint looked far from fresh, and dust and grime seemed to rest in every corner and along every windowsill. The carts and equipment we passed on the way to my father's room were scratched and dented, the furniture old and scarred. This hardly looked like a place for complicated transplant surgery.

But all my concerns about the facilities fell away when I walked through the door of my father's hospital room. He was sitting up, obviously waiting, his smile huge when he saw us.

※ ※ ※

The wait had left everyone feeling fragile and spent, but now the day was upon us and the mood turned anxiously hopeful. Kinza and I stayed for as long as we could, talking and hugging and telling stories, and then it was time for all of us to go back to our relatives' house and for my father to rest.

The next day everyone met again in Papa's hospital room, awaiting his evening surgery. When the orderly finally arrived to take my father into the operating theatre, Papa waved the wheelchair away.

"I can walk," he said proudly.

My mother, my sisters, and my uncles followed my father, stopping at the surgical waiting area. For four hours, we sat looking expectantly at the doors that led to the operating rooms. After a couple of hours, we were surprised to see an orderly approach us with a tray of biryani, curries and naan. But much to our alarm, he walked right past, disappearing into the operating-room area.

"What are they doing in there?" asked my uncle. "Having a picnic?"

A few people chuckled, but it didn't mask the anxiety in the room. The hospital hardly seemed clean, never mind sterile, even without snacks in the operating theatre.

It was about one in morning when the doors swung open and a stretcher bearing my father appeared before us. The surgery, the doctor told us, had been a success.

※ ※ ※

In the days that followed, Papa seemed to get stronger and stronger, and his test results came back indicating that the new kidney was functioning well. My relief was quickly followed by bone-deep exhaustion. Advancing pregnancy, the stress over my father, the crowded living conditions in my relatives' house and now the daily trips to the hospital were draining. So it was mid-morning when Warda, Kinza and I finally made it to Papa's hospital room about a week after his surgery. As we came into the room, I noticed that his bed was empty. My mother and Uncle Aziz were sitting in the chairs, crying quietly.

"Your father had a heart attack in the middle of the night," said my uncle. "He's in the ICU now."

My sister and I looked at one another in disbelief. I couldn't stay in the room. I took Kinza by the hand and fled to the prayer room. Collapsing onto the prayer rug, I begged Allah to spare my father.

※　※　※

The following day Papa was back in his room; the day after that, his colour had returned, and he seemed tired but much himself again. While everyone fussed over him, he turned his focus on me.

"Samra, you look worn out," he said to me. I had returned to his bedside after taking Kinza for a short walk outside the hospital. "What are you still doing here? This is all too stressful for a pregnant woman. You should go back to Canada where people can take care of you."

"No, Papa," I said. "I want to stay here with you."

"Don't be so stubborn, Samra. It's too crowded at the house. You need a place to rest, a good bed to sleep in."

I shook my head. He tried another tack. "And so many people here, in our relatives' house. I'm worried about them, too. This has been a terrible inconvenience."

I simply couldn't imagine returning to Canada, being so far away from my frail father and my weary mother. Finally, however, I agreed that I would take Kinza back to Karachi, where I could have my own room and perhaps get a little more rest. My father seemed satisfied.

Two days later, Kinza and I stopped by the hospital to say goodbye to Papa before heading for the airport. As I stood at the bottom of his bed, rubbing his feet, everything in my heart told me that I shouldn't leave. Kinza was leaning against me. She had grown very fond of her grandfather since our arrival in Abu Dhabi three months ago. But when we entered the hospital room, she didn't run to him like she usually did. She knew that he was not himself yet.

"Why is he always lying down now?" she asked me. "Why does he have so many tubes in him?"

"Beta, come here," said my father.

"Be gentle!" I warned her as she ran to his side. She paused and put her head softly on his chest. "Nana, I'm going to miss you."

"Don't worry, Kinza," Papa said. "I'll be out of here in no time. And I'm going to come to Canada to see you." He was stroking her hair. Then he kissed her lightly on the forehead.

My mother got up from her chair and came over to Kinza. She took her hand. "Come with me now. Let your mother talk to her father."

Once we were alone, I moved closer to him and took his hand. "I'm scared, Papa," I said. "What if something happens to you?"

My father tried to reassure me, just as he had Kinza, but I was shaking and inconsolable. "This is the fear in you that I've been try-ing to get you to overcome since you were a child," he said gently. "I wish you could see what I can see in you. You don't need me. You don't need anyone else."

I didn't want to let go of him.

"You can do anything, Samra," he said. "You just have to recog-nize your own strength." I stood by him for a few moments longer, squeezing his hand, unable to move. Finally, he dropped my hand and nodded towards the door.

As I walked out of the hospital my heart was breaking. Once we got to the airport, it was all I could do not to tear out of the boarding lounge and take a cab right back to him.

※　※　※

I had been in Karachi only one day when the world fell apart. I was in my bedroom when I heard my aunt cry out and start to weep. I rushed into the living room. Uncle Ali handed me the phone. Uncle Aziz in Lahore was on the other end. He told me that Papa had had another heart attack. He was now on life support.

For the next two days, I was on and off the phone with my sister Saira in Lahore. Her reports were grim. Papa was paralyzed, couldn't talk and wasn't able to eat. But, I told myself, he had bounced back after the surgery, had regained some strength after the first heart attack. He would overcome this, too.

On the morning of March 22, 2006, I awoke to the sounds of my aunt wailing. I leapt out of bed and ran to her. When I found her, I knew what she was about to say, but I didn't want to hear it.

The news she had to share simply didn't make sense. It was impossible. I needed light and air to help me think. I stepped out onto the balcony outside the living room. Gripping the wrought-iron railing, I looked down. The street below me was rippling and out of focus; I felt my knees begin to buckle.

And then a voice: "Mommy?" Kinza's small hand grabbed mine, pulling me back to myself again. I straightened and shakily led her back inside.

※　※　※

My father's death was something that refused to become part of my reality. I would approach the truth of it for a second or two and then fall back into denial.

One of the first times my mind did this little dance, I was with my aunt, sitting on her bed with her, hugging. We had just finished packing our bags for our flight to Islamabad, where my father's funeral would take place. We hadn't spoken much since that morning's phone call, moving through the necessary arrangements like automatons. Now, in this quiet moment, I begged her to tell me what I wanted to hear.

"He's fine, right?" I could only just form the words.

"Yes, he's fine now," she replied. "The soul never dies."

The tears that came at the sound of those words made me incapable of speech for hours after.

※　※　※

We arrived in Islamabad in the inky darkness. A minivan was waiting in the airport parking lot, spilling forth my aunts and uncles, my sisters and my mother. We hugged and clung on to each other before Uncle Ali shepherded us into the seats.

We were on our way to the hospital to see my dad, or so I told myself. But of course it wasn't a hospital. It was a morgue.

When we arrived, everyone climbed out of the van. I hung back as they headed into the building. Aunt Nasreen took my hand. "Come, Samra."

"I don't want to know," I said.

"You need to see," she replied. "You need to do this."

She led me into the building, down a dimly lit corridor, to a bright chilly room where the rest of my family was waiting. One wall was lined with small, square doors. A white-garbed attendant tugged one of the handles and pulled out a drawer. My father, grey and motionless, slid out on a tray before us. White cotton was stuffed into his nostrils. I gasped.

I wanted to tear the cotton out so he could breathe. I wanted to get him out of the room. He must be so cold, I thought. And then my mind went blank.

I don't know how long I had been standing there when I felt a hand on my arm. "Time to go," someone said. But how could I leave? Papa would be so scared to be left all alone in that room.

I stood my ground but was quickly engulfed by a riot of voices. One of them was mine. I was shouting "No!" Then the touch of hands on my arms, my shoulders, my back. I don't remember moving my feet. It was as if my family was somehow propelling me out the door.

※　※　※

The next day my father's casket was brought to a relative's house in Islamabad. From there, the men escorted it to the burial grounds while the women stayed behind, continuing to mourn at home. My sisters and I were weeping and distraught as we stood on the road, watching as the hearse disappeared from view. My mother had remained inside. As we walked back into the house, our arms wrapped around each other, we tried to calm ourselves. We were beginning to realize that our fully exposed grief was only causing my mother more pain.

It was late afternoon, the men back from the burial, the women wandering around holding out plates of pulao and korma, trying to get people to eat a little. Warda's new husband had arrived from Karachi in time for the burial. He was sitting with my sister, holding her as she cried on his shoulder. I couldn't stop myself from looking over at them again and again. My brother-in-law was murmuring softly to my sister, blanketing her with words of comfort. My sorrow was now edged with envy. How I needed that kind of attention and affection right now.

A short time later, my Uncle Aziz came into the bedroom I had retreated to, with his cellphone in his hand. "It's for you, Samra," he said.

I put the phone to my ear and heard Ahmed.

"He's gone," I said, starting to cry. "Ahmed, my papa's gone."

"I know, jaan, I know." I let the soft kindness of his voice wrap around me. "Everything's going to be okay," he said. "I'm coming. I'm in London right now. I'll be in Karachi when you arrive tomorrow."

"Tomorrow?" I sniffed. I was falling into Ahmed's long-distance embrace.

"Don't worry, Samra, love. I'll be there soon."

I had never wanted to see him as much as I did right then.

※　※　※

Ahmed put his hand gently on my head and pulled me into an awkward side hug. We were back in Karachi, alone in my aunt's living room, but we knew that any intimacy would be seen as inappropriate in such public space. Instead of lingering in each other's arms, we moved to the couch.

Ahmed listened to me patiently as I talked and cried. I was comforted to have him near. Since the news of my father's illness, I had felt a visceral need to be with him—the way I had when we were first married. I craved his tenderness and his love, the affection and support he had showered me with in our early days together. But we couldn't be truly alone right now. My mother and his sister Fatima were at the house as well. I got up to find Fatima and say hello. Ahmed came with me to give my mother his condolences.

Mama and Fatima were in one of the bedrooms. After chatting briefly, Fatima suggested that I go back to her house for a while. "You can have a nap there," she offered. "We will take care of Kinza while you rest."

I looked over at my mother. As much as I wanted to be with Ahmed, I didn't want to leave my family.

"Don't worry," said Fatima. "We'll bring you back this evening."

At her house I gratefully climbed the stairs and disappeared into Ahmed's bedroom. The room was quiet and the bed soft. I curled up under the covers. Then I heard the door open. It was Ahmed. He crawled into bed with me, and I rolled over into his arms.

This was what I had needed for weeks—the comfort of a long hug, of being held in my husband's arms. I needed to talk to him, now that we had privacy, about the weeks of my father's illness. And about how I felt now that he was gone. I needed to be listened to.

But Ahmed pulled out of the hug after just a few seconds. His lips found mine, his hands began to move across my body. During our five years together, we had spent months and months with absolutely no physical contact. But when Ahmed came to me, I never turned him away. I had been told what a wife's duty was, and I had always complied.

But at this moment, I simply couldn't. I pulled back from him. "Ahmed," I said, "I don't think I can do this right now."

He moved closer to me again and returned his hands to my hips and breasts.

"You can't blame me," he said. "You've been away for three months."

The quiet comfort I had felt since talking on the phone with him just a couple of days before was utterly gone in that instant. In its place—a shattering sadness and a frisson of fear.

Ahmed began to remove my clothes, and I didn't stop him. Tears coursed down my face. Suddenly he stopped. "Are these scratches on your breasts?" he asked, the familiar sound of jealousy and anger in his voice.

"I'm seven months pregnant," I reminded him. "They're stretch marks."

I didn't say another word. All my energy was focused on trying to numb myself as I lay still beneath him.

The following minutes were the worst of my entire life. Worse than any of the shouting or pushing or hitting. As Ahmed satisfied himself, waves of despair washed over me. And each time I closed my eyes, all I could see was my father's grey face, the cotton sticking out of his nostrils.

When Ahmed was done, he moved off me and settled onto the other pillow. "So," he said. "How are you? Do you want to talk about your father?"

I couldn't believe he could now ask this. Everything between us had just changed. It was as if we were standing on opposite sides of a huge canyon. There was no way my voice could broach that distance, no way to share my thoughts and feelings about my father's death with him.

"I need to take a shower," I said, getting up from the bed.

"Yes, best you do that. It looks bad for me to be up here too long while baji is downstairs," he said, getting dressed quickly and leaving the room.

Standing in the shower, I turned the water on full blast, hoping the sound would cover up my wrenching sobs. Why had I thought that my neediness would bring Ahmed back? Why had I expected things to be different? I had lost my father—and I had fooled myself into thinking I had someone else to lean on.

※ ※ ※

I spent one more night at my aunt and uncle's house before joining Ahmed at Fatima's. I didn't want to go, but I couldn't resist the pressure from Ahmed and his sister. We spent a few quiet days there, Ahmed bringing me back and forth to visit with my family, before he became restless. He began to arrange days out with his friends—shopping trips, meals and other entertainments. Chit-chat and laughter were simply not in my command, but Ahmed couldn't understand why I was unable to have fun.

"Why have you always got such a long face when we're out?" he complained.

The social activities Ahmed arranged for us meant that I had less and less time to spend with my family, less and less time to grieve the way I needed to. One day, when he announced "our" plans for the afternoon, I finally let my frustration out. "I thought you came to Karachi to support me," I snapped, "not to have a vacation!"

"You're being selfish, Samra," he said. "You're only thinking about yourself."

"I just lost my father," I said. "I'm thinking about my family."

My words seemed to have some effect. The next day, Ahmed offered to take my mother, my sisters and their husbands out for dinner to cheer us up. Mama opted to stay home—she wanted to observe iddat, the Muslim tradition that prohibits a widow from leaving the house for four months after her husband's death. We brought home some food for her instead.

The evening was a much-needed break from the sadness that was consuming our lives. But being with my sisters only underlined the contrast between how I felt when I spent time with my family and how I felt with Ahmed's. When he started talking about the two of us returning to Canada, my certainty about remaining with my family returned full force.

"I want to stay with my mother," I explained the next day. "She is going to have to move from Ruwais. She'll need the help."

Now that my father was gone and my mother was not working, she would not be allowed to remain in the United Arab Emirates. That meant she would have to pack up the house and move back to Karachi.

"You're coming back!" Ahmed said. His voice was hard. "This isn't your home. That isn't your family anymore. Your home is in Canada. Your family is back there now."

"That's not true."

"And where would you give birth?" Ahmed demanded.

I had thought of this. "We won't have to leave Ruwais right away. I can have the baby there. The baby will be a Canadian citizen no matter where it is born—because you and I are."

"You're pregnant. And you'll have a tiny baby soon. What help can you be? You will just be a burden to your mom."

I hesitated. There was some truth in that, but it didn't change how I felt. Before I could rally any more arguments, Ahmed turned towards the bedroom door. He knew he had scored the point.

"We'll talk later," he said as he disappeared from the room.

❋   ❋   ❋

The next time we spoke of my return to Canada we were with my mother, at my aunt and uncle's house. Ahmed knew I hadn't changed my mind. He had dispatched Fatima to talk to me after our initial conversation, and despite her insistence that my in-laws were now my real family and that I had been raised without sufficient guidance about my wifely duty, I stood my ground.

We assembled in my mother's bedroom in order to have a little privacy. My mother and I were sitting on the bed as Ahmed stood stiffly nearby.

"Knock some sense into your daughter," Ahmed said to my mother. Any gentleness he had been adopting around my grieving family was gone. My mother looked over at me, clearly startled by his tone.

"What's going on, Samra?" she asked.

I glanced at Ahmed. His face was stony. I summoned my courage. "I don't want to go back," I said quietly. "I want to stay with you. To help you pack up . . ."

"Your daughter is being so difficult," Ahmed exploded. "Her priorities should be with her husband and his family."

I turned to my mother. I could see how troubled she was to be caught in this conflict. My mind went back to the Mississauga condo bedroom, when Ahmed had upbraided her about my behaviour. My offer to help her was a weak excuse to stay, and I was exposing her to Ahmed's temper once again. But if we could just get through this, I rationalized, I would make up for it once he was gone.

"I just need to be close to you now, Mom," I confessed to her. "Please don't send me away."

My mother sighed. She looked drained. "But you're pregnant, Samra," she said. "You can't be of much help to me in this state. Maybe you should listen to Ahmed."

"Listen to what your mother is saying, what everyone is trying to tell you. You are thinking only of yourself. You are being so stubborn, so immature, so selfish!"

It was hopeless. I looked down at my hands folded in my lap. I could feel tears filling my eyes. I willed them not to spill down my cheeks.

"Why aren't you saying anything?" Ahmed demanded.

There was nothing left to say. I was silent, refusing to look up.

I felt Ahmed's hand under my chin. He was jerking my head up, his face hovering over mine. "Say something!" he shouted. "Why don't you say something?" I didn't open my mouth. I closed my eyes so that I wasn't looking at him.

I felt his hand leave my chin, and then my head snapped back. Ahmed had just jabbed two fingers in the middle of my forehead.

"Ahmed, that hurt!" I called out, tears spilling down my cheeks.

"Then why didn't you answer me, bitch?" As his words struck me, so did his hand. Two blows across the side of my head. "Look at the daughter you raised," he spat at my mother. "I'm so fed up with this woman."

And then he was gone, the door slamming behind him.

Shaking, I got up from the bed and sank at my mother's feet. "Please, please, Mommy," I cried. "Don't send me back. I'll tutor, I'll clean houses, I'll clean toilets. I won't be a financial burden. I'll work five jobs, I'll support you. Please don't make me go."

My mother was crying now, too. "Your father is gone, Samra. I have two more daughters to care for. I just can't take responsibility for you." She sounded as desperate as I felt, but I just couldn't stop myself from begging.

"You saw the way he treats me. Please . . ."

"Go back to Canada," my mother said. "Use your rights there to leave him."

Our sorrowful exchanged lasted another hour. My mother, still deep in her own loss and mourning, simply could not consider complicating her life any further. If I remained with her, pressure and harassment from Ahmed and his family would surely follow. There might even be legal action. And at a time when my mother and sisters needed the support of our extended family, my separation from Ahmed, even if it were presented as an attempt to help my mother, would likely create talk—and disapproval. My mother encouraged me to find a way to protect myself in Canada. When we ran out of words we sat next to each other on the bed, our bodies leaning into each other and our fingers entwined.

Eventually, Ahmed came back into the room. "What have you decided?" he demanded brusquely.

I let go of my mother's hand and looked to the floor. Every part of me was screaming "No!" But I didn't say that. Instead I took a deep breath.

"I'm going back with you," I said.

PART THREE

CHAPTER 11

IN BUSINESS

Another drive to another airport. The last leg in a series of excruciating advances and retreats on this trip home. A flight from Abu Dhabi back to Canada waited for us.

Ahmed sat rigid in the front seat of the cab while Kinza and I slumped in the back. My little girl leaned against me, sedated by the hum of tires and racing landscapes. I was somewhere far away, trying to numb myself with memories of happier times. The hum quieted, the landscapes slowed. Our cab was pulling into a gas station. I leaned my head against the window and closed my eyes. The image of a glass cabinet flashed through my mind. Well, not really a cabinet. Just shelves, pieces of glass, hinges, a pile of screws, all laid neatly across the living-room floor. It was what my mother, sisters and I had first seen when we entered my parents' house in Ruwais after the funeral. A cabinet that my father had started to assemble before we left for the wedding. Now just an unfinished project. A project that would *never* be finished. A mute testimony to a life interrupted. Like the cabinet, we were left undone.

I opened my eyes. Ahmed was getting out of the cab. "I'm going to get some cigarettes," he said. I nodded, lost in thought. Then a few seconds later, a loud crack against the glass next to my head. He was rapping on the window. "What are you staring at?" I could hear his voice booming outside the car.

Startled and confused, I rolled down the window. "What?" I asked.

Ahmed's anger blew through the window. "What man are you looking at?" I stammered out a few words, but nothing could convince him that I had not been scanning the gas station parking lot for men. "You need to keep your eyes under control," he barked, throwing the empty soda can he was holding onto the ground and stomping off to the convenience store.

Ahmed had been possessively suspicious of me whenever we were out in public since the early days of our marriage. But now that I had made it clear I was ready to give up on married life, his scrutiny of my public behaviour was intensifying to the point of sheer paranoia. After he joined me on the trip, I had donned my hijab again. I had also started to wear an abaya. The long, robe-like dress was becoming fashionable in the United Arab Emirates, although it wasn't mandatory for women as it was in some Arab countries. But the loosely draped fabric was relatively cool and had the advantage of effectively hiding my seven-months-pregnant body. Covered in yards of fabric, I was hardly making my individual presence known in public, but Ahmed was not reassured by these acts of modesty. And he seemed intent on misunderstanding even my most innocent gestures.

When Ahmed got back into the car, he sat in stony silence. We had hours of travel before us, but I was already in familiar territory.

※　※　※

Ahmed, Kinza and I arrived back in Mississauga on April 11, 2006. As I got out of the car and walked up to the door of the salmon-coloured house, I felt myself sinking in disbelief. How could I be here? It was just over a year since I had first returned to Ruwais thinking that I was escaping this place—and my in-laws—for good. And yet here I was, back at square one.

Amma and Abba had met us at the airport. Amma gave me a hug, and Abba put his hand on my head in a gesture of fatherly affection. I started to cry. I wanted to believe that now my father was gone, they might be kinder to me. But only a few minutes after Amma and I had settled into the back seat of the car, her sympathy gave way to curiosity. She began to pepper me with questions about my father's illness and final days. I could see Ahmed glaring back at me in the rear-view mirror—my answers were brief to the point of rudeness—but I simply could not go back to those painful days for Amma's entertainment.

Once we were in the house, Amma and Abba made it clear that "welcoming me back" was itself an act of kindness and compassion, one that necessitated no other delicacy.

Everything Amma said to me in the next few days seemed to be tinged with triumph and condescension. When I asked her to move from in front of the refrigerator so I could get some milk for Kinza, she smirked and said, "Why, of course. I don't want to upset you. You might run away again!"

And she made plenty of not-so-subtle allusions to what I had "put the family through."

"Everyone asks me how I can forgive you," she said to me one afternoon, "after everything you've done. But I tell them that I can't hold grudges. That's just the way I am, the way my heart is."

But there were also dark overtones to the veiled accusations. My misbehaviour had caused people to suffer emotionally *and physically*. "Of course, I wouldn't have this high blood pressure and diabetes if it hadn't been for the stress," Amma would say after commenting about her powers of forgiveness.

Abba as usual was more taciturn, but when he did speak, it was devastating. One day I walked into their bedroom to give them my customary morning salaam. Amma was sorting out her pills for the day. Abba was getting ready to go to the kitchen for his tea. First, however, he glanced over at Amma and then at me.

"Look what you've done to Amma. Because of you, she's now on all of these medications." But he wasn't done with me yet. "It's a parents' job, of course, to instill the proper values. Yours failed to do that. But Allah is always watching, and he always shows us who is right and who is wrong. And then, he punishes."

Abba's message was clear. My bad behaviour had led to my father's death.

※　※　※

A little over a week after we got back, Ahmed wished me happy birthday before he left for work in the morning and Amma gave me the usual small gift, but the occasion was marked in no other way. It was one of the blackest days since my return.

The loss of my father seemed to sweep the solid earth out from under my feet. Back in Canada, I continued to stumble around, as if I were walking half blind, half deaf, through shifting mud. The only thing sharp and clear and solid was the pain in my heart.

But gradually, my father's words began to break through: "You don't need anyone else."

And then an idea appeared along with that thought, an idea that helped me push aside some of my despair. I didn't seem able to bring about the happy marriage I had hoped for, but maybe I could fashion a reasonably happy *life* for myself. Part of that had to be a university education, but another part lay in a certain amount of autonomy and control over my affairs. No more treading water—I had to swim. And no one was going to help me. I had to find a way to move forward on my own.

I thought back to my encounter with the man in Tim Hortons. The key to taking control of my life was money. With Kinza to care for and another baby on the way, I couldn't possibly go out to work, even if I could get Ahmed to agree. But re-establishing the daycare I had run in the apartment would be easy now that I could offer the indoor—and outdoor—space of a comfortable suburban home. And throwing myself headlong into running a business might just keep my misery at bay.

Ahmed raised no objections, but Amma was concerned. She didn't want the place overrun with toys and clutter.

"What about my dinner parties?" she asked.

I suspected that once more money started coming into the household, her resistance would weaken. When Amma left to visit her son and daughter-in-law in California shortly after I returned home, I recognized my chance to act.

This time, I wasn't just trying to earn a bit of extra money to buy plane tickets. This was going to be my career for the time being, and I decided to approach it in as professional a manner as possible. I didn't bother with flyers on telephone poles. Instead, I put ads on Craigslist and Kijiji. And as prospective clients contacted me, I explained that I wasn't offering hourly babysitting but a quality, daylong program on par with licensed institutional daycares—at a more affordable price. I researched contracts online and put together my own agreement outlining my services and responsibilities and establishing working terms with the parents. I developed daily menus for the nutritious breakfasts, lunches and afternoon snacks that would be provided. And in the months to come, I would get my police background check done, arrange for insurance for the daycare and earn my CPR certification.

I built up an impressive inventory of toys and craft supplies. As I began to earn money, I re-invested some of it in outdoor play equipment—a slide, a swing set, a sandbox and riding toys—transforming the backyard into a little park. And I created a weekly schedule to share with the parents, listing our daily outdoor activities, circle time for music and stories, craft and educational activities and, of course, nap time.

By the time Amma returned from California, I was still in the midst of developing the business, but I already had three children signed up. Creating a home business that was going to be both economically beneficial and sustainable would take one more important step. And that was Amma herself.

When she had objected to the prospect of her home being upended by children, I had begun to think about how best to limit her push-back. I remembered all too well her complaints about caring for Kinza when I worked at Zellers, and I knew that for everything from cooking to household chores to grocery shopping, Amma was only happy if she was in charge. The solution was to give her that kind of authority—at least in part. If she ran the daycare with me and was able to make her own money, I reasoned, she wouldn't try to shut it down.

As soon as Amma got back from her trip, I laid out the financial details. When I told her how much I was already making, her eyes grew wide. If she joined me in the daycare, I explained, she could take on two children and keep all of the money from those contracts. I would do all the planning and organization for our little business, and since my English was fluent I would deal with the parents if she wanted. We could share various tasks, like meal preparation and activities. But as far as diapers and other upkeep—we would each be responsible for our own charges.

"And don't worry, Amma," I reassured her. "Ahmed says we can store all the toys and equipment in his den. Your house will look lovely for your dinner parties."

Abba was still working part time as a security guard. And even though Ahmed was paying the mortgage, there wasn't a lot of extra cash. While Amma was a formidable force in the household, like me she was in many ways hampered in her ability to do as she pleased by a lack of funds. She didn't hesitate to sign on to the daycare.

❋ ❋ ❋

Before we brought in Amma's daycare kids, my second child was born.

The evening of June 15th, 2006, I began to have contractions. By the morning, I was ready to go to the hospital. Ahmed drove me and sat by me in the delivery room. After eighteen hours of labour, our second daughter came into the world. A few hours later, the baby and I were alone in my hospital room. As I cradled her in my arms, I could see a lively, cheerful spirit in her surprisingly bright and beautiful eyes. When I slowly caressed her delicate, heart-shaped face, she smiled ever so slightly and two tiny dimples creased her cheeks. I gasped in delight. I'd always found dimples adorable. And my lovely little daughter had them! I leaned down and kissed her silky hair. I no longer had any illusions that a new baby would bring Ahmed and me closer together, but I took comfort in the knowledge that this new little person would be a source of love and joy all on her own. I silently promised to do everything I could to provide a happy home for her.

Both the labour and the days that followed were easier and calmer than they had been with Kinza. Amma was attentive, bringing homemade soup to the hospital and then cooking only mildly spiced food for me when I got home. But there was hardly a pause in the bleak rhythm of my marriage. A day after our daughter was born, Ahmed was with me in the semi-private room. I was attempting to get the baby to nurse. As I struggled to get her settled, the blanket I had draped over my shoulder slid off. Just then, a man who was visiting the woman in the next bed peeked behind the curtain separating the two areas. I'm sure he was just curious to see if anyone was in the other bed, and he certainly moved away quickly when he realized someone was, but Ahmed was furious. With me.

"You have to be a whore in the hospital too?" he spat in Urdu.

I was still stinging with humiliation and Ahmed was still angry when we got home from the hospital the following day.

Luckily, however, his dark mood didn't move him to oppose me when we met around the kitchen table to settle on a name for the baby. I had wanted "Saarah" for our first-born but had been vetoed. I decided to suggest it again. Perhaps if the baby had been a boy, the discussion might have been more heated, but no one seemed to have any particular interest in choosing a name this time. I was allowed to name her.

I took a week off after the birth—the parents of my daycare children had been happy to make other arrangements for a while. And then, with my seven-day-old newborn, I started back to the daily routine I would have for the next couple of years.

※ ※ ※

The workday started early, with the arrival of our first child at 7:30, and ended at about 6:30.

With up to five toddlers (not all the children were with us for the full week), as well as baby Saarah, Amma and I had our hands full during the day. Amma usually took care of the meals, while I ran around with the kids in the backyard, read them stories, taught them songs, played games and did crafts with them.

When I first got back to the house with Saarah, I had asked Amma and Ahmed if I could move out of my upstairs bedroom and into the finished basement. I told them that now with two children, I could use the extra space. They agreed. I suspect everyone was somewhat relieved to know that the crying newborn would be several floors beneath them at night.

I relished the privacy my basement room gave me, but the physical distance between me and the rest of the family underlined that Ahmed and I were living separate lives.

After the daycare children left the house at the end of the day, everyone had dinner together. Then Ahmed would disappear into his den or go out with his friends. I would clean the kitchen and help Kinza with her homework. Next was bedtime for both Kinza and Saarah, and then I too would disappear into the basement. If I had any energy left at all, I might log on to Facebook to chat with a few old high school friends I'd gotten back in touch with. Or I'd do some studying on my last correspondence course. Some evenings, I paid the bills and did our banking.

Now that I was bringing in a significant amount of money each month, Ahmed had decided that I should manage our bills and keep track of our money. Even though in practice this meant I had to use my daycare money to pay the Visa bill if Ahmed ran it up by dining out with friends or making purchases we couldn't afford, taking over the accounts gave me a sense of security, both in the knowledge of our financial state and in the control it gave me. And it allowed me, finally, to do something I had been asking Ahmed to do since the girls were born—set up education savings plans for them. (He had always said, "What's the point? They're girls. They'll just get married when they finish high school.")

Running the daycare certainly gave me a greater feeling of agency. And while Ahmed tended to hover by the door during pickup time, making sure my conversations were short and that I wasn't too friendly with anyone—particularly the fathers—dealing with the parents was always a boost to my confidence. But it was challenging to run an in-home business when I had to wait for Ahmed to come home to take me grocery shopping or to the stores to buy other supplies. I needed to rid myself of this dependence. I needed to be able to *drive*. And there was only one way.

"Amma," I said one day while we were cleaning the kitchen after supper, "wouldn't it be so much easier if you and I could take the car out at night or on the weekend to get groceries for the daycare? Have you ever thought about driving lessons?"

"Driving lessons are expensive," she replied.

I was prepared for that objection. "Yes," I said, "but I've been saving money. I think I could afford to pay for lessons for *both* of us, if you were interested."

Amma didn't say anything, but I could tell she was intrigued. The next day, while we were feeding the children breakfast, she looked over at me. "So, how do we do this? How do we get our learner's licences?"

My heart skipped a beat. We would be learning to drive!

As the cooler temperatures blew in and the leaves began to fall, Amma and I took the test for our learner's permits. I found a female driving instructor who spoke Urdu for Amma so that on the weekends, or while the daycare kids napped, Amma and I could take turns driving through the wintry streets of Mississauga while she taught us to parallel park or showed us how to avoid sliding on the icy roads. Once the snow had melted, I went for my test and got my licence. Amma, however, didn't pass; and I didn't offer to continue paying for extra lessons.

☀ ☀ ☀

As the summer months rolled into view, I made my next move. I began to talk to Amma about buying a car.

"If I had a car," I said, "we could go shopping whenever you wanted"—Amma loved to shop—"or we could take the kids to the park for a change of scenery."

Since Amma seemed pleased with the idea, I brought it up again when Ahmed was with us. I had been saving my daycare money carefully for over a year. While I'd also been paying some of the household bills, the only major purchase I made was a laptop so that I didn't have to use Ahmed's computer when doing our banking or working on a course. I knew that having the money to pay for a car would make all the difference to him.

"I have enough money to buy a used vehicle," I suggested to him. "If we could find a cheap second-hand minivan, I wouldn't have to use your car."

Ahmed agreed to help me look for something.

After a few weeks of visiting used-car lots, we found a four-year-old dark-green Dodge Caravan. It was, in truth, a tired-looking family van, but to me it was the most beautiful vehicle I had ever seen.

I proceeded with caution in the early days. Since I didn't want to be accused again of "roaming around," I made sure always to take Amma with me wherever I drove. But as the family got used to my driving, I began to go out on my own—to the grocery store or to do little errands—pushing my boundaries bit by bit.

It was an extraordinary feeling to navigate the busy streets that used to frighten me so much, to park the car in a lot and stride into a grocery store with my debit card in hand, knowing I could make my own choices, that I could even buy myself a treat or two without anyone at home raising an eyebrow. I had been right; earning money had finally given me some leverage in the family and made at least some personal freedom possible.

I still felt a little pang every time I spotted one of those blue-and-white University of Toronto signs. But at least now, I thought, I was sitting in the front seat as I passed them.

※　※　※

We were on our way home from a dinner party thrown by family friends. As we got in the car, I could tell Ahmed was fuming about something. My heart began to race. I had no idea what he might be angry about now.

After everything that had happened in Karachi and Ruwais, I no longer looked to him for affection, support or comfort. And I had given up the idea that we might fall back in love. The fact that I no longer looked to him for anything, even money, seemed to put Ahmed more at ease in the house, and his rages became less frequent. But they did not stop entirely. I still walked on eggshells whenever he was around. So it was a relief to see his back as he headed out the door to work in the mornings or to hang out with his friends in the evening.

In fact, these days what I wanted from him was absence. An absence of anger, an absence of violence, an absence of suspicion. And yet here we were again. A perfectly pleasant evening with friends had mysteriously ignited something in him.

Ahmed didn't say a single word the whole drive home. When we got in the house, I said good night to Amma and Abba and went down to my room in the basement. Ahmed followed me. As I began to take off my hijab and get undressed, he grabbed me by the arm and spun me around to face him.

"When are you going to stop being a whore?" he shouted as he slapped me across the face.

"What are you talking about?" I said, holding my hand to my stinging cheek.

"You were hugging in front of men."

When we left the party, I had given a couple of women a hug goodbye. "They were women," I said.

"All the men could see your chest pressed against their chests. They were probably getting hard-ons."

I protested: it would have been rude to have refused to hug. This is how women say goodbye. This is how Amma says goodbye to her friends.

"I don't care what other women do. They aren't my property. I don't want other men to look at my property. It's your job to protect my honour." With that he stormed out of the basement.

※　※　※

While my relationship with Ahmed settled into a chilly détente, life with Amma was better now that we were truly dependent on one another because of the daycare. She told me repeatedly that she considered me her daughter and sometimes accompanied these words with acts of genuine affection. For my most recent birthday, she had presented me with an eyeshadow compact she had noticed me admiring on one of our shopping trips. It was the first time I felt that one of her birthday gifts had been chosen specifically for me. Still, from time to time, she seemed to find it necessary to needle me or to comment about my lack of wifely behaviour.

She sometimes brought up information that she should have had no way of knowing. "So, you still want to move out, do you?" she said to me one morning as we got breakfast ready for the daycare kids.

I sputtered some sort of denial.

Another time, she sniped, "Why do you want Ahmed to get more certifications? Is his job not good enough for you?"

At first, I was baffled. How did Amma seem to know the content of my rare private conversations with Ahmed? And then one day I looked over at her sitting on the couch, cuddling up next to Kinza. Their heads were close, and Kinza was whispering in her ear. My heart dropped.

Amma adored her granddaughter, I knew. But it seemed that wasn't going to prevent her from using Kinza to get information. I was angry that Amma would turn my daughter into a pawn in her battle to keep Ahmed and me under her control. But I also felt guilty— guilty that my children were trapped in an unhappy marriage along with their parents. I hadn't been able to prevent them from witnessing the fights and the violence, but I would have to try my best not to expose them to anymore than I had to. And I would be careful what I said around them—for their sakes and mine.

❋ ❋ ❋

By spring 2008, the daycare and our daily routines were well established. Despite the house expenses, I had managed to save several thousand dollars. It had been two years since my father died, two years since I had truly realized that the only changes in my life would be those of my own making. I had looked at the university website from time to time, but now there was only one day left to apply for the fall term. I decided to fill in the form once again. This time, I didn't ask Ahmed's permission.

And then, in July, a treat: Saira and Bushra came to visit. Other than my mother, when she stayed with us at the condo, none of my family had come to see me. When I discovered that two of my sisters would be able to get away in the summer, I dug into my savings to buy them plane tickets.

Ahmed took two weeks off work, and the six of us—Ahmed, Kinza, Saarah, Saira, Bushra and I—hit all the tourist spots in the Toronto area. After visiting the CN Tower, the zoo and Niagara Falls, we piled into the minivan and drove east—to Ottawa, Montreal and Quebec City—all of us filling the car with song as we spun down the highway.

I was so glad to be again in the company of my sisters, but there was much more reason for happiness. Ahmed was his most charming, generous self. He chauffeured us everywhere without complaint, cracked jokes and bought dinners. He entertained Kinza and Saarah and listened patiently while my sisters and I chatted and reminisced. And then, one night in our hotel room in Ottawa, he looked at me with such love and affection that I felt my heart stir.

"I know I haven't been a good husband to you, Samra," he said. "It's just that I love you so much that I can't stand it if I think you are disrespecting me in any way. I'm going to try harder. I promise."

A few days later, the six of us were sitting on folding chairs in front of Montmorency Falls, outside of Quebec City. The velvety night sky was being painted again and again with the iridescence of fireworks. It was as happy a moment as I had ever had.

It was impossible not to hope that this joy would last, that Ahmed and I had turned a corner.

The rest of my sisters' visit flew by. Driving home after dropping them at the airport, I felt as if I had spent the days in some bigger, brighter universe. Yet I could sense the weight of life in the salmon-coloured house hovering in the distance. As I walked through the front door, it began to descend. And then my eye caught sight of something.

On the hall table, on top of a stack of mail, an official-looking letter with my name on it. As I picked it up, I noticed the University of Toronto logo and address. I kicked off my shoes and went downstairs to my bedroom. Sitting on the edge of the bed, I ripped open the envelope. It was an offer of admission.

As tears began to rise, so did another sensation—a cool, steely feeling. Resolution. This time, no one was going to stop me.

※

CHAPTER 12

SCHOOL AT LAST

There was no time to waste. I had applied late and so my university acceptance had come just three weeks before classes were to start. The day after the letter arrived, I got in the minivan and drove to the Mississauga campus of the University of Toronto. I didn't need to look at a map to get to UTM. I knew exactly where it was. I smiled as I passed the blue-and-white graduation-hat signs, one after another. They were finally leading the way.

I parked in the lot nearest the registration office. I got out quickly, but then stood by my car, unmoving. Looking all around me, I was awestruck. The campus lawns were the dusty green of late summer, the trees heavy with leaves. In front of me I could see a sweep of modern buildings—expanses of glass, steel, concrete—everything new and full of purpose. It might have looked pedestrian to just about everyone else. But to me, it was a magical scene.

A few people were walking along the paths, backpacks slung over their shoulders. I shivered. In just a few days, I was going to be one of them. None of it felt real.

I gave myself a little shake and looked down at the letter I had brought with me. I needed to get to the office and sign up for my courses.

A few minutes later, I was settled in a vinyl chair in a tiny, businesslike office. I had been accepted into the Bachelor of Business Administration program, but when the academic counsellor checked her computer for the courses I needed to take, she discovered that both Economics and Introduction to Management were already full. I knew I could take only two courses to start as I still had to operate the daycare, and I needed to get those required courses started.

"You applied so late," she said, shaking her head. "All the other offers and acceptances for your program were finalized months ago. Now there are long waitlists for those courses."

I had no idea what to say. Panic was rising in my chest.

"Do you have your high school transcript with you?" she asked.

I dug in my bag and handed her the paper. The counsellor scanned through my marks. "Well, I can see why they made you an offer—even with your late application. And who are we to stop you?"

With that, she got back on her computer and bypassed the waitlists, enrolling me in both courses.

A few minutes later, I was walking back to my car, my tuition paid in full and a shiny student card in my hand. I knew I was grinning like an idiot, but I couldn't stop myself. By the time I got into the van, my smile had given way to tears of joy. I cried all the way home.

Before I left the house, I had told Ahmed about my acceptance. He had congratulated me and then asked how I would pay for it all. But he had not challenged me.

Once I was home and announcing my plans to Amma and Abba as well as Ahmed, however, the real questions started. But I had been thinking about how I would manage everything ever since I applied in the spring. I had enrolled in one night course. The other course took place one afternoon a week—at about the time the daycare kids would be napping. I offered to pay Amma for her time on duty alone. And if that didn't work, I would find other solutions. I was not going to back away from school.

❊ ❊ ❊

During the next three weeks, a brittle uneasiness descended on the house. Abba was largely silent, but his gloomy expression radiated disapproval. Amma muttered and grumbled continually.

"You're a married woman. Why aren't you happy with what you've got at home?" she asked me over and over again.

Ahmed's early acquiescence gave way to bitter displeasure as well. "Don't talk to other students," he warned. "Don't try to make friends. Canadian people are so corrupt. They will try to make you un-Muslim."

Not only was all social interaction to be avoided but classroom participation was also out of the question. "Never raise your hand in class," Ahmed instructed. "Don't answer questions. Don't draw attention to yourself."

He wanted me to be a ghostlike presence on campus—invisible and unrecognized.

I tried to ignore the clouds that Ahmed and Amma were casting. It wasn't difficult. My excitement and nervousness had me floating through my household duties and daily interactions, my mind racing ahead to my suddenly bright future. Whenever I could, I got online—memorizing the course outlines, reading the bios of my two professors and checking a dozen times a day for messages on my university portal in-box. I also treated myself to a shopping trip to Staples, where I loaded up on precious luxuries: new pens, crisp notebooks and colourful binders.

❊ ❊ ❊

Finally my first day of university arrived. My economics class was from 7:00 to 9:00 on Monday night. I said goodbye to my last daycare toddler, fed Kinza and Saarah, and changed into a fresh kurti, jeans and hijab. Then I was out the door.

I arrived at the lecture hall at about 6:30. The cavernous room was empty. I walked down the aisle until I was in the centre of the banked seats and then slid into the centre row. Sitting in the very middle of the room, I looked down at the lectern and chalkboard. I had never been in a classroom this big before. Grand and imposing, the very room seemed to hold a potent promise.

I could not quite believe I was here. Eight years after leaving high school in Pakistan, eight years of disappointments and struggles, of dashed hopes and bitter setbacks, I was finally at university. I was, at twenty-six, finally realizing my dream. I let my tears flow freely, a big, goofy grin on my face. *I did it.*

After a few minutes, I could hear footsteps. The other students were beginning to arrive. I stood up quickly, checking my hijab and straightening my kurti. Then I scuttled out of the middle row. Head down, I made my way to the back corner. As much as I had tried to ignore Ahmed, his words dug their way into my thoughts. These young people were all strangers. I was nervous that they would notice how much older I was and how different, and would treat me with disdain. But I was frightened, too, that they might try to engage me and that Ahmed would find out. I could not let them put my schooling in jeopardy.

Once the professor walked in and started to talk, I forgot all about the other students. While the first class was essentially only a review of the course outline, which I knew by heart, I couldn't stop myself from taking notes furiously. I was so anxious to get started. The two hours flew by.

On the way home in the car, happiness flooded through me. A Backstreet Boys song was playing on the radio. I cranked up the volume, tapping out the beat on the steering wheel, dancing in my seat. The street lights sparkled along with me. The entire drive felt like a celebration.

My management course started a few days later. I put Saarah and all the daycare kids down for their naps before I left the house. When

I got to the lecture hall, I stationed myself in the back corner again and got my notebook and pen ready. Like economics, the first class was just an introduction, but the professor, a man named James Appleyard, was so witty and entertaining I found myself laughing all the way through.

My spirits were high as I walked back through the door of the house several hours later. The kids were all up from their naps. Saarah was toddling over to me. I picked her up. As soon as my arms wrapped around her, I could feel liquid leaking through the seat of her romper. Her diaper was soaked through, so wet and heavy it seemed about to give way. I had no doubt that she hadn't been changed since I left. I looked over at Amma, but she only shrugged and turned away. My cheerfulness evaporated. She couldn't stop me from leaving the house, but she wasn't going to reward my selfishness by making it easy for me.

☙ ☙ ☙

It happened again and again as the weeks passed. I would come home to find the daycare children fed, changed and happy, but something amiss with Saarah.

I wasn't paying Amma to look after my baby, but I suspected compensating her financially wouldn't make much difference—she wanted to give me a reason to abandon school. And even if payment did get Saarah a bit more attention, I would still be in Amma's debt for the care she was providing. It just wasn't worth it.

The next Monday, I made sure that Saarah didn't have an afternoon nap, so I could put her to bed before I left the house in the evening. Then, later in the week, I signed her up at a daycare near the university. It wasn't easy leaving her that first day. Her face crumpled at the unfamiliar surroundings, and I could hear her wail as I left for my class. I had a hard time focusing on Professor Appleyard's lecture.

But after a few days, Saarah began to enjoy herself at the daycare. When I picked her up she chattered away happily in the back seat of the car, telling me about the other children and the games they had played together. If chicken nuggets were served at lunch, she was especially pleased with her day.

Although she needed to be at the centre for only a little more than an hour, two afternoons a week, she had such a good time I decided to put her in for two whole afternoons. Amma's small act of sabotage had done both Saarah and me a favour.

❈ ❈ ❈

Running the daycare had boosted my confidence. Being in school again, even in the early months, returned me to myself in an even bigger way. The past ten years had chipped away at my sense of who I was and left me feeling incompetent in so many fundamental ways—as a wife, a mother, a woman. But here, in the classroom, I felt capable and accomplished. I knew my worth. And I wasn't afraid to claim it.

When I thought an assignment had been marked unfairly by a teaching assistant, I didn't hesitate to make an appointment with the professor.

While he re-marked my paper, Professor Appleyard asked why I was taking so few courses. When I told him, he lifted his head and looked me in the eye. "Wow," he said, "you're doing an awful lot. But you might think about applying for scholarships—so you don't have to work so hard to earn money for school." He offered to be a reference for anything I applied for.

First, the academic counsellor in the registrar's office had helped me. Now, a professor had offered to come to my aid. (He would continue to support and encourage me throughout my coming years at U of T.) When my father died, I had felt as if I were on my own. The university was proving that wasn't necessarily true.

And then another affirmation. It was the end of October, and my economics professor was handing back our first mid-term test. Before he did, he made an announcement. A few students had scored 100 percent. He looked in my direction and congratulated me by name. I felt all eyes in the room turn towards me.

I had studied as if my life depended on this test, but I wasn't able to enjoy the payoff. Instead, I wanted the ground to open and swallow me whole. I had done my best to slide in and out of class unnoticed, to follow Ahmed's directives and protect my privacy. And now everyone in the class knew who I was.

And then something amazing happened. Despite the students' clapping, despite the smile that was beginning to transform my face, despite the joy creeping into my heart, Ahmed did *not* appear in the lecture hall doorway to wipe it all away.

And when I got home, no one commented about the attention I'd garnered. I had been seen and acknowledged—and nothing bad had come of it. It was as if I had been holding my breath and finally exhaled. There was no reason for Ahmed to know what went on at school.

I knew then that I was going to go to class and participate. I was going to get involved and meet people. I wasn't going to hide. And if Ahmed became aware of that, if he challenged me, I would push back.

※ ※ ※

By the time January arrived, I had fully embraced my academic routine. I had reduced my daycare hours to allow myself to pick up a third course for the second term. I was sitting in the middle rows of the lecture hall, answering questions and chatting with my classmates. Since Saarah was in campus daycare two full afternoons a week and I was paying Amma to run our daycare during those hours, I now spent a bit more time on campus. As well as going to class, sometimes I worked in the library, sometimes I attended study groups, occasionally I had a cup of coffee with a classmate.

On one of those afternoons on campus, on my way to the bookstore to pick up a textbook, I noticed a sandwich board outside the Student Health Centre:

Do you feel intimidated?
Are you living in fear?
Do you feel devalued and disrespected?
Do you feel you have lost your voice?

The sign stopped me in my tracks. I could answer yes to each one of those questions.

My university life was a source of excitement and happiness for me, but I couldn't deny that my home life was as dismal as ever and sliding into darker terrain every day. Amma and Ahmed both resented the time I spent away from home, and the time I spent at home occupied by school work. The tiniest things now irritated Ahmed, and his voice was increasingly tinged with anger. The sound of slamming doors punctuated my days.

One night he had come down to my bedroom. "Why are you down here, ignoring Amma?" he demanded.

"I have a test tomorrow," I said. I tapped the textbook that was lying open before me.

Ahmed snatched the book and my papers from off the desk and threw them across the room. He then went over to where the book had landed and began to stomp on it and kick it.

"Why are you doing this?" I sobbed.

"Because you don't know how to be a good wife," Ahmed said. He drew his fist back and drove it through the drywall. Then he dusted off his hand and pounded up the stairs and out of the house.

Another time, he picked my laptop off the bed and dashed it to the floor.

And just the previous night, he had barged into my bedroom. "What were you doing after class?" Ahmed demanded. Amma had told him I was late coming home from school. I explained that I had spent some time in the library studying.

"Why would you study there and not at home?"

"I was going over questions with a classmate," I said, almost immediately regretting my honesty.

"I told you not to make friends there, and now you are spending time with other people like a whore!" he shouted. "You should be staying home, instead of being selfish and neglecting your family."

The conversation had left me upset but also confused. Maybe I was abusing my new freedom. I had always done well working on my own. Weren't the group study sessions just an excuse to spend time with other people? An excuse for a little companionship outside the house?

I needed to talk with someone. And I wanted that someone to be as impartial as possible—someone outside my family and my culture.

※　※　※

I went to the health centre and made an appointment with a counsellor during my class time later that day. I would have to miss a lecture, but my prompt return home would avoid suspicion.

I was nervous when I entered the counsellor's office a short time later. The room was dimly lit. There was a small couch with a table beside it. A candle glowed on the table, and a tiny fountain filled the room with the soothing sound of running water. In a chair opposite the couch sat a pleasant-looking middle-aged woman. She smiled at me warmly and gestured for me to sit down.

"What brings you by?" she said softly.

I sat for a few seconds trying to put my questions into words. "I don't know where to start," I finally said.

"Just start at the beginning. Tell me about yourself."

The room was warm and inviting, but it was the counsellor's voice that quelled my nerves and drew me in. I started to tell her about Ruwais. And then my engagement. The nikah. The rukhsati. And then the floodgates opened.

By the time I told her about what had been happening at home, my conflicting emotions were on full display.

"I just don't know why I feel this way," I confessed. "Everyone tells me that I have a normal marriage. And I know that deep down Ahmed loves me. Whenever I talk about leaving, he cries. I just can't figure out why I make him angry. But if I could be a better wife, a better mother . . ."

I told her about our recent fight about my late return from school. "It was so stupid of me. I mean, it's not as if he isn't being supportive too. He helped me shop for a new laptop for school. Just the other day he gave me a big high-five when I got a good mark on an assignment. I've just got to figure out how to stop the bad stuff from happening."

By then I was awash in tears. I took a deep breath and tried to wipe away my running mascara.

"Listen to me, Samra," said the counsellor. "This is *not* your fault."

"But if I didn't push back, if I found a better way to respond to him, maybe—"

"Samra, it doesn't matter what you say to him." She was leaning towards me, speaking slowly but firmly. "This is not the right way to be treated. This is abusive. You are being *abused*."

It had been one brief hour, but that first session was a revelation. Long after I left the office, the counsellor's words continued to run through my head as if on a loop: "It's not your fault."

I suppose the idea that I was not to blame had been implied by Nuzah at the drop-in centre and by the counsellors I'd talked to there and when I was at the apartment. But I hadn't heard those exact words, and I hadn't taken that meaning from what they said. And even if I had, I probably wouldn't have believed it. Now, hearing the idea expressed clearly, bluntly and without hesitation, it had entered my consciousness. Despite my unhappiness, my complaints to my parents and my protests to Amma and Ahmed alike, deep down I'd always assumed that if I had managed things better, been a good wife, a better daughter-in-law, a more compliant woman, I could have prevented my husband's outbursts and tempered his anger. All my appeals to him over the years had been pleas to treat my faults with more patience and understanding, to be more forgiving when things weren't "ideal." I knew his jealousy was unfounded, but I felt I could have banished it from his mind—if I'd just been smart enough or sensitive enough to figure out how.

Could I have been wrong about all of that? Was the counsellor right and everyone else I knew wrong?

And I thought about the other strange thing she was telling me: "You are being *abused*."

Abuse. Until the counsellor gave me that word, it was not part of my vocabulary. No one I knew ever used it, in English or in Urdu. Abused women were ones who suffered lasting physical injury—or worse.

And Amma always reminded me that it could be worse. "At least you don't have broken bones," she had said more than once when reminding me that a woman's role was to submit to her husband and keep the darker details of her marital life from the world. Yet she never had seen the full extent of Ahmed's rages.

But now that I had a word for the pain I had been enduring, now that I could name it, did I have a defence against Amma's claims? Questions pulsed through my mind. I couldn't wait to get back to my second appointment at the health centre to talk further.

During our third or fourth session, after I had talked about how Ahmed could be violent one minute and sorrowful the next, the counsellor pulled out a piece of cardboard with a diagram printed on it. She laid it on the low table between us. The diagram was labelled "The Cycle of Abuse."

The counsellor explained how the stages of abuse formed a continuous loop. During the "tension" period, the abuser gets angry and annoyed, and communication between the two parties breaks down. The abused feels uneasy, as if he or she needs to walk on eggshells and concede to the abuser to avoid conflict. Next comes the "incident" or "acting out" phase, in which the emotional, physical or sexual abuse takes place. Following that is a "honeymoon" or reconciliation period, during which abusers often apologize for their behaviour and promise that it won't happen again. During this time, the abuser might also try to minimize what happened or make excuses, pointing out the things the victim did to provoke the outburst. Afterwards, a period of "calm" often marks the relationship—a time when the abuse abates and both the abuser and the victim act as if it didn't happen. The abused may believe or hope that the abuser has changed and that a new type of future is possible. And then the tension begins to build again.

I was stunned. It was as if someone had recorded the rhythms of my married life. I couldn't help thinking of the time when Ahmed had thrown water in my face and then taken Kinza and me to the park and out for pizza.

"These phases," the counsellor continued, "can be very short—a few days, say—or quite long, months at a time. For some victims, the honeymoon and calm stages are extremely brief or don't happen at all."

The counsellor then produced another chart. It was called "The Power and Control Wheel." In the pie slices of the circle were descriptions of the ways an abuser asserts power over the abused— from insisting that a man must be in control of everyone in his family to using coercion and threats to keep the abused in line. It noted that abusers often destroy their victims' property and make threatening gestures and actions. They isolate their victims, keeping them from family and friends. Abuse can also take the form of economic control: making sure the abused has no money and has to ask for every penny he or she needs. Children were also often used as a tool of control, the chart explained—the abuser might threaten to take them away, or make the victim feel guilty about what might happen to them in a separation. Abusers also tend to blame the victim. They minimize the abuse. They deny that it happened. Putting the victim down, humiliating her, calling her names, making her think she's crazy—these are all ways to exert power and control.

I sat looking at the power and control diagram, thinking about the way in which it captured and summarized so many things about my marriage, about Ahmed's words and actions. I felt as if I were being swept up in a powerful cyclone of emotion, twisting helplessly as I moved through anger, sadness, denial, confusion, panic, self-pity, guilt, fear.

I was almost dizzy when I finally looked up at the counsellor. "So how do I fix this?" I asked her.

"Samra, you don't," she said flatly. "You can't. The only way for the cycle to be broken is for abusers to realize that their behaviour needs to change—and to work on changing it. The victim can't do anything to avoid the abuse other than walk away."

Over the next months, I went to see the counsellor every week. I needed repeated affirmation that I wasn't crazy, that the way Ahmed and I had been living wasn't normal or healthy. And I needed time to decide how I felt about my past and my future—and what I wanted to do now.

The one thing I was becoming certain of was that somehow I had to share my new understanding with Ahmed. In the past, he had repeatedly apologized for his behaviour and admitted he hadn't been a good husband, but I was sure he didn't realize just how unacceptable his words and actions had been. I guessed he wasn't even aware of how often he'd called me names or snapped at me. I began to respond any time he flung nasty words my way.

If he called me "whore," I would return with "You don't have a right to call me that." When he addressed me as "bitch," I would snap back, "I don't deserve that!"

One night, while I was in the kitchen making lunch for the next day, Ahmed came in to tell me Amma was upset and that I should talk to her. I knew what the problem was. She was annoyed that I was now spending more time at school and had begun to tell me to close the daycare. In fact, only a couple of children were left, and I was gone for only a few extra hours each week. I thought this was just another campaign to make me leave school. I told Ahmed I would talk to her later. He was not happy with my response, but I didn't make another comment. Instead, I focused on the rice in front of me.

My silence always infuriated Ahmed. This time, he lunged at me, grabbing my upper arm and yanking me to face him. He was now holding both my arms, pinching hard.

Instead of begging him to let me go, I tried to pull away from him. "You aren't supposed to do this to me!" I shouted.

Ahmed's eyes grew even darker. "Now you're telling me what to do, you bitch?" He let go of my arms and brought his hand down across my face. "Who are you to stop me?"

There was, as the abuse cycle predicted, an apology of sorts later in the evening. "You know that it makes me so angry when you don't talk, because I love you. I don't want to do this, but you push me to it." And some fast food appeared on my desk several hours after that.

But this time, I didn't say thank you.

※　※　※

My increasingly oppositional attitude did nothing to chasten Ahmed, of course. He only became angrier. And he began to suspect that I was being influenced by people outside our home.

"Who are you talking to?" he demanded one day. "Ever since you started at that damn school, you've been different."

More and more, I felt as if I had been right all along. The only way for us to have a different kind of life, for Ahmed to truly change, was to get rid of his parents' influence. Our brief time in the apartment and the weeks in Karachi and Ruwais after my father's death had proved that simply living under a different roof wasn't enough. Ahmed needed to recognize that his attitude about marriage and about the role of a wife was misguided—that Amma and Abba and many of our family members and social circle had it wrong. He needed to understand that his behaviour was unacceptable. He needed to learn to control his anger.

One evening when we seemed to be in one of our "calm" phases, I told Ahmed I had something that I wanted him to look at. I had printed out a copy of "The Cycle of Abuse." Now I handed it to him.

He read the page quickly before dropping it in disgust. "I knew you were getting brainwashed by white people," he said. "Going to all the wrong places for advice. If you think we need help, then we should go to a mosque for advice, stay in our culture."

I shook my head. I suspected any imam Ahmed chose would only reinforce the idea that a wife should be obedient to her husband, that a husband should control his wife. At least for now, there would be no professional help for Ahmed.

※　※　※

My reluctance to go to a mosque for counselling did not mean I was comfortable walking away from everything about the culture and religion in which I'd been raised. In fact, I'd recently been concerned about my youngest sister's unorthodox behaviour.

Around the time Saarah was born, I had received troubling news. My mother was remarrying. Her wedding took place not long after the finish of the iddat, the period of a widow's mourning and waiting prescribed by the Koran. It seemed to my sisters and me shockingly soon after my father's death. Ahmed, Amma and Abba had also looked on it with disapproval. But the person who was perhaps affected most by my mother's decision was my youngest sister, Bushra, who was still living at home when not at boarding school.

Now after almost three years, she needed her own space and had moved into an apartment in Abu Dhabi. My two other sisters had lived in the city as well, but they had shared an apartment with a family—not lived alone. I admired her boldness but feared she was being reckless and creating a dangerous social isolation for herself. I was so worried, so desperate to talk with someone, that I confided in Ahmed, making him promise not to tell his parents.

❋ ❋ ❋

Amma was throwing one of her dinner parties, and I had invited a couple Ahmed and I were friends with. I was in the kitchen getting food ready with Amma and my friend when I heard my phone beep. It was a text from a classmate: *Mid-term marks were just posted. Go look. There's a surprise for you!*

I excused myself and raced downstairs to my computer. On the university portal, the professor had made a public announcement, congratulating me on a perfect score. When I got back upstairs, I couldn't contain my excitement. I told Amma and my friend what had just happened.

"Hmmmpf," said Amma. She looked pointedly around the kitchen. "You should have told your classmates that you don't do anything at all other than study. So of course you would get a good mark."

I knew that Amma's implication would be heard and understood by everyone within earshot. I was neglecting my home and my family for school.

My face was suddenly hot, humiliation driving the words from me. There was an awkward pause before my friend began to talk about something else.

For the rest of the evening I was quiet. At the table, I didn't join the conversation and couldn't manage to eat. After dinner I busied myself cleaning the kitchen, and once the guests had left I disappeared downstairs with Kinza and Saarah.

Ahmed followed me. "Is something the matter?" he asked. He had been in a good mood all night, and now his voice was warmly solicitous. Despite his ongoing resentment about school, he'd also been supportive of my academic accomplishments. I decided to be honest. I told him how happy I had been about the mark and how Amma had embarrassed me in front of my friend.

"You're right," Ahmed said when I was finished. "Amma shouldn't have said anything. She talks without thinking. But you shouldn't worry about it. You're pulling your weight around here and doing everything you need to do. Don't let her get to you."

I was so relieved to have Ahmed's support and sympathy that it almost felt worth the earlier humiliation. I went to bed feeling soothed and happy.

The next morning Ahmed and I were in the kitchen together while Kinza was in the den watching cartoons. I was feeding Saarah breakfast. Ahmed was having his morning tea. The pleasant peacefulness from the night before lingered in the room.

The sounds of heavy footsteps on the stairs preceded Amma's arrival. She walked straight over to me, her expression sour. "So, what's your problem?" she demanded. "You didn't eat dinner last night and you didn't talk to anyone, and this morning you didn't come to my room to say salaam."

I had no intention of apologizing, and I knew nothing would be gained by explaining myself. I just wanted to put the evening behind me.

"I really don't want to talk about it, Amma," I said.

"You aren't behaving properly. You have to talk to me," she said impatiently.

I tried to deflect her again, but she kept at me. Finally, I told her how much she had embarrassed me the night before.

Amma rolled her eyes at my words. "You always twist things! You always try to make me look bad. I was just trying to praise you and point out how much you do."

"Amma, I know what I heard. I know what you meant," I said.

"Are you calling me a liar?" she responded.

I moved to the table to clear up the breakfast dishes. I didn't want to continue the pointless conversation.

"Are you?" Amma demanded.

Suddenly the air was broken by a booming voice. Ahmed was on his feet. "This is no way to treat my mother! Why aren't you answering her?" The full force of his anger hit me like blow to the stomach.

"Ahmed," I said, reeling in surprise, "we talked about this last night."

Amma snorted. "Oh, you are so conniving, trying to turn my son against me!"

I could feel the earth rolling under my feet. Things would only get worse if I stayed in the kitchen with Ahmed and his mother. I picked Saarah up and headed for the basement stairs.

Ahmed was beside me in an instant, grabbing my wrist and spinning me around. "Where do you think you're going?"

"Downstairs. To my bedroom." My own anger kept my voice firm.

"Oh, you're running away! Just like your sister ran away to live on her own. You're just a family of shameless girls."

Something about Ahmed's exposing my young sister to his family like this, something about the way he had used my concern against me, unleashed in me a white-hot fury. "You have no right to drag my family into this," I screamed. "I told you that in confidence!" I kept going. "Why are you yelling at me after you were so supportive last night? How dare you? How dare you?"

Amma was standing stock-still in the kitchen, her mouth open. Ahmed looked astonished, too. They had never seen me this angry before.

I turned on my heel and fled down the stairs with Saarah, closing the door behind me. When I got into my room, I sat on the bed, still seething.

A few minutes later, they both came down to talk me. But I wasn't interested in Ahmed's excuses or Amma's sympathy. I had long ago learned that any feelings I shared with Amma would be reported back to Ahmed in a way that would cause more friction between us. Clearly, any confidence I shared with Ahmed could go in the other direction. And I wasn't going to listen to either of them tell me I was the one misbehaving. "I don't want to live like this any-more," I told them. Then I wouldn't say another word.

That was the first time that I had actually stood up for myself in that house, with those people. And it felt good.

※　※　※

With my outburst, I felt as if I had broken some sort of spell. I didn't want to slide back into old patterns with either Amma or Ahmed. But I knew that would be difficult. The only way to prevent it, I thought, was to live as separately from them as I possibly could.

I began to do whatever chores I could in my bedroom. When the daycare kids arrived, I took them into the basement whenever we weren't out of doors. There was plenty of room down there for them to play games and have naps. I bought myself a small fridge, a rice cooker, a microwave and a toaster oven. I had everything I needed to cook meals for myself, the girls and the daycare kids. Despite

Amma's grumblings, I didn't rejoin her upstairs during the day or in the evenings if I could avoid it.

By the end of the second term of school, I had carved out my own space in the house. And while Ahmed had always claimed his separate territory—sleeping in the den and spending evenings out of the house—now that I was withdrawing, he was worried.

So worried that he was prepared to do something about it.

꙰

CHAPTER 13

TIME AWAY

I was sitting at my desk, leaning forward over my laptop, when I heard the door at the top of the basement stairs open. At this time of night, it would be Ahmed. I quickly typed "got to go" and snapped the laptop closed. But Ahmed had come down the stairs quickly and seen my hand on the computer. He had a strange look on his face and his eyes were wet. He was crying.

"What are you doing to me?" he said, his voice pleading. "Why are you talking with this Fahad? Are you having an affair?"

I blanched. He knew who I had just been chatting to on Facebook. There was clearly now spyware on my laptop as well as on the family computer.

"I've told you before. He's just a high school friend," I assured him.

I had heard fear in Ahmed's voice when he called me in Ruwais all those years ago, but this was the first time I had actually seen it on his face. The absence of anger emboldened me to continue explaining myself.

"I'm not interested in Fahad at all. But I *am* sick of this," I said, waving my hand between us. And then, without having planned to, I blurted it out: "I think we should get a divorce."

Ahmed's eyes widened. "What do you mean? I love you!"

"But I don't love you anymore," I said. "There's nothing between us. It's not like it used to be. We live completely separate lives."

It was an unreal feeling—this absence of fear. I had been caught, I had told the truth, and now he would leave me. Relief washed through me.

"Just divorce me, Ahmed," I said.

He was shaking his head. "This is my fault," he said. "I haven't given you the love you need. I haven't treated you properly."

Was Ahmed taking to heart what I had tried to tell him when I showed him the cycle of abuse diagram? I wasn't sure, but it didn't matter much to me now. I just wanted out.

Over the next weeks, Ahmed came looking for me as soon as he got home from work. He stayed home in the evenings, sitting with me in my bedroom after supper or asking me to come to the den to watch TV with him.

As the heat of summer descended on us, he suggested we take Saarah and Kinza to Ottawa for a vacation. It was the first time we had ever been alone as a family. It was a calm, pleasant trip, the kind of time together that I had hungered for in the early years of our marriage. But now I could barely rouse myself to smile when Ahmed cracked a joke or said something complimentary. At night as we lay in the hotel room, he tried to talk to me about our marriage, his voice soft and low so the girls didn't wake. But when he told me he loved me, I didn't believe it—and I couldn't bring myself to say it back. All I could say was that I didn't know what to do to fix our marriage. "I think we need to separate," I insisted.

Ahmed refused to consider this. He clearly thought that more time together was the answer to our problems. After our holiday, he told his parents he was thinking about taking a short trip with just me and asked if they would take the children for a few days. It didn't happen.

Amma and Abba were incensed with Ahmed's change in behaviour. They grumbled that we were both treating them badly, neglecting and ignoring them.

"So he's your slave now, is he?" Amma hissed at me one day.

But it was Abba who let his unhappiness be known the most powerfully.

One night Ahmed and I were sitting in his den, talking. It was late, but neither of us was ready to go to bed. "Everyone's asleep," said Ahmed. "Why don't we get some fresh air?"

We left the house and drove to a nearby coffee shop. By the time we pulled back into the driveway, it was well after midnight. Ahmed slipped his key into the lock and turned the front-door handle, but the door would not open. Someone had bolted it from inside after we left. Ahmed rang the bell, and we waited. No one came to the door. We rang again, but that didn't seem to wake anyone either. Finally we phoned.

Abba was furious. Saarah had got up after we left, and her cries had woken Amma and him, he told Ahmed. He had locked the door against us to let us know of his displeasure. When the door finally opened, Abba was sitting in the living room with Amma and the children.

His face was rigid with anger. "It's not our responsibility to care for your children when you are going around town doing God knows what!" he said. Then he turned to look me directly in the eye.

"Prostitutes come home this late at night. Is that what you are?"

I couldn't believe what he was saying. But before I could make a sound, Ahmed was shouting. "How can you say that? She's my wife! If that's the way you are going to treat us, we're moving out." Then he turned to me. "Samra, take the kids downstairs."

I picked up Saarah and grabbed Kinza's hand, disappearing from the room as quickly as I could. For the first time in our marriage, Ahmed's angry words were aimed at his parents. And he was the one talking of moving out.

The next morning, however, he was beset with remorse. "He's old. I shouldn't have talked to him that way."

As I started to put breakfast together for the children, Ahmed disappeared upstairs to apologize to his parents.

※　※　※

Remarkably, Ahmed didn't seem to resent me this time for "causing" a rift between him and his parents. I had to admit, this was a change, but I couldn't tell if it was actually any different from "honeymoon" phases we had had before. The real difference was that I just didn't care. I couldn't care.

As the new school year approached, I felt as if I were walking around in a stupor, a heavy weight in my arms. Even the smallest efforts to do anything were taxing. Perhaps realizing that it didn't matter to me if Ahmed and I loved each other was more unsettling than I had acknowledged at first. Perhaps it was just the fatigue of being caught in the endless cycle of abuse that I now recognized.

When classes started in September, I was surprised to find that I simply couldn't summon up the enthusiasm of the previous fall. My counsellor remarked that perhaps my suggestion to Ahmed was a good one—what I needed was a break from the marriage, a little distance so I could figure out how I was feeling.

Once again, a family wedding offered a route away from Ahmed and our bloodless life together. Saira was getting married in the new year. She was working full time, and on the phone her voice spiked here and there when she talked about everything she needed to do to prepare for the wedding. If I were in Abu Dhabi with her, I could help and ease her stress.

I told Ahmed that I would leave with the girls in October, and he could join me closer to the wedding.

❈ ❈ ❈

Ahmed was upstairs, playing with Kinza and Saarah, and I was in my basement bedroom, sorting through the things I would need to pack for my trip. I heard his heavy footsteps move across the kitchen floor and then fall upon the stairs. Then he was in my room, lowering himself slowly onto the bed, looking sadly at the piles of clothes—Kinza's, Saarah's, mine.

Earlier in the day, he had snapped at me. Now he was clearly feeling regret.

"You know I love you," he said.

"I know." My voice was flat.

I had been thinking about what to say before I left. "When we get back, I am not coming back to this life," I said. "Things have to be different—we have to get our own place."

Ahmed nodded.

"And not like last time," I continued. "We can't pay the mortgage on this place anymore. We need our money out of this house."

"I know," said Ahmed. "I'll talk with Amma and Abba. But they can't carry this place. We'll have to put it on the market. They will have to move too."

I looked over at him. I could tell by his troubled brow that he was serious; he was imagining how this conversation with his parents would go, how difficult it would be. But he wasn't resisting. A year or two earlier, this would have made me ecstatic—and hopeful. Now these emotions were firmly in check. I would wait and see.

A few days later, I went into the registrar's office and withdrew from all my courses for the year. Then I told Amma that she could take the two children who were still my responsibility at the daycare. I knew she wouldn't object. Our little business had been hit hard by the financial crisis of 2008, and Amma had only one charge of her own. Then I called the travel agent.

Before the girls and I flew out in early October, Ahmed came to me bearing a peace offering—a BlackBerry. (In a fit of anger, he had broken my previous phone several months earlier.) I was shocked at the extravagance of it.

"I just wanted to get you something special before you left," he said.

Ahmed's unusual gesture put a little chink in my apathy. It was the first real gift he had bought me in years and years. I was touched.

☙ ☙ ☙

The girls and I had been in Abu Dhabi for three or four days, staying at the apartment my mother now shared with her new husband, when my old friend Fahad called me. We'd been chatting on MSN messenger once in a while since the winter, but now that I was away we decided to have a proper conversation.

Fahad had been one of my most steadfast friends over the years. Despite the fact that I had gone months and years without contacting him, when I did he responded with relentless good cheer. And he had always been unfailingly supportive and encouraging.

We started our phone call with the possibility of his coming to Abu Dhabi for a visit. Then we moved on to the state of my marriage. I told him about the abuse and my feelings of despair.

"You should leave, Samra," Fahad said. "Just leave."

"But how would I manage?" I said. "I'm so afraid of being alone."

"You wouldn't be alone, honey. I'll be with you every step of the way."

Just then there was a beep on the line. I could see that Ahmed was calling me. I ignored this—I'd ring him once I was off the phone with Fahad. The beeping kept up as Fahad and I tried to continue our conversation. Then the home phone began to ring, Ahmed's name flashing on the caller ID. I told Fahad I had to go.

As soon as I picked up the home phone, I was hit by a volley of questions: "Who are you talking to, Samra? Who is that guy? Why is he calling you honey and telling you to leave me? Why are you making plans for him to come to Abu Dhabi? Are you two planning to run away together?"

I was unable to respond for several seconds. "How do you know what I was talking about?" I finally asked, shaken.

"I can hear your entire conversation. I gave you that phone for a reason."

Ahmed had put spyware on my phone before I had left Canada. *That's why my phone has been working so poorly*, I thought. It had been losing its charge after only short bursts of use. The blood was pounding in my ears as Ahmed continued to talk. He wanted me to come home. I felt too sick to stay on the phone. I told him I wasn't doing that and hung up.

I immediately went online and followed the instructions to do a factory reset on my phone.

❈ ❈ ❈

Ahmed called me incessantly in the coming days, asking about Fahad, asking whether he was the reason I had come to Abu Dhabi. And then my mother started to ask me questions, too.

One morning, as I was about to run some errands, she stopped me. "Wait, Samra. I want to talk to you. What have you been up to? Ahmed tells me you've been talking to another man."

"It was nothing," I protested. "Just an old friend." Apparently I wasn't the only one Ahmed had been phoning.

"But you're a married woman! I can't believe you'd do that. I can't believe you'd be so shameless!"

I felt my face growing red. I muttered a few more excuses before I slipped out of the apartment.

I tried to busy myself in the coming days, helping Saira with everything that needed to be done before the wedding, but I couldn't get my mother's words out of my mind. I'd been able to shrug off

Ahmed's upset—after all, my relationship with Fahad was innocent, and my counsellor had reminded me that the social isolation I'd been living in wasn't healthy. If Ahmed couldn't live with the fact that I had friends, so be it. If he left me he would be doing me a favour. But my mother had gotten under my skin. Her words had made me feel culpable and my behaviour sordid.

I messaged Fahad that I couldn't be in contact with him anymore. And then I threw myself into the wedding plans with even more fervour.

※   ※   ※

By the time Ahmed arrived at the end of December, we had put the incident with the phone behind us. Although he had missed the girls and they had missed him, he insisted on time alone with me. He suggested a trip, just the two of us, to Dubai. We left Kinza and Saarah with my mother and spent a few days in the city.

It was in many ways a mini-honeymoon. We stayed in a luxurious hotel, ate in romantic restaurants, wandered the city like two young lovers. But as we nibbled on treats or cuddled in bed, I couldn't help feeling that it was all play-acting. Ahmed's tender gestures and loving behaviour seemed rote, as if someone else had scripted the lines and he had memorized them. And the purpose of the play was to keep me close and under his control. In turn, I was acting the part of the good wife. But the small flame I had kept alive for so many years had been extinguished. Was I just too afraid to hope again? Too frightened that my heart would be broken once more? Or was there truly nothing left? I just didn't know.

And then, in a flash, the wheel turned to the next phase.

Ahmed and I were out shopping for a new suit for the wedding. We had been in and out of a dozen stores, and I was growing tired. Entering a menswear shop, I trudged to one of the couches to get off my feet. Ahmed disappeared into the change room with a few suits. After a couple of minutes, he came out, ready to leave.

"Are you done?" he snapped. The anger in his voice was unmistakable.

"Done with what?"

"Ogling that guy, like the whore that you are!" He was glaring at the cashier, a man I hadn't even noticed.

This time, Ahmed's jealousy pushed me into fury instead of fear.

"Are you crazy?" I said. "What is wrong with you? I was looking at suits for *you*! I'm done. I'm not shopping anymore."

With that I stood up and marched out of the store. Ahmed followed. I hadn't cooled down by the time we got to the car. He was silent as he pulled the car onto a busy eight-lane road. "You're a psycho!" I ranted as he drove. "You're always so suspicious. You show me no respect."

Suddenly, he veered onto the shoulder and threw the car into park. "You think I'm psycho?" he said. "I'll show you what a psycho I am."

Then he was out of the car, racing into the middle of traffic. Horns blasted as cars zigged and zagged to avoid him. An enormous truck slammed on its brakes, squealing to a stop.

I was screaming—calling Ahmed to come back. He turned. Somehow he managed to make his way through the chaos of speeding cars and get back to the side of the road.

By the time he scrambled into the car, I was both baffled and livid. "Why did you do that?"

"To show you how much I love you," he said. He looked like a wild-eyed child. I felt my anger dissolve in a wave of pity. Ahmed pulled back into traffic, and we drove to the apartment in shaky silence.

When we got into the parking lot, I made a plea. "Ahmed, we're here for my sister's wedding. Let's not make any scenes. Or distract from her celebration in any way. We can deal with our issues when we get back to Canada."

By the time we all boarded the plane to Karachi for the wedding, Ahmed and I were back to playing the happy couple.

❧ ❧ ❧

At Uncle Ali's house, the last-minute work of putting the wedding together got underway in a serious fashion. Ahmed was right in the middle of it—driving my sisters and me to the florist and to the bazaars, setting up tents and chairs for the various pre-wedding parties, asking everyone what he could do to help. Whenever anyone asked him to make a decision or give a preference, he would look at me with affection and quip, "Ask Samra. She's my queen!"

My extended family were besotted with this perfect damaad, this ideal son-in-law, commenting on how generous Ahmed was with his time and attention. But I knew he was simply trying to stay close, to keep an eye on me.

A few days before the wedding, the entire family assembled at my uncle's house for a dinner and musical night. I had put on a stylish white-and-blue shalwar kameez and had my hair loose. For years, my only clothes had been either the things I brought with me when I first married or Amma's faded, baggy castoffs. And I had avoided makeup or anything that might suggest I was looking for attention. When Saira and Bushra visited Canada, I had been struck by the difference in our appearance. They looked young and fashionable; I looked tired and drab, like someone who had given up trying. But I was beginning to push back.

Back in August, I had appeared at one of Amma's dinner parties without my hijab. She and Ahmed had grumbled but had not stopped me. Once my sister's wedding festivities got underway, I decided that I would continue to embrace my new look. At a small party we held in Abu Dhabi for family and friends who couldn't make the wedding itself, I had dressed in a sari, with my hair curled loosely around my shoulders. And I had kept my head uncovered and worn clothes that were slightly more form fitting than a shalwar kameez at the parties here in Karachi. My appearance was bolstering my confidence—I was more talkative and upbeat at the social events than I had been in my previous trips back home.

So my mood was high as I ran back and forth from the kitchen to the dining room with platters of food for the music-night supper. Each time I entered the dining room I kicked off my slippers so that I didn't track anything onto the carpets, and then had to bend over to put them on again when I left. It made for an awkward dance, and at one point my uncle almost bumped into me from behind. But eventually, the table set, we gathered to eat together.

As soon as we sat down, I could tell that something was wrong. Ahmed's gaze flashed to me repeatedly, menace darkening his eyes. Sure enough, after dinner he grabbed my elbow. "Come upstairs. I need to talk to you," he said in a harsh whisper.

Away from the party, Ahmed pushed me into the bedroom and locked the door behind him. Then his hand smashed against the side of my face—so hard that I was knocked off my feet. "You whore! Why were you showing your ass to your uncle?" Ahmed was now kicking me in the side as I lay on the floor gasping in pain. "Bending over in front of him like a randi!"

Kick after kick landed on my stomach and ribs before Ahmed stepped away from me. "Don't make any drama when you come downstairs," he spat. And then he turned and left the room.

His fury took me, yet again, by surprise. I lay on the floor trying to catch my breath, trying to reach through the pain to figure out how badly I was hurt and whether or not I could sit up.

Eventually I pulled myself up and walked gingerly into the bath-room. I couldn't believe what I saw in the mirror—the bright red handprint across my cheek, the expression of pain, the ravaged hair and makeup. And yet I realized that I might have predicted this. My coolness towards him, my own outbursts, my chattiness, my loose hair, my party clothes. All of these were "provocations." They had not gone unnoticed or been accepted. Instead Ahmed had been stock-piling these insults until there was a safe time to light the match. And then he found himself in a house full of people, in the midst of a cele-bration that he knew I didn't want to ruin. And he let himself explode.

This was the most sustained violence I had ever suffered—and it was timed perfectly. Ahmed knew I wouldn't leave him just days before the wedding. He knew there was time for me to calm down, for the memory to fade, for the bruises to heal, the sting to diminish.

I leaned forward over the sink. After a decade of these attacks, I was practised at "recovery." As bits and pieces of music drifted up from the first floor, I let the tears fall for a few more minutes. Then I pulled myself together, washed my face, covered the marks with makeup and fixed my hair. I told myself to breathe deeply, to push the incident out of my mind, to pretend that it hadn't happened, to rejoin the party with a big smile. And to keep smiling until my por-trayal of a happy wife was accepted by everyone—even myself.

※ ※ ※

A few days later, I walked my sister into the garden for her nikah ceremony. Her husband-to-be, Junaid, was waiting on the dais, looking at her with an expression of such love and joy that I felt the breath catch in my throat. I was so, so happy for her, yet my happi-ness was tinged with heartache. I knew that no one had ever looked at me like that.

Saira and Junaid had been a love match. They had met through work, become friends and then fallen for each other. For weeks now, I had watched as they moved in and out of each other's orbit with an ease and intimacy that spoke of true connection. I noticed the way my sister's eyes brightened when Junaid walked into a room, and the way he broke into a smile whenever Saira spoke. It was a closeness that I could only imagine.

Ever since arriving in Abu Dhabi in the fall, I had been living vicariously through Saira. I hadn't been involved in my own wedding preparations at all, so I shared her happy excitement as she picked out her flowers, chose her dress and chatted about the coming celebration. But now, as much as I tried to focus on the beaming bride in front of me, I could no longer stand in her shoes. I was just feeling sorry for myself.

For so many years, driving around Mississauga, trapped in a back seat while the blue-and-white University of Toronto signs flashed by, I'd thought that if only I could get an education I would be happy. But I had been doing just that, and yet I wasn't content. I was beginning to realize that I wanted more. I wanted a *life*. I wanted the freedom to go where I pleased and stay as long as I liked. I wanted to meet new people and make new friends without hiding them from anyone. I wanted to trust and be trusted. I wanted to spend my days with people who respected me. *I wanted to love and to be loved*. This was the weight I'd been carrying around for months back in Canada.

When Saira and her husband left the rukhsati party and the banquet hall later that evening, everyone was crying. It had been an effervescent, magical day.

I was crying too, but not sentimental tears. I was crying because my respite was over. Soon I would be flying back to Canada with Ahmed, returning to a life that was as confusing as it was bleak. A life that I knew I needed to change.

※ ※ ※

Before we left my family in Karachi, I decided we would have one last party—a surprise for my uncle. I wanted to thank him for making us so welcome in his home for the previous couple of weeks. He loved barbecues, so I bought and marinated a huge amount of meat and spent the day cooking side dishes and getting everything ready. My uncle was delighted by the unexpected treat. After dinner, he stood up to say a few words. He thanked everyone for coming, and he praised the food. Then he looked over at me.

I was smiling at him in anticipation of his words of gratitude to me—a much-needed salve for my sore ribs and aching heart.

"I just have to say . . . " he began, "no one in this family is as *lucky* as Samra. She has such a wonderful, loving husband!"

※　※　※

In the early years of our unhappiness, I had dismissed the pushes, the pinching, the slaps and kicks, just as my mother had, just as Amma might have. This wasn't the same as being "hit." This wasn't the same as broken bones. But Ahmed's attack on me in Karachi had exposed the lie in that faulty logic. I *was* being hit. Ahmed, I now understood, thought of this violence only as a sign of his passion. He was intent on keeping us together. I was becoming more determined to separate. And yet I hadn't left. Despite what I thought all those years ago, perhaps being hit didn't make leaving any easier.

We arrived back at the salmon-coloured house in the early days of a cold and dreary Canadian February. A miasma of conflict and disquiet came with us.

But the tension was not limited to Ahmed and me.

Once we were settled, he and I both noticed something curious. It was very quiet. The house had been put up for sale in the fall, just as Ahmed had promised me. When he arrived in Abu Dhabi, he had told me that there had been a flurry of showings but so far no offers. Now that we were back, however, the doorbell was not ringing and the house was not filled with the hushed conversations of prospective buyers. Ahmed asked his parents what was going on.

"Oh," said Amma coolly, "we took it off the market. I was sick of cleaning and having to have the house look so nice. It was just too difficult."

Ahmed was taken aback. He insisted they call the real estate agent and get the process started again. Amma and Abba were incensed.

"What kind of son are you," Amma cried, "putting your parents out onto the street? All you care about is money. You're a pig. I wish I never had a son like you!"

She and Abba stormed off towards their bedroom. Ahmed disappeared into the basement.

When I got downstairs, he was sitting on the edge of the bed, weeping. I sat down and wrapped my arms around him. I had never heard him fight with his mother before. I felt a flutter of pride and a wave of sympathy for the pain he was in.

"Let's just leave," he said after a few minutes. "Let's just forget about the money and move out."

"What do you mean?" My heart was suddenly pounding. "All of our money is in this house! We've paid the mortgage for ten years. It's our entire life savings!"

"I've done all I can do," said Ahmed. "I don't want to hurt my parents. Allah will take care of us. If you love me, you'll do this for me."

Our equity in the house now amounted to hundreds of thousands of dollars. Ahmed's credit cards were maxed out, as were all the cards and loans he had taken out in my name. We had planned to pay off our debt when we sold the house and use what was left as the down payment for a new home. Giving up our investment would mean financial ruin.

"That's our children's money," I said. Now I was crying, too.

"It's just money," Ahmed said. "We'll earn it back."

Over the next few days, he returned to this idea over and over. He pointed out that we would likely be stuck for months arguing with his parents if we didn't just walk away. And we might never convince them. What's more, once I finished university, I could get a good job and our combined income would help us recoup our losses quickly.

I was both amazed and chastened. It appeared that Ahmed was willing to make a real sacrifice to get out from under his parents' influence—to save our marriage. If he were willing to do this for us, how could I refuse?

※　※　※

In early May, Ahmed, the girls and I moved into a dilapidated two-bedroom apartment in another subsidized building. This apartment was smaller than our first, so small that we didn't bother to bring all of the furniture from my basement living space.

Everything about our new life was a faded repeat of our earlier attempt at independence. Ahmed came back from visits to his parents stretched thin by their resentment and criticism. And we were both brittle from the constant financial strain. For the first few months, as well as rent we continued to pay the mortgage on his parents' house while Abba arranged for new financing. When that obligation finally concluded, our debt had swollen even further and hovered like a brimming storm cloud over everything we did. Tutoring several children in the building brought in a few dollars, but not enough to make any real difference.

After several months of being unable to make even the smallest payment on our credit cards, I saw an ad on TV for debt help. Ahmed agreed we had to do something. We applied for a consumer proposal—in my name—to consolidate and reduce what we owed. This arrangement, one tiny sliver away from full bankruptcy, would be on *my* financial record for eight years. (Ahmed had argued that because I was a woman I didn't need a good credit rating and he would always take care of me.) But it was the only way to make a fresh start.

And while I couldn't stop feeling bitter about our financial state, Ahmed couldn't curb his possessiveness, which had been re-energized by his expectation that I would be compliant in response to the big sacrifice he had made for us. Even a short trip to the grocery story was seen as an opportunity for me to indulge in wantonness. Our fights were frequent, and now that I was no longer turtling each time, now that I would oppose his opinions and decisions and on one occasion had fought back physically by slapping him in the face, some of them stretched for hours and became darkly histrionic. After one particularly nasty brawl I escaped in a cab, spending the night in a nearby hotel.

Almost as frequent as the arguments were Ahmed's tears and apologies, those emotional reversals that kept me in such a state of uncertainty.

※ ※ ※

For three months, it felt as if we woke up each morning and smashed a bright, promising day to pieces. And then, just as it seemed as if the future would hold nothing but ugliness and confusion, a burst of light broke through.

Ahmed heard from his insurance company. The claim he had made nine years ago after his car accident, a claim we had all but given up on, had been granted. They had an $80,000 cheque for us. Our very first phone call was to a real estate agent.

House hunting lifted our spirits almost immediately. And when we found our home—a three-bedroom, semi-detached brick house that backed onto a lush, green golf course—well, it was as if both Ahmed and I had been transported to another dimension. A place where we would never fight about money again, where the girls could have their own bedrooms, where we could host our *own* dinner parties, a place where we would make new friends. Most important, this house would be a place where the past could stay in the past.

As I packed up the bits and pieces of rickety furniture from our apartment, I was suffused with euphoria. I remembered a day following my nikah, before I had come to Canada. I had earlier told Ahmed that I loved Dairy Milk chocolate bars—and not long after, a surprise arrived in the mail for me. He had shipped a huge box of them all the way from Canada. It was one of the moments that made me think I was falling in love—and for days after, I floated around, tingling with giddy pleasure. Being in love made the whole world look different. My family's roach-infested apartment seemed cozy not crowded. My dull shalwar kameez felt sophisticated and elegant. Even the gritty streets of Karachi seemed like verdant promenades.

Here I was, so many years later, experiencing the same thing. I was in love.

But this time, my heart had been given to my brand-new family home—and the future it seemed to promise.

CHAPTER 14

TALAQ, TALAQ, TALAQ

I was in Kinza's bedroom, putting the final coat of paint on the walls. The shade she had chosen was a funky, bright purple—the colour of cartoon flowers and party balloons and little-girl excitement. After the last sweep of the roller, I looked around the room with a small shiver of pure pleasure. The house was beautiful—and it was *mine*.

Since moving in on the Labour Day weekend, Ahmed and I had thrown all our spare time into turning the place into the family home I had been longing for. We painted every room in warm, rich colours that delighted me. And went together to furniture store after furniture store, choosing couches and recliners, a new dining-room suite and bedroom sets for each room. I spent hours arranging it all while Ahmed cheerfully hung the paintings. The girls' bikes were in the backyard, cozy pillows festooned the family-room sofa, my china and spices filled the ample space of the kitchen cupboards.

It really did feel as if this time, our house would be a home. Ahmed seemed truly happy and hopeful, and I began to look forward to the end of each school day, when we would both walk through the door to start our evening. We often stood side by side in the kitchen, cooking together, just as we had in the early months of our marriage. After supper, Ahmed or I played with the girls or helped them with their homework. Then, once the girls were both in bed, we'd meet again on our new living-room couch, snuggling together in front of a movie. In the mornings, we would chat and laugh as we all flew about the house, getting ourselves ready for another busy day.

Amid all this domestic bustle, the rest of our new life had gotten underway as well—Kinza was enjoying grade four at her new school, Saarah had started junior kindergarten and, for the first time, I was enrolled full time in university. Unlike all those years in Amma's house, where the neighbours were as much strangers to me by the time I left as when we first moved in, I was joining my little suburban community. I was introducing myself to people and making friends along the street. I had even been invited to a ladies' lunch at a house a few doors down.

And we were opening *our* doors too. We had a big housewarming dinner party in September. In October, my mother would be arriving to spend several months in our new guest room.

Finally, finally, we had the space and the independent family life I had wanted ever since Kinza was born—a home that was comfortable, sociable, serene.

And yet, of course, it didn't last.

※   ※   ※

After only a few short weeks, stress began once again to thrum through the air. Now that I was taking a full course load, the better part of my day was spent on campus—a fact that drove Ahmed wild.

One day, I left my laptop open on the couch. When I returned, Ahmed had it in front of him and was reading my emails. One was from a new female friend. We were going to meet at the campus pub for a lunch of half-price chicken wings.

"So now you're going clubbing?" he snapped as I reached over to retrieve my computer.

"It's just a restaurant," I said with a sigh.

"A restaurant with liquor. So you can drink, too?"

"No, just eat wings and chill."

"Sure, you have time to chill, but you don't have time to text me."

Ahmed was now asking me to check in with him multiple times throughout the day. He told me to text him as I went into class and as soon as I exited. If I went to the library, he wanted to be notified—and he expected that I message him at frequent intervals while I was there. The tone of these conversations was friendly, but if I failed to let him know where I was every second of the day, my cell buzzed in my purse like a jar of angry wasps.

Things were no more relaxed when I *was* at home. Ahmed wanted me beside him at every moment.

If I was studying, he would pester me to watch movies with him. If I was too tired to stay up until the last scene, he said my sleepiness was proof I didn't love him enough. When I ran a bubble bath for myself, he sulked, saying that I was only doing so to avoid him.

"You have time for everyone but me," he said again and again.

Once my mother was with us, this churlish clinginess only got worse. While Mom's presence made our lives somewhat easier—she helped with the housework and took care of the girls when they got home from school—Ahmed was jealous of the time I spent with her. It was a strange change from all those years when he wanted nothing whatsoever to do with me.

❄ ❄ ❄

Of course, Ahmed's behaviour was not restricted to petulant moodiness. There were shoves and insults, too—often in front of my mother. And yet the domestic fantasy world I had created with the new house allowed me to minimize the friction and the violence. It was as if my infatuation were blinding me to the stark truth that nothing had changed.

And then one late fall evening, I was forced to stop deluding myself.

We had finished dinner and my mother had disappeared upstairs into her room. I was clearing the table and putting the uneaten food into the fridge. Before the meal, Ahmed had been once more complaining about how little time I had for him. Now he entered the kitchen and began in again.

"Samra, this isn't right," he said bitterly. "Your school work is taking too much time away from your family." He meant away from him.

I was exhausted, and the prospect of defending myself for another hour or more was crushing. "I don't want to talk right now," I said.

"What do you mean?" demanded Ahmed. "You have to talk!" He stood in front of me blocking my way to the fridge.

"No," I said firmly. "I don't want to. Now please let me go so I can keep cleaning up."

With that, he grabbed my arm with one hand and buried the other in my hair. Yanking my head back, he spat into my upturned face. Then spat again. "Now you can go, bitch," he said before he released me.

I jumped away from him and ran shaking into the bathroom to wash my face. Then I escaped upstairs to the guest room. As soon as the door closed behind me, I burst into tears. "I just can't live with that man anymore," I told my mother, who was lying on the bed.

Mama sat up. She had seen enough over the past months and years not to seem surprised at my words. She patted a space on the bed beside her. "You're in university now," she said gently. "You can find ways to get out."

※ ※ ※

My mother was no doubt thinking of this scene when she sat me down to talk just before her flight home in January. "Leave this man, Samra," she said. "He's not the right man for you. And people don't change."

I looked down at my lap. I was struggling with how to respond.

"Don't make the same mistake I made," my mother continued. "I didn't have the support of my family or of the law. You do."

Finally, I voiced my concern. "But what about my home? I love this home."

"This is a *house*, Samra," she said, shaking her head. "Not a home. A home isn't bricks. You don't have the love here to make a home. You *need* to leave."

I sat quietly, letting her words sink in. They were extraordinary. My mother was, after all, a woman who had been raised to believe that her own separated mother was a failure and that she herself had been forever scarred by that diminished status. And she had felt the full force of family pressure to remain in her own unhappy marriage. For years, she'd been sympathetic to my intermittent moves to leave Ahmed. But now she was actively counselling divorce. In fact, she was *insisting* on it.

※ ※ ※

My mother's words echoed in my mind for days and weeks. And it wasn't only *her* words that haunted me.

One evening I was tucking Kinza into bed. It had been another tempestuous day in the house, and I expect my sadness was evident on my face and in my voice. As I leaned over to kiss her on the forehead, she looked me in the eyes and said quietly, "Mama, why are you with Daddy?"

I pulled back in surprise.

"He isn't nice to you," she continued. "Are you staying because of Saarah and me? Because you don't have to. I will help you take care of Saarah. We could do it on our own."

I stared at her in astonishment.

"We won't be happy until you're happy." She was not quite ten years old, yet she could see clearly that things were amiss in our family. And she was offering to change her whole world for me. I leaned in and gave her a hug.

"It's going to be all right," I tried to reassure her.

※　※　※

Even with my mother and Kinza's prompting, I made no move. I was going for counselling two times a week; Ahmed and I were sleeping separately again; we argued constantly. But it was as if I were stand-ing at the edge of a cliff, unable to peer over the edge and find a safe way down.

And then one of Ahmed's outbursts almost pushed us both right off. We were in the kitchen. I was setting the kitchen table for supper, and Ahmed was again arguing about my time. He was annoyed by my heavy winter-term schedule. We were getting nowhere, but the more I tried to end the conversation, the angrier he became.

"Kinza, Saarah, dinner's ready," I called, hoping that their arrival might distract him. Instead, he began to cross the kitchen floor towards me. I pulled out my phone.

"If you raise a finger against me," I said, "I'll call 9-1-1."

Ahmed stopped in his tracks. Then he exploded.

"Talaq, talaq, talaq!"

As soon as the words were out of his mouth, he looked aghast. I stood frozen in place. We both knew exactly what he had just done. According to widely accepted Muslim law, if a man says "talaq" three times, his marriage is automatically dissolved. Ahmed had divorced me.

Over the past several years, I had asked him to do just this. But now that divorce was happening in the very moment, I was overcome with disbelief and panic.

Clearly Ahmed was as unnerved as I was. He turned on his heel and fled the house.

As I fed the girls dinner and then got them ready for bed, I tried to keep myself from crumbling. I realized that since the abuse had restarted in our new house, I'd been carrying around a little script for how our marriage might end—I would finish university, get a good job and then leave, financially able to build a life as a single mother. But that was an abstract part of the future. This was too soon, too abrupt. I wasn't ready.

When Ahmed came back to the house, his anger had vanished, as had mine. We huddled together, talking about what we needed to do now. We agreed to go to a mosque the next day to ask whether or not our marriage had truly been terminated.

The imam told us that three repetitions were three repetitions. We were no longer married in the eyes of Allah. It wasn't what either of us wanted to hear. We went to a different mosque. Shaken by the bad news from the first, Ahmed's regret was on full display before the second imam. While I sat nervously in the chair next to him, he weepily told the imam how much he loved me, how much he wanted to change, how sorry he was to have uttered those dangerous words. The imam looked with sympathy at both of us.

"This is not an ideal situation, but Allah is forgiving and merciful," he assured us. "But you must be careful. There are no second chances after this." Ahmed and I knew whose guidance we wanted to follow.

The talaq scare knocked us into another period of peace and ersatz harmony but, not surprisingly, it was short-lived. Our verbal swords were taken up again, as were Ahmed's pushing and slapping. And the facade I was trying to present to the world—the pretty life that matched the pretty home—was disintegrating. At one of the neighbourhood ladies' lunches, I arrived trembling and fragile, hoping that the foundation I'd carefully applied to my cheeks was covering up the deep-red hand mark Ahmed had put there just minutes earlier. My host, my friend, could see immediately that something was wrong, but when she inquired I put her off, telling her I would explain later.

I got the sense, however, that she already knew.

※　※　※

It had been a miserable morning. We'd been fighting since breakfast about an upcoming dinner party at Amma and Abba's house. I had an exam the following morning and didn't want to be out that night. Ahmed was insistent.

The girls were in school, so our acrimony could be given free rein. When shouting and yelling didn't move me, Ahmed picked up my laptop and dashed it to the ground. He sent my carefully ordered study notes flying around the room. Then he angrily retreated to the basement rec room. Ordinarily I would have left him alone, but after spending twenty minutes on my hands and knees, crabbing along the floor to pluck my papers out from under the furniture and put them back in order, I was too agitated to let things be. I marched into the basement and told Ahmed that I was sick and tired of his tantrums. I was ready for another fiery exchange of words. I was not ready for what happened next.

He leapt off the couch and flew towards me, knocking me hard. I tumbled back into a chair, where Ahmed pinned me, his thumbs across my collarbones, his fingers wrapping up around the base of my neck. He was squeezing hard.

"You don't listen to me!" he was screaming. "You're the one who makes me angry!"

I had been grabbed and pinched so many times, but he had never put his hands so close to my throat before. I could feel his thumbs pressing into my collarbones, just a small slip away from my windpipe. *He's going to choke me*, I thought. Fear shot through me and I reached out, slapping him. As he jumped back I sprang from the chair and made for the stairs, but before I could reach them Ahmed had grabbed me from behind. I screamed—a horror-movie scream—a long, electric peal of sheer terror. As the sound escaped from me, I hoped that it might pierce the shared wall and our neighbours would call 9-1-1. Instead, my scream caught Ahmed off guard, and I felt his grip loosen.

I pulled away, taking the stairs two at a time. When I reached the top, I snatched my car keys from the hall table and burst through the front door. Once in the minivan, I squealed out of the driveway and was gone.

I drove through neighbourhood streets as quickly as I could, looking in the rear-view mirror to make sure Ahmed wasn't following me. After I was certain I was alone, I pulled over to the side of the road, stopped the car and started to sob.

This was a new and horrifying low. I had never truly thought Ahmed would or could kill me. But sitting in the van I could still feel his hands on my skin, his thumbs terrifyingly close to my neck. I could imagine them sliding up just an inch. I could imagine them squeezing the life out of me.

I was shaking so hard I could barely hold my phone as I called the Assaulted Women's Helpline.

They advised me to tell Ahmed to move out. But first, they said, I should call the police and report the attack. "Just to warn you," the counsellor added, "you have to tell the whole story, and it won't be easy. The police will try to poke holes in it."

I hung up and sat in the van, staring out the window. It was March. The time of year when winter is on its way out but not yet gone. The time of year when the trees are skeletal, the skies undependable and the earth sodden and grey. I could see a line of little houses, much like mine, stretching before me. They looked quiet and dark, as if they might all be vacant. There was not a soul on the street. It seemed that the entire world around me was just waiting for life to start.

I was tired of waiting. I did not want to call the police. I did not want to see Ahmed arrested. I did not want to earn the wrath of his family. I just wanted it to be over.

I felt a sense of calm descend on me. I had made a decision.

A few days later, I called my mother. "I need you to come back," I told her. "I'm going to end it with Ahmed, but I'll need your help with the kids . . . with everything."

※　※　※

When I returned home after our big fight, Ahmed had looked both happy and greatly relieved. He had thrown his arms around me, buried his face in my hair and told me how sorry he was. I hugged him back, knowing that I would have to play along until my mother arrived.

But the scene in the basement seemed to hang in front of us as we moved about the house. Ahmed acknowledged as much when I told him that my mother was on her way. She would be intruding during a difficult time, he said. We had things we needed to work out in private. I shrugged at his objections. My mother was coming because she needed my support right now, I lied, and I wasn't about to deny her.

※　※　※

On April 19, 2011, my 29th birthday, my mother's plane landed at the Toronto airport. I was in the midst of exams, but we found the time to talk about everything that had happened since she left just three months earlier.

I recounted the recent abuse, including the near-choking incident. And I told her that I was worried not just about my own safety but about the girls', too. I knew Ahmed would never put his hands on them. But the counsellors had been telling me that children who witness partner abuse often either commit it themselves or accept it from others. I'd been haunted by this for a long while and was finally realizing that I had no time to lose. By staying with Ahmed, I would be causing the girls real harm—and putting them in danger in the future. We were *all* drowning. I needed to pull us out of the river.

My mother looked both sad and concerned. But when I recounted the business of the three talaqs, her expression changed. She sat up straight and her eyes widened.

"I don't think that imam you listened to was right," she said. "I don't think you and Ahmed are married any longer." She insisted we go back to the same imam.

When my exams were over, Mom and I made an appointment. This time, I told him about the abuse.

The imam looked surprised. "I did not know that. You are no longer married," he said. His tone invited no questions or challenges. Now I had a way out.

As we drove away, I couldn't stop my heart from hammering. "I don't think I can tell Ahmed," I said. "I'm afraid."

"Don't worry," said my mother. "I will tell him."

※　※　※

On April 26th, my mother descended the basement stairs to talk to Ahmed. I stayed, hovering, in the kitchen. After a few seconds, I could hear voices drifting up from the rec room. Ahmed was apparently refusing to listen to what my mother had to say. I decided I had to join them.

When I got downstairs, my mother was talking quietly and politely. "Ahmed, this is not my opinion. This is the opinion of the imam whom you went to see and whom you listened to earlier. He did not have all of the information. You have been divorced since January. You have been living improperly for three months. You can't continue that. You have to leave."

Ahmed looked offended. "What do you mean? This is our house!" He was now looking intently at me.

I felt a pang of guilt but managed to get a few words out: "I'm sorry, Ahmed, but you'll have to go back to your parents."

Ahmed's gaze changed direction. I could see emotions flicker across his face—stubborn resistance, dumbfounded shock, bitter realization. In our relationship, he had always been the defender of the faith. He worried constantly that my exposure to non-Muslims would weaken my observance and lead me away from righteousness. He even talked me out of taking an Islamic history course, worried that the Shia professor would corrupt my Sunni faith. How could he now ignore religious law—or ask me to?

He had just been caught in an inescapable trap. And it was a trap of his own making. I wasn't leaving him—because he had *already* left me.

Finally, he looked at me again. "I can't go back there," he said quietly. "I'll stay in the basement until we sort this out. I won't inter-fere with you or the rest of the family."

That evening, Ahmed moved his belongings down into the rec room.

❀ ❀ ❀

For the next day or two, Ahmed would slip silently out of the house in the morning and disappear into the basement after work.

Despite everything I'd been through, his sad acquiescence and shadow-like presence tugged at my heart. I felt sorry for him and guilty that I had made him a ghost in his own home. I wished I could have handled things better; I wished he could have changed.

On the second night, I decided to go into the basement to see if Ahmed was okay. He was asleep in his clothes on the sofa. I brought a blanket over and covered him up before heading back upstairs. I was relieved that my mother was with me. I could sense that if I'd been on my own, I would have told him to stay.

After a couple of days, Ahmed moved back to his parents' house. As soon as he did, Abba phoned me. Amma was in Pakistan, visiting family. Ahmed's father wanted to know why he had returned.

I told him that my husband had given me three talaqs, an imam had ruled we were no longer married, and we could not live together any longer. There was silence on the other end of the line. This was something Amma and Abba could understand. And they would accept that there was nothing I could now do about it.

"Well, what can we parents do," Abba finally said, "if our kids turn out this way."

※　※　※

Within a few days, Amma returned from her trip and immediately appeared on our doorstep. She was in tears. "Please, can we see the children?" she begged.

I reassured her that she, Abba and Ahmed could see the girls whenever they wanted. I had no desire to keep them away from their grandparents and their father. We made plans for Kinza and Saarah to go over to Amma's house for the day.

Shortly after that, I got a call from the imam. Ahmed had been in touch with him, and now the man was backpedalling. He told me that Ahmed's version of events differed from mine, and since he was so remorseful, Allah would forgive him and allow the marriage to stand.

It seemed Ahmed was not going to slip out of the marriage quietly after all. Mom and I decided to seek out another religious ally. We met with a different imam, a man who had written a book about Islamic marriage and divorce. He insisted our union was over and wrote a fatwa to that effect. Along with the ruling, he gave us a copy of his book.

Ahmed showed up in the driveway a day or two later, awash in tears and apologies. Seeing him so distressed made me feel weak with guilt and pity. His remorse had drawn me back so many times that I knew I needed to resist it. I held the book out towards him like a shield.

"I'm sorry," I said, making him take the book and the fatwa. "It really is over."

But the visits continued. The next time Amma showed up at my door, she was standing next to one of Ahmed's friends. I did not like the way the man's eyes travelled over me as I stood in the front hall.

In Islamic law, divorced partners can re-marry each other only if the wife has been married to and divorced or widowed by another man first.

"Bhabi"—the man was calling me his "brother's wife"—"I'm willing to help you out." He was staring at me with lecherous anticipation.

I looked at them both in disbelief. "Leave," I said to Amma. "Leave right now." Then I turned and closed the door in her face.

※　※　※

The next time Ahmed called, he seemed to have accepted our fate. "Let's keep things amicable," he offered. He sounded calm. Pleasant, even. "I don't want the girls to suffer. I think we need to sell the house, so I will have money to pay child and spousal support. I will co-sign a lease on a condo for you and the kids."

Even a few months earlier, I might have been heartbroken about the loss of the house. But now I could see it for the empty shell it was, and I was relieved and grateful that Ahmed was willing to be so financially supportive. Unemployed and with the consumer proposal on my record, I wouldn't be able to sign for a decent apartment on my own.

Ahmed couldn't bear the idea of sitting together in a lawyer's office to hammer out a separation agreement. He suggested I get a lawyer to work something out, and he would review and sign it. He would pay me back for the legal fees. I found a young woman who had recently passed the bar and got her started on the paperwork. Then I put the house on the market.

Ten days after the house was listed, it sold, the closing date a mere four weeks away.

It was a surreal time—I couldn't quite believe what I had put in motion. And while I was relieved that Ahmed was being relatively calm and cooperative, I could hardly be sanguine in the face of so much uncertainty and new territory.

For several days, I packed boxes, visited the lawyer and started a summer course that I had signed up for before I understood what lay ahead of me. But my focus was on finding a place for Kinza, Saarah and me to live. I flew around Mississauga looking for condos to rent, finally finding a nice two-bedroom not far from the university. I texted Ahmed that I had the lease and needed to meet up with him so he could sign it.

A day went by and he didn't text back.

I sent him another message and waited.

Another twenty-four hours elapsed. The landlord contacted me again. Without a co-signatory he would need the entire first year's rent up front.

That was, of course, impossible. Even if I sold all my wedding jewellery, all my furniture, every possession I had, I wouldn't be able to come up with that kind of cash. What's more, we had a thousand-dollar lawyer's bill that needed to be paid.

I texted Ahmed again. I was beginning to feel desperate. If I didn't get back to the condo owner very shortly, I would lose the unit. And with only a few weeks until our house closed, it would be nearly impossible to find a suitable place to live before the girls and I had to move out. We would have no place to go. Amma had offered to let the girls and me move back in to their house, but it didn't feel like a real option as Ahmed was living there.

I sent him yet another pleading text. *Please, Ahmed! You're the one who suggested that we didn't have to go to court. I just need the lease signed.*

This time, after a few seconds, my phone beeped.

As I read Ahmed's message, my mouth went dry. I dropped down into a chair, staring unbelieving at the words on my phone.

LMAO! Talk with my lawyer!

🌺 🌺 🌺

My mother and I spent the evening in a panic. At one point, I had to leap from my chair to throw up in the bathroom. Finally, since neither of us knew what to do, I called the Assaulted Women's Helpline once again. As always they were kind, but they said they couldn't give me any legal advice. Instead they suggested that I apply for legal aid immediately.

For the next three days, I was in and out of the Brampton courthouse, filling out pages of the legal aid application, explaining my story, pleading for help. I called my real estate agent as well, but as I suspected, there was no way to halt the sale of our house without incurring severe financial penalties. Next, I phoned a number of homeless shelters, my heart ricocheting in my chest as I did so. I'd heard many stories about the dangers of staying in these places, crowded as they were with desperate people.

My fears hardly mattered. I was put on a waitlist, but no one had space for me and the girls.

After a harrowing seventy-two hours, legal aid certificate in hand, I headed to the UTM Office of the Registrar. Now that I was separated, I hoped I'd be eligible for the Ontario Student Aid Program. But I knew that even if I received a grant, I wouldn't get the money right away—and I still had nowhere to live. As I drove to the campus, my whole body felt as if it had been caught in an electrical field, the current singeing my nerves but keeping me in frenetic motion nonetheless. I had to remind myself to breathe.

The financial aid officer was kind and supportive. She confirmed that I could now get financial assistance. But she could see that this good news did not erase the worry from my face. I explained about my impending homelessness.

"Why don't you go over to the Student Housing office and talk to them? It's a long shot—their leases usually run September to August, so they probably won't have any empty units. But you could try."

I thanked her and walked across campus.

I entered the housing office holding my breath. It was all I could do to explain myself and what I needed. The receptionist smiled at me kindly, but she didn't look hopeful. She buzzed the housing supervisor for me. Like the financial aid officer, the housing supervisor's tone was warm and reassuring. When she heard my story, she looked thoughtful.

"You know, I might actually have something. Let me go check." With that, she disappeared back into her office. She reappeared a few minutes later with a smile on her face. She took my hand in hers. "Someone just broke their lease," she said. "Let's go over and look at the unit right away."

※　※　※

Two days later, I was sitting in the middle of my new apartment's living-room floor, staring at the set of keys in my hand. The place was tiny, much like the last apartment Ahmed and I had shared. And to describe it as shabby would be entirely too kind. The walls were painted a glossy yellowish-white—the colour of soured skim milk. The corners of the room were stringy with cobwebs; the windows, set high in the walls, were grimy and small. Thin, stiff dark-green commercial carpet stretched out in front of me. The kitchen, no bigger than my clothes closet back at the house, was outfitted with dated and dented miniature appliances. There were baseboard heaters but no air conditioning. It was only June, but already, intense heat pulsed through the stale air.

And yet the place was a true gift. The university housing office had told me I could move in as soon as I wanted. They would be happy to wait for the rent until OSAP, my financial aid, came through and my teaching assistant job started. The five days in which I'd thought the girls and I were going to be homeless had been the scariest of my whole life. I looked around my cramped little apartment and burst into tears of sheer relief.

I had found a place to start again.

PART
FOUR

CHAPTER 15

ON MY OWN

I was in my bedroom, stuffing clothes into green garbage bags. I'd hired a couple of university students to help me move my furniture into the apartment. There wouldn't be a lot—I had sold my sofa in order to help pay the lawyer's bill that Ahmed was obviously no longer willing to cover.

But I couldn't afford to pay the students for more than a couple of hours of work. In the end, it would take me five days and ten trips in my old van to hump the rest of our stuff into the apartment.

It was while I was still packing up my clothes that I began to think again about what the counsellor had told me when I called after the near-choking incident. I needed to report the assault, she insisted, in order to protect myself.

I had actually already called the police once. Just after Ahmed sent me the LMAO text (LMAO means "laughing my ass off") he had showed up at the house to pick up the girls. When he pulled into the driveway, I went out to meet him, holding the separation papers the lawyer had drawn up. He might not have signed the lease, but I was hoping he might still sign these. I was going to have dinner with some neighbourhood women later. The sight of me in a dress, with my makeup done, holding the papers, set Ahmed off. He laughed at my request that he take the agreement.

"Where are you going, dressed like a whore?" he demanded.

I tried to reply as calmly as I could, but he wasn't going to ease up. "Do you think you're some kind of hotshot, that you'll survive on your own? Within weeks you'll come crawling back."

He threw the travel mug he was holding on the ground and started to kick the garage door. Then he hustled the girls into the car and squealed out of the driveway. I was rattled. Even though we were living apart, we would have to continue to interact because of the girls. But now that I had left him, what reason might he have for self-control? What if he didn't leave next time? What if he managed to get into the house, to get me alone? And what if he took the kids and didn't return them?

I got into my minivan and drove to the police station. Once there, I explained to the officer at the reception desk what had just happened. The officer asked if I wanted to press charges.

I shook my head. Why had I come? What did I want? I had no idea. I just knew that I was frightened. It was only a matter of time before Ahmed lost his temper again.

"Would you like us to go talk with him, give him a warning?" the officer suggested. I nodded.

After the visit from the police, Ahmed had been more restrained when we talked to or saw each other.

But ever since then, I couldn't stop thinking about the lengths he seemed willing to go to, to break me emotionally—even if the result was that his own children didn't have a place to live. Of course, I was worried his actions might turn physical again, but it was more than that.

I had suffered at Ahmed's hands for nearly a decade, and yet despite the hurt and humiliation I had protected his image with my extended family and his. I had acted the good wife with all his friends. I had done what I was told. But why should I continue to pretend? Why did he deserve this kind of compassion from me? I had been told by the helpline and my counsellors that reporting abuse was important. Now I wanted to do the right thing.

I finished tying up the garbage bag I'd been filling and went to tell my mother that I would be going out to run an errand.

※ ※ ※

When I got to the police station, I recognized the officer I'd spoken with the first time. "I want to file a report," I said, "to make a full statement about what I've been through."

The officer explained that if I did make a statement, the police would have the authority to press charges—and I would not be able to stop the process.

"Are you sure you want to do this?" he asked. "You've been separated for several months, and you don't have bruises now, so there's no way for you to prove what happened."

"I understand," I said. "It's up to you if you want to press charges. I just want the story on record. I just want to have my version of events out there."

The officer nodded and told me to follow him.

The interview room was stark—just a table and a few chairs. One wall was covered with a mirror. I knew it was a two-way mirror and that other officers were likely to be behind it, watching and recording what I had to say. The officer sat at the table across from me. He had a notebook in front of him.

"When you're ready," he said.

I started in, recounting every time Ahmed had hit me or kicked me. Every time he'd shoved me down or slapped me. Every time he'd broken my things or threatened me. Every incident of abuse I could think of. At times, I felt oddly detached, as if I were talking about someone else's life. At others, I experienced a rush of relief, as if holding Ahmed accountable was allowing me to let go of the lingering feeling that I had somehow deserved it all. That it was my fault.

All the while, the officer in front of me nodded and gave me smiles of encouragement. A few times, much to my surprise, anger creased his face as I described Ahmed's actions.

Wow, I thought, *even a man thinks that what happened was wrong.*

At the end of three hours, I was exhausted. The officer looked at me kindly. "The problem here is that all of this is historical. Does anyone else know? Did you tell anyone?"

I mentioned that I had talked with both my family doctor and the counsellors at the university health centre. He asked if I would sign a consent form, allowing them to look at those records. I was happy to do that.

As the officer walked me out of the interview room, he took my hand and gave it a squeeze. "You did the right thing," he said. "That was very brave of you."

※　※　※

When I got home and told my mother, she was both shocked and deeply unsettled. She repeated the familiar refrain—what will people think? She worried about Ahmed's future. She insisted that even if I was getting a divorce, my duty was to protect the family honour. The pride I had felt about telling the truth quickly withered in a gust of fear and guilt.

Those feelings only grew the following morning when I heard that Ahmed had been arrested and charged with four counts of common assault. Since it was Saturday, he would remain in jail until his bail hearing on Monday morning. Victims Services of Peel had called to inform me of the development and to let me know that once he was released, a restraining order would be put in place, prohibiting Ahmed from coming within five hundred metres of me. Also, a

Children's Aid Society worker would be coming to the house to talk with the children. It was all terrifying and utterly surreal.

※ ※ ※

By Monday, Saarah and Kinza were asking to see their father. Despite my reluctance to talk with anyone from Ahmed's family, I called Amma. She was hostile but relatively quiet, no doubt scared by the police involvement in our lives. We agreed to meet in a grocery store parking lot, so she could take the kids for the afternoon.

When my mother, the girls and I got out of the car a few hours later, it was clear this would be no calm transfer of the children.

Amma came towards us screaming: "My poor son. They hand-cuffed him and took him away!" Then she turned to Kinza and Saarah. "Look what your mother has done. She has put your father in jail!"

The tirade went on until both girls were crying uncontrollably, refusing to go with her. Amma and I agreed to drive to a nearby park to see if the girls would calm down. For almost an hour, we sat on the bench while she vented her outrage. Finally, she coaxed the kids into her car and took them off to see Ahmed.

The drive back home with my mother was silent and tense. Once in the house, I could do nothing but sit watching the clock, terrified that Amma would not return the girls. She'd always said that Ahmed would get custody of them if we separated. I'd been educated by my counsellors to understand that this was not true, and came to regard the threat as a scare tactic to keep me in the marriage. But it was dawning on me that Ahmed and his mother could force me to fight to keep the children.

I did get a call from Amma a few hours later, telling me to come and pick up the girls. But almost as soon as I hung up the phone, it rang again. This time, it was the police. Ahmed had reported *me*, claiming that my plan to come to the house to pick up the girls was putting him in danger of violating the restraining order.

"But how am I supposed to pick up my kids from his house then? And how do I get them there for visits?" I asked.

"Just be careful," the officer said before hanging up.

He had talked to me kindly, but his pointedly unhelpful answer seemed proof that my effort to move forward was not so much a bumpy road as a dark and almost impenetrable thicket. How was I going to manage it?

※　※　※

Since telling Ahmed that the marriage was over at the end of April, I'd been buffeted relentlessly by doubt. But the day I had to hand the house keys over to the real estate agent, remorse crashed into me like a tsunami. I'd waited for my own home for twelve years but had ended up in it for only seven months. I spent the morning walking through the empty house from room to room to room, while the same thoughts looped through my mind: *I shouldn't have made him angry. I shouldn't have reported him. I shouldn't have separated the girls from their loving father. I shouldn't have given up.*

By the time I'd done the circuit several times, I was convulsed with tears and churning emotion.

"Please call Ahmed," I begged my mother. "Please apologize for me. Tell him I want him back. I'll quit school. I'll be quiet. I don't want to leave," I continued, rambling and incoherent, until my mother actually slapped me across the face.

"Samra, what are you talking about?" she said, frustration tightening her voice. "This is just a house. I've seen what he's done to you. Pull yourself out of this."

I stopped beseeching her but refused to move, sitting in the middle of the living-room floor, staring at my lap as I let the tears wash down my face. Eventually my mother gave up talking with me and called one of the neighbours I had become friends with. The woman arrived at the door a few minutes later, and the two of them, my mother and my friend, each took one of my arms and dragged me, still sobbing, from the house.

❋ ❋ ❋

It was a summer of soaring temperatures and staggering humidity, the kind of weather that makes walking down the sidewalk feel like moving headfirst through a bowl of stew.

And while the heat made travelling outdoors unappealing at best, the atmosphere inside my new apartment was worse. Even in the early morning hours, the air was hot and viscous, a fungal scent hanging like a mouldy veil. It reminded me of my parents' apartment in Pakistan but without the sanctuary of the air-conditioned bedroom.

In the first few days, I continued to plead with my mother to intercede with Ahmed—to help me somehow return to my former life.

My mother was clearly discomfited by both my emotional chaos and the stifling apartment. After two days in the new place she announced that she needed to return home.

"Do whatever you want, Samra," she said, "but do it on your own. I'm not going to help you with this madness!"

Before she left, I got her to do one last favour for me—to accompany me to the Students' Union office so I could ask about bursaries.

I'd been a student at UTM on and off for three years, but I'd never crossed the threshold of the Student Centre, which housed the union. The centre was a gathering place—that I knew—and as such it was the kind of place that Ahmed considered rife with temptation and cultural corruption. Now that I was free to go there, I found myself intimidated and ill at ease. I'd interacted with a few students when the social glue was academic work, but I had no idea how to be around the general population in other situations. I wanted the security of being accompanied by someone I knew, who would be there if things went sideways.

Trying to look as inconspicuous as possible despite my pink shalwar kameez, I slipped into the vast, window-lined atrium of the centre and followed the signs to the Students' Union, my mother quietly following my lead. As I walked into the office, heads turned towards me. I felt as if I had interrupted a conversation between the young men and women who were lounging in the reception area.

"Hi there," said one of the men. "Can I help you?" He sounded friendly enough, but I was still nervous. I explained that I wanted to apply for a bursary.

"Oh, I'm sorry. The person in charge of all that isn't here right now."

Everyone was watching me. Feeling strangely exposed, and relieved to have an excuse to make a fast exit, I thanked the young man, turned on my heel and hurried out of the room.

As my mother and I made our way through the sun-soaked atrium, I heard a voice ringing through the air. It was the fellow I had just been talking with in the office. He was running after us.

When he caught up, he was holding out a business card. "Hi. My name is Abhi. I'm the VP of part-time students for the Students' Union. Is there anything I can help you with?"

I told him that I was starting again in the fall as a full-time student but I needed financial help. My nervousness and self-consciousness must have inflected everything I said. I could see that Abhi understood things were not as simple as that. "Well, listen, the Students' Union is here to assist with all kinds of things. You can call me whenever you need help. Day or night."

I hadn't been back in the apartment for more than a couple of hours when I decided to call. My mother was out visiting an old friend who had moved to Mississauga. Alone with my thoughts about the coming year, I was sliding into full-blown hysteria. How was I ever going to manage once my mother left? Abhi had offered assistance. I had no idea what that might mean, but I knew I needed some kind of help.

⁂ ⁂ ⁂

The next afternoon Abhi was settled on my living-room couch, and I was telling him every sorry detail of my current circumstances.

"Listen," he said once I'd finished, "come back to the Students' Union tonight. We have a council meeting. I want to introduce you to people. You don't have to go through all of this alone. We'll help you."

I didn't know it at the time, nor would I fully appreciate it for many, many months, but that call and my subsequent talk with Abhi were perhaps the most important things I did once I was on my own. They opened up a new world to me, a world that would both support and sustain me in the coming years. Ahmed was right. I would never make it on my own. But that phone call ensured I didn't have to.

That evening I was back at the Student Centre, this time with Saarah and Kinza in tow. As soon as I walked through the door, Abhi began to introduce me to the other students who were milling about. Walied, the executive director, asked me a bit about my life, and like Abhi he insisted that the group at the Students' Union would support me. A woman named Cherri told me how much she loved kids and how happy she would be to help with Saarah and Kinza if I needed it. But the person who made the biggest impact on me that evening was a woman named Saba.

When I first walked into the office, Saba was stretched out on one of the couches that lined the walls. She appeared to be of South Asian descent—it turned out she was Pakistani—but she was wearing Western clothes. What struck me, however, was not her dress but her demeanour. There, in a crowded room of men and women, she was sprawled unselfconsciously across the furniture, as relaxed and at home as if she were in her own bedroom. Even when she sat up and approached me, everything about her calm confidence said that she belonged. I simply couldn't imagine feeling that way. But I knew that I desperately wanted to.

The meeting, and the entire evening, flew by, and I left feeling hopeful and excited. In the coming days, Abhi, Walied and the others were true to their word. Ruba, the person in charge of the bursaries, came by my apartment to talk to me, so I didn't have to trek down to the Student Centre with both kids. And others offered to take the girls whenever I had court dates or meetings with my lawyers, which was depressingly often. Frequently, this child care took place in the Students' Union office, which my girls soon discovered was as good as any playground or amusement park.

One afternoon, I returned to the office to pick up the girls and found Saarah squealing with delight as she was propelled around the place on a wheeled chair. While Saarah enjoyed her ride, Kinza was at a desk with a stack of paper in front of her. One of the union members, Matthew, was sitting in front of her, posing while she sketched him. The table held half-eaten cupcakes and cans of pop. The only thing missing from the party was balloons. Saarah and Kinza didn't want to leave.

The union office became a refuge for me and for the girls, one that I returned to again and again as I struggled to adjust to my new single life. I was taken aback by how thoughtful and supportive everyone was to a near stranger and her two small children—and how hard they worked to include me.

One afternoon, I was having coffee with my new friends when someone suggested going to a movie later in the day. They assured me that it was a kid-friendly film and told me I should bring the girls. There was no way I could spare that kind of money, so I mumbled a few excuses about other things I had to do. Saba disappeared from the office and then walked in a few minutes later with four printed movie tickets—one for her and the rest for me and the girls. "You're coming with us. I'm not taking no for an answer." When I started to protest she told me that I could repay her by cooking her a meal.

Indeed, over the course of the summer, whenever my new friends popped by, I tried to repay their kindnesses by feeding them. I also let everyone know that they were welcome to stay at my apartment whenever they wanted. As many of them lived a distance from the campus, they started to take up my offer—whether it was for a quick midday nap on the spare mattress I kept propped against the living-room wall or overnight when they had a class or test early the next morning. I loved the company and the social energy. For the first time since high school, I could make friends freely. For the first time since I'd started school, I wasn't checking my watch constantly when I was on campus. For the first time in my life, I could open the door to my own home and welcome others into it. It was extraordinary to feel a part of something beyond my family. By the time the fall term was underway, my tiny, stuffy apartment had been dubbed the Union Station of UTM. I puffed with pride at that.

My connection with the Students' Union gang also helped me overcome one of the biggest hurdles I faced during those early months of separation. Even though the campus housing organization was allowing me to defer my rent payments, my financial situation in those summer months was nothing short of perilous. The small amount of equity in the house would not be divided between Ahmed and me until our separation agreement was finalized. In the meantime, he was paying only a tiny amount of child support, and it didn't come close to covering groceries, gas and my cellphone payments. My OSAP and teaching assistant position wouldn't kick in until the fall. Michelle, a friend from the Students' Union office, helped me apply for Ontario Works government assistance to tide me over, but that too would take time to arrive, and my cupboards were literally bare. She suggested that I visit a food bank—which seemed to be my only option until my first government cheque arrived.

So one hot July evening, I put both girls into the minivan and drove to the little church where the food bank operated. As we descended the stairs into the dank basement, my heart sank. A table stretched across the room, a line of metal shelves filled with cans and boxes behind it. A sour-looking woman put her hand out to take my Ontario Works registration information. After glancing at the papers, she gave them back to me and without a word began filling a paper bag with various items. She was about to drop a can of tuna into the bag when I stopped her.

"Oh, no thank you," I said. "I'm afraid my girls won't eat that."

Her hand hung in the air above the bag as she looked at me in disbelief. "You come to a food bank and then you're going to tell me what you want?" She put the tuna back on the shelf and then thrust the half-filled bag at me. "Have a good night," she said, dismissing me.

As Kinza, Saarah and I retreated up the stairs, I tried to keep my eyes from filling.

"Mommy," said Kinza, reaching for my hand. "I don't want to come back here again." She needn't have worried.

The next morning, I returned to the Students' Union to see if anyone had ideas about where I might find a part-time job. Walied suggested I apply for a shift at the info desk in the Student Centre.

As I went through my closet looking for something to wear to the interview, I let out a little sigh. I hoped that I might squeeze a few dollars from any future paycheques for some new Western clothes. I had acquired a few loose, unfashionable pairs of jeans and shirts when I started university, but now I wanted a whole new look. I didn't want any of the South Asian outfits that Amma and Ahmed had expected me to wear. I'd already given away all my hijabs.

The interview itself was nerve-racking. Other than my job at Zellers, I'd never worked outside my home, and as I sat in front of Ruba and Walied, I was quite sure that Walied was regretting his suggestion. Besides, how could someone so desperately in need of help herself possibly answer questions and give assistance to others? In my favour, however, I was interested in a shift that few people wanted: 8:00 p.m. to 2:00 a.m. It seemed a perfect time to me—I could be in class or at the library during the day, come home, feed the girls and put them to bed, then come to work. I figured that shift would also be the quietest, and therefore allow me to study while I staffed the desk.

I was able to take that late-night shift because I'd just found a foreign exchange student, Maria, who was willing to take the second bedroom in my place. (I was happy to squeeze Saarah and Kinza in with me if I could make a bit of extra income.) We struck a deal that she would receive meals as well, and in exchange pay a small amount of rent and provide me with child care during the evenings and on other occasions as needed. So when I got the job, I was ready to go.

All these bits and pieces of income kept our stomachs full until the fall started. And by the time classes got underway, I had started earning a little extra money in yet another way. Abhi had become an enthusiastic fan of my cooking, and one day he suggested that I start to provide dinners for students—for a fee. He would spread the word if I were interested. I immediately stocked up on cheap plastic containers and started to cook massive portions of everything. Before long, I had a loyal group of customers who would show up once or twice a week and purchase dinners for the coming evenings. When they came back for refills, they'd return my containers.

※ ※ ※

When the fall 2011 term began my schedule was bursting. I had a full course load, I was a teaching assistant, or TA, and I was working part time at the info booth. But of course I was also making sure that Kinza and Saarah were fed, cared for and off to school each day. I was taking care of my little home while running a small catering business out of it. I was volunteering at the university's Accessibility Centre and the Afghan Women's Organization. And I was finally enjoying a university social life.

Through it all, my new friends shored me up and cheered me on. I can't adequately express how important these extraordinary people were (and still are) to me. They threw me a buoy when I was sinking, and they continued to be a lifeline for me in the coming years.

As I read through everything I've written in the last few pages, I'm struck by the upbeat energy of it all, the sense that my first six months on my own were a frenetic push forward marked by enthusiastic industry and remarkable good luck, by a new-found community and much-enjoyed freedom. All that is true. But it is a far cry from the whole truth.

The reality of those first months was far more uneven, a pockmarked landscape that had me living as much in the shadows as in the breaking daylight. Eventually those shadows almost undid me.

CHAPTER 16

THE WAY FORWARD

Those summer months of 2011, when everything was new and frightening and when my work and study schedule had not yet filled every minute of my day, I was often immobilized by intense loneliness and despair. On some days when Kinza and Saarah were with Amma or Ahmed I would go back to bed as soon as the girls had departed, lying there hour after hour until it was time to pick them up again. But even in the autumn, once the pace of my life intensified, days and weeks disappeared into darkness.

My new friends, as wonderful and helpful as they were, simply could not understand why I would miss my old life, or Ahmed, but I did. Intensely. At times my married past seemed to disappear into a dense fog, and all that broke through were bright beacons of occasional happy times and sporadic kindnesses.

During these periods, all my bold acts—protesting loudly when Ahmed grabbed me or called me names, telling everyone I wanted a divorce, calling the police—no longer looked like acts of bravery, dignity and self-possession but instead the self-defeating tantrums of a spoiled child. Why hadn't my previous life been good enough for me?

Ten-year-old Kinza, wise beyond her years, continued to save me—just as she had years ago when I collapsed on that prayer mat, ready to let go of everything.

One evening, she and I were driving to McDonald's to treat ourselves to a junk-food dinner. As I was thinking about what we would bring back for Saarah, whom we had left with my tenant at the apartment, a picture floated into my mind—Ahmed tiptoeing into my basement room, clutching a paper bag, a soft look on his face as I turned to him. Since our rukhsati, other than the diamond ring and the booby-trapped BlackBerry, Ahmed had never given me gifts. But fast food had been his quirky language of love. It was his way of apologizing after a fight. It was his thoughtful offering when he knew I had struggled through another dinner of his mother's spicy food. It was the mark of each honeymoon period, each period of peace and relative happiness. As the bright red-and-yellow McDonald's sign came into view, I felt my throat grow tight and painful and the tears pool under my eyes. In that moment, nothing seemed as romantic to me as those late-night visits, announced by the comforting smell of hot French fries and savoury burgers. Ahmed had been kind. He had loved me.

"What have I done?" I said out loud.

I felt a small hand on my arm. Kinza was giving it a little shake. She knew exactly what I was talking about. "Mommy, if you go back, it will only be worse because everyone will want to punish you for leaving. Look at how much progress you've made. You've got real friends now. It will get better. We can do this."

We held hands in the car all the way home.

⁂

It wasn't just the loss of Ahmed and my marriage that made me ache. It was the evaporation of the entire community I had lived in. What social circle I had formed was through Ahmed and Amma. All my old friends were the wives of Ahmed's pals, and they wanted nothing to do with me now. I tried to phone a few of them at first, but no one would take my calls. I soon realized that was perhaps a good thing.

I was delighted one summer afternoon when I saw a familiar number pop up on my cell. It was one of those wives. "Is it true?" she asked after I'd said hello. "Everyone says you were cheating on Ahmed and now you've left so you can live with some guy." She sounded thrilled by the scandal, and after making a few ignored denials I gave up. I knew I wouldn't be able to convince her.

My family was an ocean away, but more than physical distance separated us. I was not in touch much with my sisters, and I knew Warda and Saira were both unnerved by my separation. Warda hadn't even been able to tell her husband. While my mother had been supportive during the past few years and I could reach out to her in a crisis, our long-distance phone calls did not make me feel as if I had a kindred spirit to help me through the quotidian struggles of my new life. ("How am I ever going to make it without a man in my life?" I asked her one day. She murmured sympathetically, but I could sense her unspoken response: *You can't.*) What's more, given what I knew of my extended family's feelings about divorce, I did not expect to be welcomed into their lives now.

My alienation stretched beyond the people I knew. Even strangers from my community were often hostile and threatening once they found out that I was separated from my husband.

One day in midsummer I answered my phone and was met with a voice I didn't recognize. The man was speaking Urdu. "Hello, Samra Zafar? I am calling in response to your daycare ad."

I was taken aback. I hadn't run any online ads for the daycare for almost two years now. "I don't run a daycare anymore," I told the man. I did need money, however. Perhaps this was an opportunity. "But if it would help, I could provide some daycare for your children until September," I offered.

"Well, where are you living?" the man asked. "Who lives with you?"

These were the standard kinds of questions I was asked by people phoning about the daycare. I told him I was living on the UTM campus with my two children.

"You're divorced then?"

"I'm separated," I responded. "How old are your children?"

"Oh, they're not my children. I'm just calling for a friend."

I felt the hair on the back of my neck prickle. "Ask your friend to call me," I said, trying to sound as coolly professional as I could.

"I've heard about you," the man continued, "that you were separated. My wife is in Pakistan right now, and I'm lonely. We should get together. Have coffee and chat and maybe more . . ."

My breath caught in my throat. "How did you get my number?" I said.

"You're not that hard to find."

"Please don't call me again."

"Oh, come on. Don't be that way." The man's tone was slippery and smug.

I hung up. My phone buzzed again. It was the same caller. I blocked the number and then tried to go about my day. But I was deeply unnerved. What if he showed up at my door? *You're not that hard to find.*

More than one encounter in stores and restaurants in the coming months reminded me that I was now considered fair game by many men in my old community.

After I'd moved into my own place, I started shopping at a nearby family-run Pakistani grocer for all of my meat and spices. Over time I became quite friendly with the woman who ran the shop and often ordered meat by phoning in advance.

"Why does your husband never come with you?" she asked me one day. I explained that I was separated and in the process of getting a divorce. She seemed surprised but didn't say anything.

After that conversation, I noticed that the man who ran the meat counter seemed especially attentive. Whenever I asked him the price of anything, he would smile and say, "Why are you asking me the price? If it was up to me, I'd be giving this to you for free!" At other times, he would wink and say, "Save a little of your stew for me!"

One day, I ran into the store to pick up my meat order. I was going out to the movies later, so I was more dressed up than usual and had paid special attention to my hair and makeup. I could tell immediately that the butcher noticed. He handed me the brown-paper package of beef and gave me a leering smile. As I was getting into my car, a text popped up on my phone.

You look very, very pretty right now. I wish I could hug you.

There was only one person it could have been from. I had not given him my phone number. I never returned to the store.

I was so rattled by the incident, the earlier phone call and other responses I'd been getting that I eventually went to the campus police to ask them to do more patrols around my apartment. And I put their number on my fridge and in my cellphone. But I wasn't ready to give up my cultural community. I wanted desperately to find a way to stay connected and be accepted. In the early months of my separation, I sought some spiritual guidance from various imams and started taking Koran classes at the Al Huda Institute, a non-profit Islamic education organization. There I met a young Pakistani woman, Maya, who invited me to her family home for dinner one evening in August. Maya's family had come to Canada from Saudi Arabia a few years before. Her parents were extremely traditional, but they welcomed me with warmth and kindness, even though they knew that I had broken all the rules they believed in. I was grateful to them for their tolerance.

I ended up at their dinner table on many weekends when Saarah and Kinza were with Amma and Ahmed. They plied me with delicious Pakistani food and tried to give helpful advice about my future.

The only real way forward, as far as they were concerned, was to find me another man. And they set out to do just that.

One afternoon when I arrived at their house, Maya's mother approached me with a wide smile. "Good news, Samra," she crowed. "We have a marriage proposal for you! He's very rich, in his sixties, and his children are all grown."

I couldn't quite make sense of it. "Aunty," I protested, "I'm only twenty-nine!"

"So what?" Maya's mother said. "You're divorced now. You should consider yourself lucky. Do you think it will be easy to find a man your age? Even men in their sixties can get eighteen-year-old virgins!"

I stood my ground, but I understood the truth of what Maya's mother was telling me. And so I agreed to go on a date with a couple of other, younger finds. But as much as I wanted to prove to them, to myself and to the world at large that I could still attract a man, in particular a man close to my own age, none of these matches worked out.

Maya's mother grew increasingly concerned about my man-less state. One evening in December, she reminded me that time was not on my side.

"You mustn't wait much longer, Samra," she warned. "Once you are over thirty it will be so hard for you to meet anyone." I thought back to my aunt Nasreen in Pakistan. She would certainly have agreed with this assessment. But then Maya's mother served me a far more devastating blow.

"And you must remember, *no* man will ever accept Kinza and Saarah except their father."

I returned home that night feeling sad and desperate. She was right—I was damaged goods. And despite what my university friends might tell me, in the world I was most familiar with, the world I called home, women just weren't complete without a man. What had I been thinking? Why was I going out on dates and meeting new men when there was one who already said he loved me? Why would

I bring a strange man into my life when my daughters' father was within reach?

※　※　※

Restraining orders were of course in place, keeping Ahmed and me away from each other. Amma and Abba picked the girls up for visits with him and dropped them off after. And yet I hadn't given up contact with Ahmed altogether.

In the spring, when we were newly separated, I'd got a number of calls from his friends, urging me to return. Missing my husband and desperate to hear news of him, I took the calls. I resisted the temptation to tell them I would go back, but I couldn't stop myself from wanting to see him. I missed him, yes, but I was also tortured by the question of whether or not he felt remorse. Finally I called him from a friend's cellphone and suggested that we meet clandestinely.

The first time we got together was in the summer, in a deserted parking lot late at night. Ahmed was unrepentant—the name-calling, the pushing and pinching, the spitting, none of it really hurt me. He was, he weepily insisted, the one in pain. He was the one who had been left, who had been forcibly separated from his children. We met a couple more times in the fall, but with each encounter Ahmed made it clear that if there was any fault to be assigned in the failure of our marriage, it was mine.

But now, with the dark winter months before me and Maya's mother's words ringing in my ears, I felt every bit of resolve and every ounce of confidence melt away. Without marriage, without Ahmed, my future would be a disaster. And worse still, my children would be condemned to the same miserable and bleak existence I had fashioned for myself.

I called Ahmed and asked him to meet me once again. We agreed to connect in the parking lot of a nearby strip mall.

❋ ❋ ❋

As soon as I slid into the front seat of his car, I started to beg. "Please, Ahmed, I made a big mistake. You were right. I can't do this anymore. I want to get back together."

"What's happened, then?" Ahmed's voice was cool. "You've been so high and mighty these last few months. I don't even know if I want you back. Look at everything you've done to me—you sent me to jail."

I had my hand on Ahmed's leg and was leaning towards him. "I know, I disrespected you. I disrespected your parents. Let's just forget everything that's happened. I'm still your wife. I will do anything you say. I just want to be with you."

I leaned closer and put my arms around him, but when his hands began to move across my body, I flinched.

Ahmed pulled away. "You don't care that I have needs. You're probably getting your needs fulfilled elsewhere." And then, "You're still my wife, right?" His look was easy to read. I leaned into him and let his hands go where they pleased.

At the end of the strip mall was a sad-and-neglected-looking Motel 6. Ahmed let go of me, turned on the ignition and drove over to the front door.

I got out without saying a word.

❋ ❋ ❋

An hour later, Ahmed drove me back to my car. I felt utterly hollow, as if every drop of blood had been drained from my body. I wasn't sure how I found the strength to open the car door and stand up. But I looked over at him before I walked away.

"Are we back together now?"

"I don't know," Ahmed said. "I'll think about it."

As his car sped off across the empty parking lot, I put the minivan into drive, my hand trembling as I did so. What had I done? I had given Ahmed just what he wanted. I had humiliated myself in front of him, reduced myself to something worse than nothingness. I had just thrown away everything I'd fought for, had shredded every scrap of self-respect I'd claimed in the last years and months. The hollowness I had felt was now filled by fiery self-loathing. I would never recover from this.

I was barely conscious of where I was going as I drove towards campus, but as the asphalt spooled underneath me, the guardrail caught my eye. I was driving along a raised road bordered by low strips of corrugated steel. On the other side of the rail, the pavement fell away abruptly.

It could be over so soon. All I had to do was sit still, and I would never have to feel this way again.

My front wheels were on the shoulder, the guardrail speeding closer and closer until the grey steel was just inches from the right side of the car. And then it was as if I could feel the first shards of impact and hear the sound of crushing metal and splintering glass. I gasped, jerking the steering wheel to the left just in time to avoid impact. As I pulled the car back into the lane, my fingers tightened around the hard plastic. I needed every ounce of strength and concentration I could summon to keep the car on the road. My whole body was shaking. I couldn't believe what I'd almost done—to Kinza, to Saarah, to my family, to myself.

When I finally walked through the door of my apartment, Cherri was sitting in the living room, reading a book. She looked up at me and then immediately sprang to her feet.

"What's wrong, Samra?"

I saw Cherri moving towards me, alarm sketched on her face. Then the floor began to tilt up, and I ghosted away.

After Cherri brought me around, I tried to explain what had happened. "I don't want to live," I whimpered.

Cherri left my side and returned with a framed photograph of Kinza and Saarah. "Look at these two. What will happen to them if you're not here? Do you want them to be pressured into marriage too? Do you want them to be abused like you were?"

Worried about my mental state, Cherri insisted on taking me to the hospital. I stayed for the day, talking to counsellors and gazing at the picture of Kinza and Saarah, which I had brought with me. I couldn't help feeling that I had failed them—in my marriage and in my recent actions—and that someone else might do a far better job of raising them.

And yet Cherri's words had hit a chord, summoning a disturbing scene. It happened after Ahmed had given me the three talaqs but before I finally resolved to leave him. In a fit of anger, he had thrown me down on the bed. Saarah was in the room with us, and when Ahmed got on top of me and began to slap me, my frightened four-year-old pleaded with her father. "Stop it, Daddy, please stop it." Ahmed's only response was to yell at her to get out. Instead she scrambled, crying, into the bedroom closet.

The image of Saarah hunkered down in the closet, praying for her mother's safety, just as I had done as a girl, was shattering. Cherri was right. The only way I could prevent the girls from travelling the same road I had was to stay in their lives.

If I wanted them to have a different future, I needed to show them the way.

⁂ ⁂ ⁂

By the time I got back home from the hospital, I had come to a conclusion. The temptation of the guardrail and the deadly plunge was like a piercing shot of clarity. The truth, my truth, was that there were only two real choices—lightness or darkness, energy or defeat, happiness or despair. I was choosing happiness.

I had lived for over ten years in the murky half-light of "what if" and "if only" and "maybe in the future." But there was only "right now." What I did and how I lived in the present.

I decided to make some changes.

During that first summer on my own, I had started doing some volunteer work while the girls were visiting Ahmed and their grandparents. At the UTM Accessibility Services office, I was paired with a sixty-five-year-old woman who was blind, almost deaf and confined to a wheelchair. She was completing her degree with distinction. As I typed up her assignments and wheeled her from class to class, I realized that what she was teaching me about resilience and determination was far more valuable than the help I was giving her. I also started tutoring at the Afghan Women's Organization. Focusing on others kept me from lying in bed ruminating about my life and feeling worse about everything. I was still volunteering as the winter began, but now I committed myself wholeheartedly to purposeful distraction. The second my thoughts drifted to Ahmed, the second I felt my spirits slip, I was on the move—on a walk, to the library, or running errands. My schedule had been busy—but now it was non-stop.

I also decided that Maya's family, as lovely as they were, fed my greatest insecurities. In the coming months, I would visit them less and less often, eventually dropping them from my life altogether. I felt bad turning my back on people who only wanted to help, but I couldn't risk succumbing to feelings of unworthiness and hopelessness again. And with that came the end of dating for a while. I simply didn't want to think about men or marriage. I needed to build myself up first.

In place of fretting about my relationship status, I began to focus even more seriously on my studies. School had always been my safe place. In my childhood it had provided a steady peace when home life was unpredictable. Then, and in adulthood, it was a source of enjoyment and self-confidence, a place where I found both success and a sense of belonging. So while I'd always worked hard at my studies, now I intended to take it up a notch.

My legal aid lawyer also had to go. He had not yet served Ahmed with the separation papers—the fellow wasn't even returning my phone calls. The few conversations we had always ended with the same words, "Be patient, Samra. These things take time." I didn't have any more time. I fired him early in the new year and found a young female lawyer who kick-started the work on my legal separation.

※ ※ ※

The coming months were tough ones—Ahmed seemed intent on drawing the process out, making endless adjustments and amendments to the agreement, costing me money, time and mental anguish with each change. After every meeting and every call from the lawyer, I reminded myself that this trouble was only temporary. I had to spend my energy on things that would last: my girls and my education.

My new commitment to moving forward and staying positive could only take me so far, however. By late May 2012, I was exhausted by the seemingly endless negotiations—by Ahmed's refusal to agree to the provincially suggested support levels and by his demand for joint custody. It was time to cut my losses. I agreed to joint custody, putting in a clause stating that the children's primary residence would be with me. That, and the fact that Ahmed had never been the one to make daily parenting decisions, reassured me the informal arrangement we had been following would remain unchanged.

I also told him that I would accept any amount of spousal support he thought was fair.

Around that time I got a call from Ahmed's parole officer to tell me two of the assault charges had been dropped but that Ahmed had pled guilty to the remaining two. He had been given a year of parole and then would be pardoned after three years. I wasn't surprised a deal had been struck. Earlier in the year, I had written to the Crown Attorney to say that while everything in my initial statement to the police was true, I wasn't willing to testify. I told them that he was the father of my children and I didn't want him to go to jail. But it was more than that. I had talked with my lawyer about the case. The Crown wanted to go to trial. But my lawyer pointed out that a successful prosecution might mean Ahmed would be sent to jail. If that happened, I'd get no child support, never mind any spousal payments. I knew I couldn't put Kinza and Saarah's futures at risk.

So, on June 12th, I walked out of my lawyer's office with the signed, executed court order for our separation. I was jubilant. It had been just over a year since I ended the marriage, but it felt like a lifetime.

※　※　※

The separation agreement and the financial security it brought allowed me to make some significant changes the following year. I stopped running my little catering service, and I quit the info-desk job. It was a relief to know that during the upcoming year I would have time for more than four hours' sleep each night. My promotion to head undergraduate TA also meant a little extra cash to make up for the jobs I was relinquishing, and I'd been awarded a number of bursaries and scholarships that eased my financial burden as well.

I also switched from the Business Administration program to Financial Economics. That not only meant lower tuition but was also the right undergrad program to prepare me for the master's degree I had decided to apply for. I took summer school and enrolled in an extra course in the fall term and two extra in the winter term in order to graduate with my cohort in June.

My final undergraduate year, my second year living outside of marriage, was one of slow, steady progress. Standing in front of a class of first-year students, teaching and sharing everything I'd learned, I couldn't help thinking of how far I'd come since creeping into that first lecture theatre four years ago. Here I was, wearing Western clothes, all eyes on me, and the earth wasn't opening up to swallow me whole. Nor was I nervous as I left the classroom, wondering if my boldness would be found out and punished. What's more, the students were responsive and engaged—each day of teaching boosted my confidence a little further. That change was underscored by the fact that the professor whose teaching assistant I was, Gordon Anderson, had been one of my first instructors. Then, I had been so dazzled by his reputation that I hadn't been able to approach the lectern to ask a question without trembling from head to foot. Now I walked into his office on a regular basis, confidently requesting words of guidance.

My social circle continued to widen, and with it, the sources of support and encouragement—as well as the good times. I spoke more and more frequently with my professors and academic advisors, continuing to be awestruck by this network of brilliant people who were dedicated to helping others succeed. And the many brave people I met through my volunteer work continued to inspire me.

Now that the idea of being a single parent was no longer the terrifying spectre it had been just a year before, I could relax and *really* enjoy my little family. Many evenings, the girls and I would hunker down in front of the TV with a big bowl of popcorn to watch one of their favourite movies. Or on weekends when the girls weren't at

Ahmed's, we might all hop into the minivan for an impromptu drive to Niagara Falls or Wasaga Beach. Kinza continued to be my rock, Saarah my entertaining and lovable baby girl.

Everyone in my old community referred to us as "a broken family." Yet the girls and I had never felt so complete and happy before.

CHAPTER 17

FREEDOM

One December morning in 2012, walking across the campus, I received an email. Ruby Mack, the Department of Economics academic advisor, was inviting all students to apply for the John H. Moss Scholarship for graduate studies. The award of Moss Scholar went to the most outstanding graduating student across all three University of Toronto campuses, based on academic excellence, leadership and community work. A few minutes later, I was knocking on Ruby's door. She smiled as soon as she saw me. "I knew you'd be in," she said.

I took a seat across from her. "I just came in to ask you if you think I meet the criteria. Do you think I have a chance?"

"Why not?" said Ruby. "Your grades couldn't be better. You had leadership experience through the TA position. And you do so much volunteer work. You're a great candidate!"

I could tell Ruby was rooting for me and that stirred hope. If she had faith in me perhaps I should have faith in myself too.

The application required a written personal statement about the student's academic and career goals. Ruby offered to review whatever I wrote. A number of my professors graciously provided the required reference letters. I submitted all the documents and waited, hardly daring to hope that I'd hear back.

In early January, I got an email telling me that I had made it to the final phase. I was thrilled—but also apprehensive. The six short-listed applicants were required to undergo a daunting panel interview. Mine would be on February 6th, in the last slot. The chair was John Rothschild, then the CEO of Prime Restaurants, Canada's largest restaurant chain. The other committee members were likewise accomplished—company presidents and CEOs. Reading their bios on a computer at Robarts Library, I was both filled with admiration and terrified by the thought of facing them.

During the past couple of years, I'd learned to advocate for myself—something I had known how to do as a schoolgirl but had largely forgotten in my married life. Writing the personal statement had required me to think about the future, but now I had to be prepared to answer any questions the judges might throw at me, including ones about my relatively late-in-life, stop-and-start undergraduate attendance.

The interview took place at the main campus, in downtown Toronto. I arrived a full hour early, finding a spot to park the minivan. It was the first week of February, and as soon as I turned off the engine, cold air began to seep into the car. I sat behind the steering wheel, shivering, trying to calm my nerves. I had a copy of my personal statement in my purse. I took it out and read it. Then I read it again. And again. I was trying to beat back the needles of doubt. I was trying to remind myself of who I was *now*. And who I wanted to be. Eventually I got out of the car and walked towards the interview room.

A few minutes later, I was taking a seat at a large square conference table in an elegant, window-lined room. I looked at the ten awards committee members facing me. Their expressions were friendly, and John Rothschild started the interview with some generous words about my academic record, which helped me breathe a bit easier.

One of the first questions was what leadership meant to me. I had been a TA and run some classes and groups at the Afghan Women's Organization, but these were not the experiences I wanted to stress. Instead I told them that I thought the most powerful type of leadership was leading by example. As a mother, I was striving to do that. I wanted my daughters to know that they had a right to every opportunity in the world. I remembered Cherri's words.

"I'm trying to show them that through my actions."

One of the next questions made me pause. "Who is the person who has taught you the most? Who has been the most influential?"

I was about to say my father, but I stopped myself. If I were being honest, I had to admit that wasn't true. I took a deep breath and forced myself to answer.

"My husband," I said.

I glanced around the table. Face after face registered shock and disbelief. In my personal statement, I had mentioned briefly that it had taken me many years of struggle to get to university because I had wed as a teen and been stuck in an abusive marriage. My answer had clearly struck everyone as bizarre.

"My husband taught me how *not* to treat people," I explained. "He showed me what I didn't want to become. In a way, he taught me how to be strong because he forced me to be strong. Because of what he put me through, what I had to rise above, I learned what I was capable of."

While I wouldn't wish my experience on anyone else, I might never have known the truth of my strength or discovered its dimensions if Ahmed had not driven me to it.

The final question, however, was the one that unnerved me. "With everything that you've faced, what is it that keeps you going?"

The cool, professional facade I'd been trying to maintain through the long round of questions started to crumble. I could feel my throat constrict. When I started to speak, my voice was wobbly.

"Every day, I feel I should give up," I admitted, "but every day I make myself get up and keep going. I need to respect myself and my dreams, to live with dignity and freedom. But it's more than that. I keep going because of my daughters. I want things to be easier for them. I want them to be able to pursue *their* goals and their dreams. Everyone should have the right to do that." With that, I thanked the judges for their time and for the opportunity they had given me.

※   ※   ※

All the way home in the car, I played the interview over in my mind, thinking of better ways I might have expressed my ideas or other things I should have said. I prepared myself for disappointment. When I got into the apartment, I put my phone away and told myself not to think about whether or not a call would be coming.

But only a few minutes later, my phone was ringing. I picked it up with a trembling hand and sat on the edge of the bed. Kinza and Saarah squeezed in beside me. Celina Caesar-Chavannes, one of the committee members, was saying hello.

"Are you sitting down?" she asked. And then: "Congratulations. You are our winner this year!"

I burst into tears of disbelief and happiness and thanked her profusely.

"You've struggled so much, Samra," Celina continued. "It's time to get recognition. You deserve this more than anyone." Then she asked to speak to my daughters. I put the phone on speaker mode. "You should be very proud of your mother," she told them.

By the time I hung up, Kinza and Saarah were both jumping up and down on the bed in giddy celebration. I dropped my phone on the bedside table, climbed onto the mattress and joined them, the three of us bouncing and laughing and crying until we collapsed in a heap, thoroughly dizzy with joy.

※ ※ ※

The ceremony was held on April 11, 2013. Before Kinza, Saarah and I left the apartment for the event, I examined myself in the mirror. I was wearing a modern black-and-white dress. I had straightened my hair and applied my makeup meticulously. I looked nothing like the scared and shabby student I had been just a few years ago.

The award came with the biggest financial scholarship at the university, but in all honesty I had never really thought about the money. More than anything, I wanted to be recognized. I was growing more self-assured by the day, but I thought winning would be a powerful reminder that I could make a success out of my life—and that I truly belonged in graduate school. Indeed, the woman in the mirror looked as if she could take on the world.

Standing with the girls in the beautiful Great Hall of Hart House, just before the ceremony was about to start, I let a gentle pride wash over me. To think that I not only belonged in grad school but that I belonged *here*, in this prestigious place. Then I felt a tap on my shoulder. It was John Rothschild.

"I didn't want to miss this. I wanted to congratulate you in person, Samra," he said.

A few minutes later, my name was called for the award presentation. During my acceptance speech, I thanked Kinza and Saarah for being my inspiration, for giving me courage and strength. But I also acknowledged so many others.

"I want to thank all of my professors, friends and mentors who have supported me," I said. "I would not be here without you." I truly meant it.

※ ※ ※

Two months later, I attended the University of Toronto Mississauga campus graduation reception. Here I received another gratifying validation: the award for the top student in economics. As I headed to the stage to receive that award, I took Kinza's and Saarah's hands so they would come with me. Words of thanks were not enough. After all, these awards were just as much theirs as mine.

At the end of that ceremony, my friend Farah and an older woman came over to where Kinza, Saarah and I were standing. Farah congratulated me and introduced her mother. Ilmana was a columnist for the *Express Tribune*, a prominent Pakistani-Canadian online newspaper. She asked if she could write an article about me. I had been interviewed for a few articles about the Moss Scholarship, so I didn't feel as awkward as I might have even a few months earlier. I would be happy to talk with her.

"But I want the whole story," Ilmana said. "Would you be willing to talk about everything, including what happened in your marriage?"

I felt the colour drain from my face. "No, no," I said quickly. "It's so embarrassing. I'd be ashamed."

I could see Kinza staring at me, a question on her face.

"Well, I understand," said Ilmana, "but imagine how many women you will be helping, women who may be suffering the way you were. Please think about it."

I nodded, and Farah and Ilmana moved on.

Back home, twelve-year-old Kinza took me to task. "If every woman thinks it's too shameful to talk, how is anything going to change? I think you should do it. If anyone can do it, it's you."

I gave Ilmana a call and agreed to tell my story.

On June 10, 2013, Kinza, Saarah and I drove to Toronto to attend my convocation ceremony. Just before we left the apartment, my phone buzzed with a Facebook notification. An old friend from Pakistan had posted the *Express Tribune* article on my Facebook wall. "So proud to call you my friend," she had written above it.

I froze. Now it hit me that my private life was truly exposed to the world. I tried to put that thought out of my mind as I drove into Toronto. It was time to get my degree.

※ ※ ※

By the time I was standing in the wings of Convocation Hall, waiting for my name to be called, I'd forgotten all about the article. I couldn't quite believe I was here. I thought back to all the times I had pictured this, had pretended that the mortarboard was on my head, the gown draping over my shoulders. All the times I had walked around my bedroom, pretending that I was moving towards a university provost offering a hand and a diploma. And now it was better than I had ever imagined. As I crossed the stage, I could hear Saarah and Kinza hooting and hollering from the audience. I wished so much that they could have been joined by my mother, my sisters, my father. Papa had always said, "One day, my daughter will be a top student at a top university." If only he could have seen his prediction come true.

But I was too excited to be truly sad. I was thirty-one years old, and I had been waiting for this moment for almost my whole life. Tears were tracing down my cheeks as a diploma was placed in my outstretched hand. I floated off the stage.

Out on the lawns surrounding Convocation Hall, my friends and the girls threw their arms around me. We were surrounded by hundreds of other students and their families. Congratulations were ringing through the air. I didn't want this to end. But what I didn't realize was that another sort of recognition was coming my way. And this public attention would help me to make a difference.

※ ※ ※

Kinza, Saarah and I returned to the apartment, happy but tired. The girls settled down in front of the TV. I went into the bedroom and pulled out my laptop, logging onto my Facebook account. My mouth dropped open when I looked at my page. Messages. Hundreds of messages. *Thousands* of messages. From all over the world. From people I didn't know. The *Express Tribune* article had gone viral.

Congratulations, many of them said. *Thank you for breaking the silence.*

I spent a long time in front of my laptop, reading one message after another. But one stopped me in my tracks. It was from a young woman named Amna who lived about an hour from me. She asked if we might talk on Skype. When we connected a few days later, I was struck by the familiarity of her story. She'd been raised in Canada and had attended university here while living at home. After graduation, her parents took her back to Pakistan and pressured her into an arranged marriage. Almost immediately, the abuse began—both by her husband and by the mother-in-law she was now forced to live with. After a number of years, she became pregnant and fled to Canada to have the baby. But it had been agreed that once the baby was born, she would sponsor her husband so he could join her. She was now back with her parents and a new baby, terrified by the prospect of her husband's arrival in Canada, cowed by his long-distance threats and bullying.

She showed me some of the emails and texts he had been sending her. I shuddered at the familiarity: *haramzadi, bitch, whore, you will never survive without me, you will be damaged goods.*

Despite everything, the thought of leaving him—and of the social stigma that would bring—terrified Amna. She was certain she would never survive on her own. As she talked, I couldn't help thinking, *This was me five years ago. I can't let this happen to her.*

"I want to see you," I told her. "In person."

The next day I drove out to her home in Waterloo to talk to her and her mother. I poured my heart out, telling them all the things I had learned in counselling: abuse is never okay; it's never your fault; you deserve better; raising children in an abusive home is damaging. I pointed out that she had her whole life ahead of her, and there was no point in staying in a bad marriage.

"Just because something bad happened doesn't mean your entire life has to be bad. You deserve so much better. I had no education. You do. I had no friends. You do. My kids were older. Yours is a newborn who won't remember any of this. If I can do it, so can you."

I told her I would go with her to the lawyer's office, and that she could call me any time of the night or day. "I'll be there for you," I assured her.

I was holding her hand, and she was crying while I talked, but three weeks passed before I heard from her again. When I did, she told me she had made a decision.

"Samra, I had lost myself in the midst of all of this," she said. "When I met you, I found myself again. I'm filing for divorce and enrolling myself in a master's program."

In the years to come, she would become a good friend and I would watch with excitement and pride as she got her master's degree and then a great job. At one point she said to me, "Samra, you saved my life."

"No," I replied. "*You* saved your life. I just showed you it was possible."

※ ※ ※

The *Express Tribune* article blew my world apart—but in a good way. Many of the messages that poured in from that and other small media appearances encouraged me. They made me feel that I was not alone in my journey; that I was, instead, part of a community of survivors and supporters. What's more, they showed me that I had a part to play in this community. Telling my story could, as Ilmana had assured me, help others. In a few more years, I would figure out a way to make the most of that.

That summer was filled with of all sorts of new beginnings. After I graduated, feeling more confident about my finances because of the scholarship, I found a bright, spacious condo to rent and moved out of campus housing. I'd believed the golf-course house was the first place I could genuinely call my own, but that had been a delusion. Both the apartment and now this condo were true homes, where there was no shadow of abuse. Homes where my girls could grow up happy and free.

While the condo cheered me, a new connection gave me an even greater sense of possibility. After I won the Moss Scholarship, I had emailed John Rothschild to express my gratitude. I asked if we could meet for coffee so I could thank him in person. Instead, we went out for breakfast, and at the end of our meal John asked if he could do anything to help me. There was so much I could learn from him. Without a second thought I blurted out, "Would you be my mentor?"

"You've got it," he said.

After that breakfast I met with John every month, as I continue to do. He has become a trusted friend, and his academic and career advice have been invaluable.

In those early months of grad school, he encouraged me to think about pursuing a career after my MA rather than a PhD. He agreed that financial independence should be my primary goal. Further, he encouraged me to connect with other people in the business world. My graduate advisor put me in touch with Halina von dem Hagen, a senior executive at Manulife. When I met her, she hugged me and said, "The worst is over, Samra. It's only up from here." She offered to contact other executives for me. One of those people was the head of Asset Based Lending at the Royal Bank of Canada, who interviewed me in December 2013 and then offered me a part-time job right away, with a full-time position once I graduated with my master's of economics in the spring of 2014. The day I walked into my own little office at RBC, wearing my brand-new Banana Republic business suit and clutching a box of business cards with my name on them, I could barely believe what my life had become.

I couldn't help thinking of Ahmed's taunt: "Now you think you're some kind of hotshot!" *Yes*, I thought, laughing to myself as I pinned photos of Kinza and Saarah to the cubicle walls, *I guess I am*.

❀ ❀ ❀

I wouldn't want to give the impression that I found my past easy to shed. My route out of marriage wasn't fast, and it wasn't linear. Even while I was trying my hardest to change direction, it was a painful little dance, the emotional steps so incremental that it sometimes appeared I wasn't moving at all. Even when it seemed as if I had made a big leap, I could find myself pulled down.

Back in the early spring of 2013, before graduation, I'd been asked to give a short speech at the Pakistan Republic Day celebrations at the University of Toronto. The organizers wanted me to talk about winning the John H. Moss Scholarship and my journey to finish my undergraduate degree. Mindful of the audience, I donned a sari and did my hair and makeup with a modest touch. I was crossing the campus, checking my emails as I walked, when I noticed one from my lawyer.

My divorce had been finalized.

I stopped dead on the sidewalk. I was about to stand in front of a sizable audience as a divorcee—a flawed woman. Damaged goods. I managed to make it to the Students' Union office before collapsing in a fit of wailing, as if I were keening for the death of a loved one. My worried friends rallied around me and managed to calm me enough that I could take the stage and give my very first talk.

Despite having pushed hard for this divorce and living as a single woman for almost two years, I continued to grieve for months after receiving those final papers, often finding that feelings of shame, defeat and regret swept over me in unguarded moments. Indeed, all my academic and career success couldn't banish the sense that I was a miserable failure in my personal life.

❀ ❀ ❀

While the shame of my failed marriage has been remarkably tenacious, as the years have passed my confidence has grown. Whenever that sort of negativity flickers through my mind, I remind myself that it is not what I really believe—it is only the remnant of flawed cultural conditioning. With that assurance has come something precious. I have begun to find my voice once again. The Facebook messages - and through them my connections with women—inspired me to join the boards of various women's shelters and anti-abuse organizations. And I began to speak about what I had experienced with numerous media outlets, organizations and schools.

But then another opportunity came my way to help others and voice my perspective. In January 2016, John Rothschild and I were having one of our monthly breakfast meetings.

"How's your time these days?" he asked.

"I'm busy, but it's manageable," I said.

"Would you be interested in applying to the Governing Council for the University of Toronto?"

My jaw dropped. I understood a little about the university structure. The Governing Council is U of T's most senior governing body and oversees all the academic, business and student affairs of the university. The fifty-person council is involved with all major decisions at the university and provides guidance to the senior administration. Governors are either appointed by the Ontario Ministry of

Education or elected by one of the university's constituent bodies: staff, faculty, students and alumni.

John explained that he had been asked by the Alumni Association to approach me about applying to fill one of the three alumni governor positions open at the time (out of a total of eight).

I knew that all the alumni governors were extremely successful professionals and executives. I was just at the beginning of my career. I couldn't imagine I had much of a chance. "It's so flattering that they have asked me to apply, but I don't want to make a fool of myself," I told John.

"When has that stopped you before?" he asked. "You are one of the bravest, smartest women I know. I think you should put your name forward. Besides," he added, "the alumni body has been following your career and volunteer work. They're interested in hearing from you."

The university had done so much for me over the years—the administration, the faculty and the students had all been instrumental in helping me turn my life around. I wouldn't be sitting here, with my career and my independence, without U of T. If there was an opportunity to give back to the institution and to help other students, I wanted to take it.

※ ※ ※

The application process was extensive, but in contrast with the Moss application, I approached it with hopefulness devoid of anxiety. When the interview came, I was struck by how much more confident I was than I had been at the scholarship interview. Sitting at an enormous circular board table in the gold-decorated council chamber being interviewed by over twenty members of the university's College of Electors, all a great deal more accomplished than

I was, I realized that I had things I wanted to say, ideas I wanted to share. What's more, I felt that my opinions had value and were worth expressing.

When one of the interviewers asked me what the biggest challenge facing the university was, I was quick to answer.

"I believe education is not a privilege but a right. I would like to help ensure that it is accessible to everyone—people of all economic backgrounds, genders and races. Education is what helped me change my life. It opened my world. I would like everyone to have that opportunity."

A few weeks later, I got an email informing me that the College members had voted. Two of the three seats had been filled by governors who were up for re-election. I had been elected for the third spot.

※ ※ ※

As I walked into the impressive circular council chamber for the first meeting, I felt a small flutter of doubt. *Do I really belong here?* It was an odd thing: I had been one of the oldest students when I started my undergraduate degree, and now here I was, one of the youngest people ever elected to the Governing Council, surrounded by a cohort of truly impressive academics and professionals. And yet I *did* feel I belonged. The university needed to hear from people like me. My experiences were different from my co-governors' but they were equal. And they mattered. My voice mattered. I was thrilled that I had been given the opportunity to use it. Five years ago I'd been afraid to raise my hand in class or approach my professors. But now I was ready to speak.

That realization—that I had at last found my voice—led me to take one more step, in many ways a much more daunting step, in my personal journey.

＊＊＊

After that terrible afternoon at the Motel 6 five years ago, I had begun to let my marriage go, literally and figuratively. With each passing day, I found myself missing Ahmed and the social "security" of my married state less and less. By the time I was fully immersed in graduate school, my former state of mind seemed like the thoughts of some fictional character I had once read about.

As I healed and regained strength, Ahmed took up less and less space in my world, until he was simply the father of my children, the man whom I needed to deal with about visits with the girls.

And yet, those small points of contact refused to become easy or to feel benign. Whenever I had to get in touch with Ahmed, I did it by text or email. The thought of hearing his voice or catching a glimpse of him filled me with dread. That fear became muted over time but it was always there, quickening my pulse whenever his name popped up in my in-box or when I had to send him a message. And then, in the spring of 2016, at the age of thirty-four, just after I'd accepted my seat on the U of T Governing Council, something changed.

Around the time the divorce came through, Kinza had begun to protest her weekly visit to Ahmed, Amma and Abba's house. She would cry and fume before she was picked up for the weekend and return sad and frustrated on Sunday nights. She admitted that Ahmed and his parents said nasty things about me, which angered her and made her feel defensive. She talked with me, but she also confided in her school counsellors. Eventually one of the counsellors advised that I not send her—even if legally I was supposed to. Kinza would be able to make that determination for herself when she turned thirteen, but in the meantime, the counsellor recommended, it was worth defying the separation agreement if it spared Kinza the weekly trauma.

Ahmed wasn't happy when her visits stopped, but he never took action. Now, at fifteen, Kinza seemed more open to the idea of seeing her father again. I didn't want her to go through life without her father, and I knew he was desperate to renew the relationship. The only way to do so was for me to act as a liaison. And that couldn't be done by text.

My latest accomplishment seemed to give me the shot in the arm I needed to face this personal challenge. I gathered my courage and sent Ahmed a message offering to meet him at a local coffee shop to talk about how he and Kinza might connect again.

On the day of our meeting, I arrived a little early and took a table near the window, overlooking the parking lot. A few minutes after I sat down, I saw Ahmed's car pull in and park. It had been four years since I'd set eyes on him. As his door opened, I waited to feel my heart start its raucous tap dance. It didn't happen. As Ahmed's black hair and tall frame took shape outside of the car, I felt . . . nothing. The anxiousness I had wrestled with during the drive over seemed to have evaporated. I watched calmly as Ahmed crossed the parking lot. As he approached my table, my breathing was steady. I smiled easily at him as he took his seat across from me.

To my surprise, the first words out of his mouth were ones of sheepish gratitude. "I cannot believe after everything that you're still willing to help me with this."

"Of course," I said. "Kinza deserves to have her father in her life. But there have to be some ground rules."

And then I began talking. I talked and I talked. And Ahmed listened.

Through all the years of our marriage, it had been Ahmed who did the talking. I had had no voice in our relationship. But those times were truly past. I was no longer afraid, but what surprised me more, I was no longer angry. All the resentment, the hurt, the humiliation had somehow slipped away. And in its place—a peaceful confidence and the power of forgiveness.

As we got up from the table an hour and a half later, Ahmed thanked me. I waved it away.

I walked to my car smiling, my eyes rimmed with tears of joy. It was an extraordinary feeling.

I was free.

EPILOGUE

O ver the years, reflecting on my journey, I've realized again and again that my story is not just mine. It is the story of millions of people, especially women and girls, from all around the world. Indeed, during the past five years, I've received hundreds of thousands of messages from people who have shared their heart-wrenching stories of abuse and survival.

The fact that my story is only one iteration of an all-too-common experience is borne out by the sad statistics. The US-based National Coalition against Domestic Violence reports that one in three women and one in four men have faced intimate-partner violence at some point in their lives. A 2014 Statistics Canada survey found that 4 percent of both men and women had been physically abused by a partner in the last five years, with the most severe types of physical abuse being reported by women. What's more, the study found that in 40 percent of the cases violence continued after a breakup, and almost half of those reporting post-split violence noted that it had become more intense than previous abuse. Of these assaults, both before and after the relationship, only 30 percent came to the attention of the police. Furthermore, these statistics often represent physical violence only. When you add the unreported cases, as well as emotional, psychological, financial and other forms of abuse, the numbers are far worse.

※ ※ ※

Although I share my experiences with many others, one of the challenges of telling my tale is that the circumstances of my marriage and eventual separation can seem strange and exotic to the mainstream Western population. To be sure, any community that encourages women to wed when they are very young, forces arranged marriages on couples, and makes divorce taboo will likely create an environment in which domestic abuse is difficult to address. But I hope that people will not assume my story is representative of only a certain community, that it is about the flaws of a particular culture—that it is, in a word, unusual. Nothing could be further from the truth.

Victims and abusers come from all cultures, all races, all religions, all socio-economic backgrounds and all walks of life. Time and again, otherwise powerful, professionally successful men and women have found themselves in violent, dysfunctional relationships with no idea how to get out.

And despite my experience, and the experience of many of the women who write to me, the vast majority of domestic abuse occurs between men and women who began their relationships as love matches. And conversely, I know many couples who have found respectful and loving partnerships within arranged marriages.

Indeed, while physical and verbal abuse may be easy to identify, emotional and psychological abuse can be insidious—it can creep up on you, disguised by the trappings of love. And that is one reason why leaving can be so hard. On average, an abused woman returns to her abuser seven times before she is able to make the final split.

And, of course, many victims never manage to leave at all, or die at the hands of their abusers.

That may be especially true of victims of non-physical abuse. Without the tangible evidence of bruises and broken bones, many are convinced by their abusers that they are overreacting or imagining harm where there is none. I've often heard people say that they wished they had been hit, so they would have a reason to leave. The memories that haunt me still are not slaps and kicks but the name-calling and all the demoralizing, demeaning comments that wormed their way into my head over the years. (Although the sound of a slamming door can still leave me rattled for hours.)

For victims, thoughts tend to follow a strikingly common pattern: *I'm afraid of being rejected. No one will respect me. No one will want me. I feel like a failure.* Almost all victims of abuse share the same fears—of rejection, of shame, of judgment and of financial constraint, and the biggest of all, fear of isolation.

※ ※ ※

Sometimes I wonder why I was able to succeed beyond my wildest dreams in the face of abuse. I know I'm smart and capable. But the messages and letters I get from women who have not yet found a way out make it clear that I'm not alone in that.

The real game changer for me was the support system I found: the friends who watched my children when I went to court, the professors who wrote my scholarship letters, the mentors who championed me and advocated for me. All the people who loved and supported me because they saw me as an equal who was working hard to build a better life.

The restraining order and my supportive university community helped me to avoid returning again and again to my marriage: helped me, in other words, to escape being part of the statistical average. I was lucky to have university—it gave me a concrete goal and a path out. More than that, it provided an almost instant community and support network when I needed it. If it hadn't been for all those who rallied around me in the early days of my separation, I don't know if I would have made it.

That is why the fear of isolation can be positively debilitating. After all, we are in this world for connection. As human beings, that is our basic need. Many victims stay in abusive situations because they fear losing their families and their communities. Women often leave only to find themselves intimidated, overwhelmed and alone. Walking out of a marriage with no community to join is akin to taking someone who has lived in prison for a long time, putting her in the middle of a big city and saying, "You're free!" That person is likely to have no idea how to begin creating a new life. Some of those who try to leave lack life skills—knowing how to pay the bills, how to get a car fixed, or how to find a job. All lack the feeling of connection and support that invisibly keeps each of us going in our daily lives.

In my years of serving on the boards of women's shelters and organizations, I've seen many women arrive at a shelter to start a new life, only to fall back a few months later into the same pattern with their previous abuser or with a new abuser. That world, after all, is what they know. It's the same reason why some prisoners reoffend. The new is scarier than the old.

What survivors need—beyond shelters, police and counselling—is a sense of belonging. A community of support. Someone to hold their hand and say, "It's okay, you can do this. I'm with you." Someone to teach them how to walk so that they can eventually run and fly.

※ ※ ※

Amna is not the only abuse victim I've been able to reach personally. Since then, several local women have contacted me after hearing me speak at an event or watching one of my videos or TV appearances, or reading one of my posts on a friend's Facebook timeline. I've had countless coffees with women from all walks of life.

One woman was working two minimum-wage jobs to support herself and her three children after her husband fled the country when she threatened to report him for abuse. She wanted to go to school but didn't know how to balance her responsibilities and education. I helped her apply for bursaries and scholarships and then find ways to structure her classes so she could pick up a few campus jobs and be present for her children. Today she works at a major accounting firm, enjoying a six-figure salary.

After a TV appearance, I was put in touch with a nurse who had lost her entire community and social circle when she left her husband. Years of abuse had ripped her self-esteem apart. I started taking her with me to movies, networking events, even spa days. Within a few months, I could see her confidence blossom and her happiness in her single life grow. She started to build a bigger, more satisfying life of her own.

And after I published a magazine article, I met a very successful business executive who admitted that he had been the victim of abuse at the hands of his wife for over a decade.

There are many other stories, but the pattern is the same. All the people I met changed their own lives. But what they needed was someone to believe in them and to show them they were not alone.

That first encounter with Amna, and the others that followed, led me to an idea. If I could make an impact on women's lives with my own, imagine how many lives could be changed by a network of support and mentorship for abuse survivors. At present, I'm working with a small group of dedicated people to create such a program. We're hoping to build an organization that will match women who have come out of abusive relationships with a mentor, ideally from their own community, who can help them through the early years of their new life. Our aim is to help create a world in which no woman has to compromise her self-respect, independence and dignity in order to be accepted. In which no woman feels alone in her struggle.

※　※　※

Most of what is done to address abuse, including my project, is reactive. While shelter services, counselling, support and mentoring are absolutely essential, they occur after the abuse has taken place. But what can we do to prevent abuse before it starts? I believe the answer lies in education, providing everyone with a knowledge of what abuse looks like and how one can find oneself in an abusive relationship. We also need to teach people how to prevent themselves or loved ones from becoming victims.

That means teaching our children that they are worthy of love, respect and belonging. It means educating them about healthy relationships, healthy boundaries, early signs of abusive behaviours and tendencies. We also need to underline the importance of empathy and compassion. Only with this knowledge can young and old alike build (and demand) authentic connections with others. Giving back, paying it forward, asking and receiving help should be considered life skills: skills that everyone approaching adulthood has and practises on a regular basis.

Finally, we need to share our stories, and we need to listen to others.

I try to do all of that in my increasingly frequent speaking work. During the last several years, I have addressed high schools, universities, corporations and banks. I've delivered two TED Talks and made a Yahoo! video that has reached tens of millions of people worldwide. I've also been interviewed by dozens of publications and written a piece for *Toronto Life* magazine. The response to that article was tremendous, reminding me once again that people both want and need to hear stories by people who have successfully escaped abusive situations.

Of all the speaking engagements I've had, one was especially meaningful to me. Last year, I joined thirty-four other RBC employees on a corporate volunteer trip to rural Kenya organized by a charitable organization. Outside of the group itinerary, I was asked to share my story with hundreds of high school girls in a particular village. I was told that they faced many of the same challenges I had—they lived in a restrictive culture, and the chances were high that they would be forced into child marriages and become victims of domestic violence. As I stood in front of them sharing my journey, I felt as if I were speaking to a teenaged Samra, telling her the things she needed to hear. I told them how the power to change their lives lay within them, not around them, and how they could make choices to pursue their dreams—the key was never to give up. But with success comes responsibility. They would be carving a path not just for themselves to walk but also for others to follow.

After my speech, I heard a voice saying, "Thank you for inspiring me. I am going to become a doctor." Then another voice: "I will be a lawyer." And the little exclamations continued.

There was an extraordinary power in all those young voices expressing their hopes and dreams. And as I hugged the girls who embraced me, I found myself hoping with all my heart that every one would be able to make her words come true.

※ ※ ※

Amid the encouragement and support I get every day from all over the world, I sometimes experience backlash—stark reminders that some people perceive me to be a failure. I receive numerous messages telling me I am a "shameless woman" and a "home wrecker" who

331

is defaming her culture and community for self-promotion (including, sadly, some from my extended family). A number of friends have confided that their families want them to stay away from me and my bad influence. While these barbs only convince me that I need to keep telling my story, they used to bother me as well. But I'm growing a thick skin. Humour has become one of my favourite deflection tactics.

One day last year, I was in the elevator of my condo building with fifteen-year-old Kinza and an older South Asian woman. I had just returned from work, so was still dressed in a corporate skirt suit. I noticed the woman giving me the once-over.

Finally, in Urdu, she said, "How come I never see your husband around?"

"Oh, Aunty," I replied, "I'm divorced."

She smirked at me. "Ah, no wonder," she said, her voice dripping with disapproval. "Well, you never know when men will get their fill and leave their women. I guess it's just your bad luck."

Instead of letting it go, as I would have just a few years ago, I gave her a sweet smile. "Oh, Aunty," I said, "actually *I* got my fill and left. He just couldn't satisfy me anymore."

With that, Kinza and I sauntered out of the elevator. I could see the woman's flabbergasted expression out of the corner of my eye. Kinza was laughing. "Mom, you're such a badass!"

I can chuckle about this now, but there was a time not too long ago when I would have felt deflated by that woman's judgment. I would have been reminded that many people think I have tarnished both my character and my family's honour. The episode would have had my mind whispering, "You're useless. You're worthless." And despite everything I now know, those thoughts would have unsettled me deeply. While the physical wounds always mended quickly, the psychological ones have been harder to heal.

The girls and I have done a lot of work to recover from the

trauma of our previous life, and I do deeply regret not leaving earlier, not saving them from some of that pain. While I hope they will model their choices and behaviour on the way I lead my life now, not on what they witnessed early in life, I've learned that I have to allow them to make their own decisions—especially when it comes to how their father figures in their lives. Despite the fact that I want only the best for them, that I would save them from heartache and mistakes if I could, I know I must allow them independence and agency.

As a mother, I struggle with feelings of guilt about the past. And occasionally, as a divorced woman and an abused wife, I still fall prey to the imposter syndrome and to feelings of shame. But I resist *those* feelings with everything I've got. After all, we need to put the shame where it belongs, with the abusers. There is no honour in silence. My honour lies in my freedom to be me—unapologetically.

And being me is a pretty good deal.

One of the wonderful things about my new life is that I've embarked on an extraordinary journey of self-discovery.

I've come to understand that while I am an empathetic person—and while I genuinely believe that compassion, vulnerability and empathy form the cornerstone of healthy, functional relationships (and a healthy, functional society)—I've had a little trouble balancing this with personal honesty. My desire to be liked has sometimes made it hard for me to say no or to express what I want and need from others. My fear of being abandoned has at times prevented me from standing up for myself or creating boundaries. I've discovered, however, that by giving voice to my opinions and my truth, I can actually forge more loving and supportive relationships.

Indeed, I'm discovering the value of knowing my own self-worth. When I was young, I yearned for awards and prizes. During and after my failed marriage, my need for these types of external validation only intensified, as though academic and professional success might "redeem" my personal shortcomings in the eyes of the world. At the same time, I found myself downplaying my accomplishments in romantic relationships. And I accepted partners who didn't inspire me and who didn't share my interests or my drive because I thought this was all I could expect, all I warranted.

But I've learned that diminishing my own fire does no one any service. I will get from my life what I feel I deserve. And if nothing else, I'll be happier being myself than trying to fit into a box to satisfy others.

✻ ✻ ✻

Through all of this, I am embracing the things that make me truly happy. I have returned to various childhood enthusiasms, including tennis and squash. But I've also found many new ones.

After all those years of being isolated in my marital house, I find nothing more exhilarating than meeting new people and making new friends. While I am invigorated by public speaking, attending conferences or getting involved in volunteer organizations, the best part is connecting with the people I encounter there.

I entertain whenever I can. I've always enjoyed cooking, and now I can gather friends—old and new—in my home and share my culinary efforts with those I love.

I adore travelling, both with my girls and by myself. I've cycled and hiked in the Austrian Alps on my own, ziplined through the Mexican jungle with Saarah, and explored the museums of New York with Kinza. I've gone scuba diving in Cuba—even though I've not yet mastered the art of swimming. I've spent mornings watching lions and giraffes move across the African savannah. I've whiled away afternoons in Parisian cafes, sipping café au lait and watching the world go by. And I've enjoyed evenings in the vibrant jazz clubs of New Orleans. It fills my heart with joy each time I experience the magic of this big, beautiful world.

But there's more to my love of travel than that. Just recently, I was in Gainesville, Florida, for a speaking event. It was a quick trip but I had a couple of hours free one morning, so I decided to explore. I went onto my laptop and found a hiking trail not far from my hotel. I hadn't brought any hiking clothes, so I set off in an Uber wearing flip-flops and a summer dress. At the entrance to the trail, I bumped into two couples. Perhaps my unusual appearance piqued their interest. "Are you on your own?" they asked. When I said I was, they invited me to join them. We talked steadily for the entirety of our two-hour hike and parted as friends. To me, that's the very best part of travel—making serendipitous human connections.

Simply being on the move gives me a thrill, too. I've been known to get in my car during evenings without the girls and just drive. More than once I've barrelled down the highway all the way to Niagara Falls before turning around. Watching the miles flash by, lost in thought, I find that driving gives me the time to enjoy my own company and reminds me I can now make my own way in the world.

※ ※ ※

Freedom to travel, both near and far, has been a great gift, but there is no greater gift than my wonderful family. My daughters are my best friends, my pride and joy. We talk about everything under the sun and support each other unconditionally. Kinza terms us the "perfectly unorthodox family." Saarah calls us "The Power Girls." (Saarah once said to me, "I think Daddy's family picked you because you were only sixteen. They thought you were just going to do whatever they told you to do, and they'd be able to make you into whoever they wanted you to be." She paused and then added, "Man, they picked the wrong girl." I may not have felt like a Power Girl when I was sixteen, but I love Saarah's faith in all three of us.)

Kinza continues to amaze and inspire me. She has become a

wonderfully talented artist, something completely outside my own abilities. I'm continually blown away by the beautiful work she produces. She is an extraordinary young woman, and one who is carving her own path for herself.

Saarah's generosity and big heart make my own heart swell. Over the last few years, she has repeatedly won the HERO Empathy award at her school. Most recently, she was recognized for befriending a boy who was being bullied. He blossomed largely due to her support. I couldn't be prouder of her.

And my delightful family has a great home. Canada seemed a strange and frightening land when I first arrived, but I've come to love this country with all my heart and am beyond grateful for everything it has given me. I'm as proud a Canadian as anyone could possibly be.

❊ ❊ ❊

I value the incredible love I have in my life from my children, my friends, my mentors and so many people around the world. I'm grateful for every interaction, every experience, every breath and every moment of existence.

Of course, I don't have a perfect life, but who does? Even with my wonderful girls and my satisfying work, I have my ups and downs, my triumphs and struggles. I still often feel like a misfit, and confusion and uncertainty sometimes creep in. That said, I am truly happy—the happiest I have ever been. I love my mistakes because I have the right to make them. I lean into challenges because that's how I know I will grow. I will fall and I will fail, but I will not stop living. I have come to embrace this truth: *I am enough*.

I'm committed to letting my past make me better, not bitter. I strive to forgive Ahmed, his family and my parents, not because what happened was okay—it can never be okay—but because giving resentment, anger and hatred any place in my heart will only leave less space for love, joy and happiness.

I strive for the day when my past will serve only to provide me with strength and wisdom and will not waylay me with occasional pitfalls and self-doubt. But I will never relinquish it. I will keep raising my voice and speaking up. Because it's necessary to break the silence. Because millions of silences are still waiting to be broken. And because, sometimes, just telling my story can prevent it from being repeated.

In the spring of 2017, after the *Toronto Life* article appeared, I received an email from a man in Pakistan. He told me he had a seventeen-year-old daughter. He and his wife had arranged a marriage for her that was supposed to take place in a few months. "After reading your article," he wrote, "I have decided to cancel the wedding."

Instead, he was sending his daughter to university.

ACKNOWLEDGEMENTS

Two people without whom this journey would have been impossible are my teammates and biggest cheerleaders—my lovely daughters. I was nervous and scared when I became a young mother. Little did I know your presence would so empower me and give me a renewed drive to live life to the fullest and make a difference. You are my world, my pride and my joy. Every choice I make is to ensure you both get all the opportunities to reach your potential and dreams, and to pay it forward and help others. By carving a path for yourselves, you are paving the way for others to follow. My heart swells with pride and love when I see the kind, wonderful young women you are. I am so incredibly proud of the bond we share.

This book would not have happened without my dream team! Samantha Haywood—my wonderful agent who worked so hard to bring my message to the world. My amazing editors Kate Cassaday and Julia McDowell, who really understood my vision to make a difference in people's lives, and worked tirelessly to make it a reality. And of course, my co-writer and partner in this book, Meg Masters, for putting my words to paper and bringing this book to life. I will always miss those hours on your couch, Meg!

Three of my mentors deserve special mention: John Rothschild, who has already appeared in these pages. I would not be who I am today if it weren't for his support and guidance. John is one of those people who have taught me to have faith in myself by expressing *his* faith in me.

Harvey Botting, a fellow alumni member of the U of T Governing Council. He took me under his wing when I first joined the board, arranged meetings to introduce me to key people at the university and has given me immense guidance personally and professionally, especially on my journey with this book.

Professor Gordon Anderson, who was one of my first teachers at the University of Toronto and is now one of my dearest friends. He has spent countless hours guiding and inspiring me to believe in myself and my dreams and will be always an instrumental figure in my life.

The presence of my mentors continually reminds me that there are good men out there—the kind of men I want in my life.

A special thanks to my mentor Halina von dem Hagen, for not only opening the door to my first job, but also being a constant source of inspiration and support for so many years. Halina, your warmth and love mean more than you will ever know.

This journey would have been impossible without all the incredible support I have received from my second home, the University of Toronto. The moment I stepped foot on that campus in 2008, as a mature student and mother of two, my life changed. There are countless people who supported me along the way, from my professors to my friends, and I will always be grateful to all of them. Professor James Appleyard, for writing my first ever scholarship reference letter. Professor Rob McMillan, for supporting me wholeheartedly in my academic journey. University of Toronto Mississauga ex-principal Deep Saini, for his valuable guidance. My amazing friends who have been there for me through all the ups and downs, from spontaneous 2:00 a.m. Niagara Falls trips to hugging me as we drowned our sorrows in monstrous ice-cream sundaes.

A special hug to my wonderful ex-colleagues and friends, Justin Schurman and Eric Turner, for your constant kindness, support and motivation.

To my entire Brave Beginnings team and partners—thank you for all your wonderful support on this journey.